Reaping the Benefits
of Mergers and Acquisitions
In Search of the Golden Fleece

John Coffey, Valerie Garrow and Linda Holbeche

BUTTERWORTH
HEINEMANN

OXFORD AUCKLAND BOSTON JOHANNESBURG MELBOURNE NEW DELHI

Butterworth-Heinemann
Linacre House, Jordan Hill, Oxford OX2 8DP
225 Wildwood Avenue, Woburn, MA 01801-2041
A division of Reed Educational and Professional Publishing Ltd

ℛ A member of the Reed Elsevier plc group

First published 2002

British Library Cataloguing in Publication Data
Coffey, John
    Reaping the Benefits of Mergers and Acquisitions: In Search
    of the Golden Fleece
    1. Consolidation and merger of corporations – Case studies
    2. Corporate reorganizations – Case studies
    I. Title   II. Garrow, Valerie   III. Holbeche, Linda
    658.1'6

ISBN 0 7506 5399 X

For information on all Butterworth-Heinemann
publications visit our website at www.bh.com

Composition by Genesis Typesetting, Rochester, Kent
Printed and bound in Great Britain by Biddles Ltd
www.biddles.co.uk

Contents

Acknowledgements

The authors would like to thank the managers of Articon-Integralis for their support in producing this book. In particular the extensive contribution of Martyn Webster, the ex-CFO and the valuable support of Gunter Fuhrmann, the joint COO and Jenny Robb, the Corporate Development manager.

Our thanks also go to the other members of the Roffey Park mergers and acquisitions team, Wendy Hirsh and Marion Devine, without whose detailed research this book would not have been possible. Many of the companies mentioned in this book provided case studies for the original research and we are grateful for their time and willingness to share their learning. Thanks are also due to Samantha Allen for her careful checking of facts and to Bob Green for his helpful suggestions.

For the detailed preparation of the book we have relied on the efforts of a dedicated team at Roffey Park and in particular Debbie Beaney, Claire McCartney, as well as the Learning Resources team. Val Hammond, Chief Executive of Roffey Park, has kindly supported this project.

Finally many thanks to all the organizations that have given us permission to use illustrations of tools or processes from their own experience of mergers and acquisitions.

Figures

Part One

CHAPTER 1

Mergers and acquisitions – in search of the Golden Fleece

Jason, who was in the vigour of youth, and of an ambitious soul, cheerfully undertook the expedition to obtain the Golden Fleece, and embarked with all the young princes of Greece in the ship Argo

Merger and acquisition strategy

Will the early years of the new century continue to witness the huge growth in merger and acquisition activity that marked the end of the twentieth century? The chances are that they will – witness the value of deals carried out by the top five investment banks in the first quarter of 2001 alone ($456.2 billion). The quest for the Golden Fleece is alive and well.

Will the vast majority of mergers and acquisitions (M&As) continue to fail to achieve their potential value? Again, the chances are that they will – have we learned nothing from the past? This book is about breaking out of the cycle of grand strategy, great prospects, poor implementation, lost opportunities. We do believe that it is possible for M&As to realize their value – and more.

But bringing home the Golden Fleece involves more than just setting sail in quest of riches. It's about understanding the destination/end-game and working out the most appropriate route. This involves identifying the key ingredients of a successful journey which have to be managed. Latter-day Jasons need to be able to plan and implement intelligent approaches to managing the process of merger from start to finish. They need to learn how to avoid sea-monsters and make friends who can help them reach their desired destination. They need to evaluate their success and share the learning about how to succeed. Only then can they hope to realize value. Just setting sail is not enough.

Though mergers are increasingly common, managers are unlikely to be buying and selling businesses every day and therefore lack experience of handling the kinds of change involved in mergers and acquisitions. Managers are generally very influenced by their advisers and there is an entire industry of consultants willing to advise you on various aspects of M&As. We would not wish to play down the value of advice, especially from real experts in the field, but we aim to provide some of the information you need to make the most of any advice you receive. We shall be looking at what needs to happen before and after the deal to help realize its value.

No merger or acquisition is the same as another. That's why no single blueprint for success will work in every case. So rather than go in for the 'Ten Top Tips' approach, our intention in writing this book is to provide a broad map of the territory, to highlight some common stumbling blocks and to suggest a framework which should be helpful for most M&As. The book does not aim to be comprehensive or specifically tailored to your organization's merger – that's for you to do. However, we believe that the tools we supply throughout this book will be helpful if applied at the right time in the way that's right for your organization. Our aim is to prevent your organization becoming just another statistic in the merger failure category.

We'll start by defining terms, looking at the various reasons why organizations embark on M&As and why they so often fail.

Mapping the voyage

Defining terms

So what are mergers and acquisitions? In our research into the human aspects of M&As we used a not-too-original distinction between mergers, acquisitions and joint ventures. M&As represented a 'marriage', while joint ventures meant 'cohabiting'. Although mergers and acquisitions are generally treated as if they are one and the same thing, they are legally different transactions. In an acquisition, one company buys sufficient numbers of shares as to gain control of the other – the acquired company. Acquisitions may be welcomed by the acquired company or they may be vigorously contested.

A merger on the other hand is often agreed in cooperation between two partners. However, the degree of cooperation differs and mergers are not always a marriage of two equal partners. In either case, there will be degrees of integration. Integration refers to the combining of processes, markets and activities of the acquiring and acquired organizations. It can take place at a variety of levels – ranging from merging financial and management information systems alone to a complete integration of the brands, staffing and management.

Throughout this book, the terms 'merger' and 'acquisition' are used interchangeably. This is to some extent licence on our part reflecting common usage. The strange facts of the matter are that even in the case of a true merger, employees in one organization or another may feel that they have been taken over. In some cases, even when a company has been acquired, they refuse to act as if they lack power, prompting impressions of a 'reverse takeover'. The ideal scenario is that even when one company has effectively acquired another, employees in each company feel empowered to give of their best and be valued for it. This aspiration is often reflected in the use of the term 'merger' by chief executives, even when this is not the case. The use of either term in any merger scenario will reflect not only the financial realities but also people's assumptions and experience of the merger process.

How this book works

Because we believe that it is possible for mergers to succeed, we have written the book with practitioners in mind, suggesting tools and approaches that we have used ourselves as consultants or learned from companies through our research. We have tried to point out the classic merger pitfalls, while indicating what can be done to increase the chances of success. In Part One we provide an overview of the merger process and set out some of the key elements of success – getting the business strategy right and understanding what needs to be managed on the people side if you are to stand a chance of implementing your strategy.

In Part Two we focus on the nuts and bolts of managing the integration process – from transition to full integration. We illustrate the integration process through a detailed case study of Articon-Integralis AG, the leading supplier of IT Security Solutions and Services in Europe. In Part Three we look at some of the themes which can make or break mergers – creating the culture of the new organization, communications, retention and the roles of line managers and HR. Each section contains checklists which should be helpful whether you are a novice at the merger game or an expert.

The boom in merger activity

M&A activity appears to be on the increase, especially in mature sectors such as manufacturing and financial services which are ripe for consolidation. The late 1990s and early 2000s has seen the whole field of M&As becoming more focused and strategically driven. Mega-deals are on the increase, with Goldman Sachs reporting on being instrumental in 55 deals in the UK alone, worth in total £311 billion in 1999. Industry-specific restructurings in sectors such as telecommunications, media and technology, banking, pharmaceuticals and chemicals reflect the ongoing quest for consolidation, growth and global reach. The Glaxo Wellcome and Smith-Kline Beecham merger alone was worth $78 billion.

The slow-down in merger markets, combined with lower trading volumes following the rout of the UK stock market in April 2000, left many investors worried about the impact on profits at top banks, investment houses and on-line brokers. However, it looks as if some of these fears were overdone. Financial soothsayers predict that the fall in the spectacular number of deals which took place in the first quarter of 2000 ($1172 billion) is no more than a temporary blip.

It is notable that many companies continue to consolidate within their domestic markets before they look for partners in other European countries. According to JP Morgan's head of M&A research, Paul Gibbs, 'Regulatory intervention is becoming an increasingly common obstacle to M&A deals in Europe, although the number of deals that fail to proceed due to European Commission intervention is still small'.[1] Indeed, cross-border European deals are on the increase since the landmark Vodafone acquisition of the German firm Mannesmann in 2000.

Gone are the bad old days when acquisitions looked like a needless exercise in debt creation. This was an image brought about by many over-inflated deals and some spectacular failures. There appears to be a general consensus among M&A experts that deals in the heady days of the 1980s, when the whole business world appeared to be involved in merger activity, were often unrelated acquisitions, whereby conglomerates simply expanded their portfolio of activities.

Gone, too, are the days when acquisitions seemed at times to be driven by pure greed. In the 1980s and early 1990s, many a struggling company became easy prey for asset strippers. Some of course still are and arguably rightly so. The acid test seems to be – if the parts are worth more than the whole then sell them off. If the whole is worth more than the sum of its parts, this organization is being well or strategically managed and may be worth acquiring for its expertise and brand strength.

Now, mergers and acquisitions are viewed as a respectable and legitimate tool for effecting change. Today's deals are more complex and teams of advisers are likely to include experts in the New Economy such as Internet strategists. Management teams are spending more time analysing suitable targets and generally thinking about strategic and cultural fit. They are making greater efforts than ever before to explain and justify their decisions to key stakeholders – not just financial analysts and institutions, but shareholders, customers and employees.

Why acquire? The strategic drivers of M&As

Investment Dealers Digest speaks of the increasing waves of 'strategic deal making' which have 'reaffirmed the role of mergers and acquisitions – regardless of size – as the preferred device of the 1990s for positioning businesses to handle the concurrent challenges of competition and ensure their survival in an often uncertain future'.[2]

The dominant logic of European mergers and acquisitions since the mid-1990s is strategic focus. Whether buying or selling, businesses are clarifying or re-defining their core capabilities and key markets. Public companies are looking at all their operations and reassessing their value in strategic terms. They are growing in confidence to restructure themselves and sell-off significant chunks of their portfolios. Nothing is sacrosanct. Analysis of deals by a number of specialist research organizations reveals that the majority of today's transactions are related or horizontal acquisitions, by which companies refocus on their core business. Leading companies in sectors such as the automotive, chemical, and pharmaceutical industries, manufacturing, telecommunications, insurance and banking have either shed non-core businesses, or bought related businesses. There is an increasing blurring between public and private markets for deals.

The classic reasons for acquiring other businesses include being able to rapidly add scale and so achieve greater economies and market reach; gain access to new markets and distribution networks; capture new product technologies and innovations; wipe out competition and emerging competitive threats; provide long-term ownership and control over value created.

Another common driver of merger activity is the desire to achieve scope, where companies such as domestic gas providers also seek to provide electricity and water to the same customers. In today's knowledge economy, a key driver of M&A activity is acquiring intellectual property and talent. Ironically, while these are potentially an organization's most valuable assets, they are also the most fragile and difficult to control since they depend on the goodwill and commitment of people.

In the UK public sector, there is government pressure on local authorities and other public sector bodies to achieve 'joined up' outcomes. This is currently leading to reshaping central government bodies such as the Employment Service through merger. Local Authority Social Services divisions are being encouraged to merge with local NHS Trusts to provide improved health and welfare provision.

Technology and the need to achieve market dominance are driving many deals in 'New Economy' companies in fields such as telecommunications, digital media and high technology. The announcement by AOL of its intention to acquire Time Warner in a deal worth $182 billion prompted a domino deal effect with on-line and traditional media companies looking at their options. However, an increasingly important driver of mergers in the early 2000s is the availability of cash from private equity providers. JP Morgan reported a 58 per cent rise in European private equity volume in 1999 leading to deals worth £45 billion.[3]

Is the sum of the whole greater than the parts?

Despite the high levels of merger activity, there is no shortage of research studies which suggest that mergers usually fail to yield their expected financial results. McKinsey's have found that 60 per cent of acquisitions fail to deliver returns exceeding the cost of annual capital.[3] One of the most significant studies, carried out by Hall and Norburn[4] over a seventeen-year period found that:

- Returns to the shareholders of acquiring firms are, at best, slight. They tend to disappear rapidly and, at worst, are significantly negative. On the day that the Royal Bank of Scotland announced its successful bid to take over NatWest, the Royal Bank's shares fell by 14 per cent

- Returns to shareholders of acquired firms are strongly positive
- Gains and losses of victims and predators become a zero sum
- In certain cases, a failed bid leads to improved stock market valuation
- Acquisitions are unlikely to reduce risk.

Ironically, rather than increasing an organization's value, M&As can cause share prices to be badly hit if they are mishandled. Conversely, the way in which organizations are able successfully to navigate mergers through problematic territory and keep the employee–customer–investor value chain intact is increasingly being seen as a form of competitive advantage. The more effective a firm is in handling all stages of a merger, the more its value will be enhanced in the eyes of the investment community. Recognizing this, some firms are embarking on small-scale acquisitions just to gain the experience!

Why do mergers fail?

Most of the effort in explaining these failure findings has gone into exploring financial fit or business portfolio fit. Several studies point out that related acquisitions are more likely to succeed than conglomerate acquisitions. This is primarily because they have the advantage of transfer of product knowledge and expertise and also offer more potential for economies of scale. Increasingly, though, the people and organizational fit is coming to be seen as the main factor why businesses fail to reap the benefits of mergers. The people issues revolve around the way the merger process is handled, the impact of the merger on individuals and the way they react to what is happening. In this section we will look at some of the main reasons why mergers fail and look at what can be done to make mergers work in later chapters.

The fact that mergers are difficult to make work successfully is leading many companies to prefer the alliance/joint venture route before they progress towards merger activity. The biotechnology sector is noteworthy for this. Making mergers work successfully requires outstanding leadership skills as well as good management skills to create an effective transition to the new organization.

1. Lack of clear M&A strategy

While people-related issues are generally thought to be the major reasons why M&As fail, other common problems stem from the lack of a structured approach to M&As. This is often demonstrated in the failure to think through the strategic logic of any specific deal. Logic suggests that management teams would typically approach M&As in the following manner:

Assess our position
↓
Strategy
↓
Acquire, Merge or Build
↓
Acquisition/Merger
↓
Realize the Value

In reality, many management teams acquire or merge businesses without really having thought through the dynamics of their market, or the more powerful and different market demands on the acquisition. They are often tempted by the strength of the equity market and the availability of capital. The desire to generate cash for other ventures or the need to impress competitors is often related to senior managers' ambitions and egos. In the excitement and adrenaline rush, which are characteristic of deal-making, important implementation issues may be missed. This alarming but all too common approach can always be identified when senior managers, three months into trying to implement rationalization or other operational changes are reported as saying, 'Just remind me why we actually bought this company!'

To avoid these dangers, SKF the Swedish international engineering company, has developed a clear acquisition process. [5] This involves the following steps:

SKF acquisition process

- Identify the target company
- Scan target company
- Develop project plan
- Evaluate target company
- Develop business plan
- Due diligence review
- Follow-up (including incorporation into SKF)

SKF considers the acquisition as only the start of the process of realizing value. They prefer to leave nothing to chance and have developed a systematic approach to managing each phase of an acquisition. Having a clear strategy generally improves the chance of a successful takeover or merger.

- The strategy will generally reflect the overall philosophy of the acquirer. Acquirers have the luxury of setting the tone for the merger, made evident in large and small decisions. So an acquiring philosophy of 1 + 1 = 1 will be evident in an over-emphasis on cost-cutting and efficiencies. This usually entails job loss, streamlining of processes and a focus on squeezing the asset. Interestingly, in many mergers among financial services organizations, the focus is on achieving cost savings. Such mergers tend to make slow progress towards achieving their objective.
- The real challenge is for management to realize the scope for greater improvement and business growth. This different philosophy of 1 + 1 = 3 focuses on revenue enhancement opportunities. This orientation is evident in the acquirer's desire to grow the value of combined companies intellectual capital – the ideas, skills, knowledge, patents, experience, processes – reflected in the intellectual property premium paid to the underlying stock price. Retaining key people in the acquired organization will therefore be a business imperative. When both types of philosophy are evident – with job losses on the one hand and new business development on the other – the effect can be temporary confusion for surviving employees.
- A clear strategy and explicit purpose, which people can buy in to, will help people make the transition to the new organization. Bringing the wrong philosophy to the right acquisition is a recipe for disaster. Clarifying your organization's M&A philosophy for any deal can help avoid expensive mistakes.

2. Misunderstanding the nature of the asset

Another of the main causes of failure is faulty logic in valuing the asset to be acquired and then being unable to realize the value of the asset. This is often evident in an inappropriate deal structure based on inadequate information. In assessing the value of any asset, purchasers need to weigh up whether the expected gains through cost cuts and potential synergies outweigh the costs of integrating the asset. Making this assessment accurately is no mean feat. First, there is the challenge of establishing the current and future value of the target company to the acquiring company's current strategic plans.

- In the past, analysts were interested largely in whether a deal could be 'earnings positive', i.e. did the deal add to the net earnings of the combining companies? Even the analysts are recognizing that the true value of a firm may be far more, or less, than what appears on the balance sheet of tangible assets. A new class of deals appears to be emerging, in which the main purpose is to grow a company's intellectual capital. In today's knowledge economy, there is an increasing focus on the so-called 'intangibles' which represent the real potential of future earnings.

- These 'intangibles' include the quality of leadership, the speed of decision-making, the flow of ideas and the quality of talent. Another important intangible is the degree to which employees share a mindset which supports the firm's strategic purpose. So, in a company whose brand image is one of outstanding customer service, any group of employees whose behaviour is not in line with that image risks destroying brand value and reputation. In a sense, the strength of the brand reflects the extent to which customers believe in and buy the brand and the extent to which employees identify with and act in sync with, the brand image. The due diligence process needs to be geared to identifying the state of these key assets, especially if they fit into the 'intangible' category. So, if retaining key people is critical to the success of the combined business, due diligence should look at the nature and location of talent and the 'soft' issues such as the interests and intentions of staff.

- This follows from the logic of the employee–customer–investor value chain which works on the basis that satisfied employees are more likely to provide excellent customer service. This in turn will lead to customer satisfaction and loyalty (or repeat business). This leads to predictable returns to investors. A number of US companies, like Sears Roebuck, for example, have refined this value chain to such a point that they can predict the impact on business results of any shift in employee or customer satisfaction. They have also worked out which elements of satisfaction seem to matter more and what therefore needs to be managed.

- So far, so good. However, M&As upset the smooth flow of this logic in a fundamental way, bringing together as they do different organizations, cultures, brand identities and loyalties. Even with good risk assessment, mergers are the joker in the pack, where the unintended consequence is to be expected. The impact of mergers on people – especially employees – appears directly to affect the bottom line of combined organizations in ways which can make executives tremble.

- Company managers usually know why they have embarked on the acquisition trail. The irony is that they are often at a loss as to how to realize their goal once they have chosen their target company and done the deal. So the second major challenge in realizing the potential worth of an acquisition is managing the integration is a way that enhances, rather than destroys, value. However clear and logical the purpose, the real challenge of mergers is being able to handle every aspect of the process so as to maximize the chances of strategic success.

- The problem seems to be that once the merger process begins, the high activity levels and sheer volume of decisions which have to be made cause people to lose sight of the strategic purpose. The very thing you need for success, such as key people to stay if you want to acquire their expertise, can backfire if the way the merger is handled causes them to leave. In other words, every aspect of the way you manage the merger will contribute to making it succeed or fail.

3. Competitor and customer reactions

Many companies have learned to their cost that customers are not as keen on mergers as shareholders if it means disrupting or downgrading the product quality or customer service they receive, or leads to price rises. Typically, customers will give a firm the benefit of the doubt once news of the deal has reached the press if they simultaneously receive clear information about why the merger is happening and how they will benefit from it. However, this benefit of the doubt does not last for long and the potential risk of competitors moving in, making the most of their uninterrupted service, is high. The danger at this time is that the organization becomes so internally focused that it stops paying attention to customers. Similarly, competitors often see mergers as a prime time to come poaching staff who have become destabilized by the merger. In a worst case scenario, vital organization information is transferred to competitors, along with key staff.

4. Inability to maximize potential synergies

Successful mergers are ones that produce maximum synergy, or fit, between the acquired business and the parent company. A major cause of merger failure is unrealistic synergies, based on inadequate information and checking in the due diligence process. All too often strategies are incomplete, focusing on the requirements of the purchaser, without integrating the different market demands on the acquisition. Tell-tale signs of strategic failure are when proposed synergies are unrealistic, the price paid is too high and competitors rally to attack the floundering giant.

- Typically, managers in the acquired organization are left powerless and unconsulted if the acquiring organization is inexperienced at handling acquisitions, is arrogant, incompetent or any combination of these. Both acquirers and acquired companies lose out in such a scenario, since valuable knowledge can be lost which can make a difference to the way the acquisition is managed.

Monsanto workshop[5]

To avoid these problems, Monsanto uses a three-day workshop with key Functional Leaders to align the company's acquisition strategy with the business strategy. This involves a marketplace comparison, discussing non-negotiables, comparing organizational culture, processes and practices, identifying and resolving gaps and major issues and developing project plans for integration. The output of the workshop is integration implementation plans. Plans are built around the '3Cs' of Integration, i.e. Clarity, Conflict Resolution and Consensus Building, with communications focused on people's everyday jobs.

---

5. The wrong type and level of integration

Of course, the questions to be answered by an integration strategy vary by the market of the business you are in (see Checklist). A key reason for failure in the M&A context is a mismatch between the level of integration required for the specific purpose of a merger or acquisition. Shrivastava[6] distinguishes three levels of integration: (1) procedural, (2) physical and (3) managerial and sociocultural integration.

- Procedural integration is maybe the easiest level of integration, including integration of accounting systems and creating a single legal entity. Physical integration involves integrating physical assets such as technologies and product lines, as well as locations. Often the time and cost of integrating production technologies, distribution systems and computer systems is underestimated. In order to achieve synergies, resources have to be shared. This usually requires concerted efforts such as communicating a long-term strategy for exploiting synergies throughout the organization.

- While integrating systems and processes is difficult enough, the hardest form of integration to achieve is managerial and sociocultural. This includes for instance selecting and transferring managers, changes in organization structure, the development of a compatible organization culture and a frame of reference to guide strategic decision-making. This involves the systems and processes of people management as well bringing together different pay scales. It can involve capitalizing on, or unwinding strategic alliances which have become conflicting and dealing with a wide range of regulatory demands. It also involves gaining commitment and motivation from personnel and the establishment of new leadership. Its purpose is to merge cultures and managerial viewpoints. The 'soft' side of integration is the trickiest since it involves people's differing beliefs and ways of working.

- However, sociocultural integration does not always take place, nor is it even necessary. Even if full integration is not required, cultural differences need to be addressed. In most mergers, integration takes place at all three levels, leading to job losses, 'winners and losers' in the job stakes, changing brand identity, new procedures, relocations, head office closures etc. Is it any wonder that employees look back with nostalgia to the 'good old days', even if they weren't?

- Similarly, the level of cooperation between acquiring and acquired organizations will affect how employees feel about the merger. In an *organizational rescue*, where the acquired organization is actively looking for help from outside, collaboration is likely and the aim is to get a good deal for both firms. Even so, employees may demonstrate passive resistance. In a more *hostile or contested acquisition*, or a perceived raid, there is likely to be a lot of resistance within the acquired firm. An *assimilation* has discrete and focused strategies which are different from the strategies of an acquisition. An assimilation usually has tangible goals such as volume and growth, where culture is considered unimportant and acquired managers are required to adopt the ways of the purchaser or leave.

- An *integration strategy* has as its goal to create synergies or to establish a new third company. The more the acquired company's value depends on the quality and commitment of the people employed, the more carefully the integration has to be handled. Managing organizational cultures is therefore seen as critical. Conflict resolution and team building have high priority. *The damaging general tendency of managers is to drive an assimilation strategy, resulting in cultural in-fighting, when an integration strategy may be called for.*

- In other cases, business managers are unwilling or unable to adapt to integration strategies which vary according to the market of the business that has been acquired. Strategy and organizational culture need to be consistent if they are to succeed. Of course companies that have amassed a good deal of cross-border merger management have a clear under-standing of merger success factors. In the case of UBS Warburg, which has grown rapidly by transformation and acquisition since the late 1980s, business strategy matches the desired level of integration.

Factors in matching strategy and integration at UBS[5]

1 How integrated will the new organization be?

- Standalone unit
- Partial integration
- Complete integration

2 How much of the organization will be impacted by the deal?

- Technology/infrastructure
- Single business unit
- Single location
- Entire company

3 Who will the controlling parties be in the new organization?

- Acquisition
- Full merger
- Joint venture

Source: Presentation at EFMD/ Roffey Park Group (November 2000)

---

6. A lack of clear process for handling the merger implementation

In many mergers, management focus is on doing the deal, rather than on making it work. Yet experience suggests that value is created by successful implementation, not through the trans-action itself. Mergers are key organizational events and perhaps more than other critical incidents, cause people to expect major change to happen. If there is a major delay between announcements or the pace of implementation is slow, people's willingness to change is eroded. Experienced acquirers move rapidly into integration activities, before the ink has dried on the deal.

Mergers are a lot of hard work for all involved. They inevitably produce a huge number of complex, interrelated tasks, decisions and implementation issues. In the mass of data, it is easy to lose sight of what needs to be achieved. Poor implementation is common for a number of reasons. There is often a lack of commitment and energy from top management to take tough decisions or to drive through merger benefits. Typically there is little understanding of the people/cultural dimension of the merger and a lack of planning or process. Symptoms of poor implementation include poor integration management, little tracking or communication, cultural differences remaining unaddressed, lack of employee support and loss of customers.

The most effectively managed mergers are those where specific responsibility for handling them is shared between different groups or work streams and where there is an appropriate framework for coordination, maintained for long enough for the new organization to start to flourish. The key lesson from companies who have developed merger experience is to treat the management of a merger as a project, with definable end points to each phase. The merger project has to run alongside a 'business as usual' approach which maintains or improves services to customers. As with any project, there needs to be a plan with clear phases and defined responsibilities for those involved.

Organizations vary in their approach to planning. Some like Whitbread plc[7] prefer to set themselves a clear time target for integrating all the relevant 'mechanics' – structures, HR, financial reporting and IT systems. They aim to get through the logistics in the shortest possible time so that the organization can settle down and develop its new way of operating. Others, like the UK's Environment Agency[7], prefer a more organic approach, dealing with one aspect of integration at a time as the culture of the new organization evolves. We will be looking in more detail at what is involved in managing the transition in Chapters 5 and 6.

Whichever approach is preferred, effective monitoring and reporting systems need to be established. There also need to be clear handovers between the people involved in different stages. By phase three (integration), line managers who may have had no control over the earlier phases may have lost sight of what the new organization is meant to achieve and may revert to their ways of operating pre-merger. They need to be kept informed and involved in the process if they are to exercise a continuing leadership role in the creation of the new organization.

Similarly, chief executives and other directors may have lost interest in the mechanics of the merger, having assumed that once the first few months post-deal have passed, the new organization has come into being. In this they are likely to be mistaken. They need to remain hungry for information about how the integration is going, how issues are being dealt with and how they need to operate to reinforce the new direction. Without an ongoing focus on what the organization is trying to achieve strategically through its merger, the chances of realizing the potential value of the deal are slim.

7. Mismanaging organizational and human issues

Typically, a strategy which is inconsistent with the culture of the new company is doomed to failure. So is one that fails to take into account differences in organizational culture which can help or hinder the achievement of the strategy. Many culture-related pitfalls are allowed to persist. Examples abound of 'silo' mentality, lack of management unity, misunderstandings and other evidence of differences persisting.

Some management teams recognize the importance of getting the people aspects of mergers right but then fail to think through how to achieve this. Tell-tale signs of muddled thinking include publishing fine-sounding value statements yet failing to provide people with adequate or relevant communication, mishandling the appointments and redundancy processes, keeping people waiting for information about location decisions, lack of visible leadership and frenzied workloads without a strategic overview or coordination.

For most employees, mergers represent the biggest change they are likely to experience in the workplace. Managers too may not have been involved in, or led, change on such a scale before. Typically, managers and employees lack the support they need to survive and thrive during mergers. Two groups of employees have a special role to play in providing this support. Human Resources professionals have a key role to play in designing appointments and exit processes, rationalizing terms and conditions and other aspects of employment contracts. Line managers have to provide support to others as well as keeping the business going while they or members of their team are involved in transition projects. We will be looking at the roles of these two key groups in avoiding these errors in later chapters.

There is often a mistaken assumption that large companies will have more experience of mergers than smaller ones, but this is not always true. If organizations are increasingly likely to go through mergers at some stage, they need to strengthen their ability to manage future change and be better able to leverage a merger to achieve growth and work with new business paradigms, such as e-business.

This book should help you avoid the classic pitfalls of merger management. Our aim is to provide you with a helpful guide to what needs to be done at each stage of the merger process timeline.

The merger process timeline ● ● ●

A basic merger process involves tailoring the approach to the merger context, setting a clear merger aspiration, identifying all the value levers and choosing the most important, addressing organizational issues, designing the integration process then executing this process rigorously. There are choices at each stage of this process. In setting aspirations, do you aim simply to capture near-term synergies and protect ongoing business, or do you want to move to fundamentally higher levels, leveraging assets beyond the combined model? Do you really want to embark on new strategic opportunities made possible by the merger?

Choices on the integration process include at the pre-closure stage, do you go for the critical actions only, or for the legal maximum. In deciding the speed of integration do you go for getting everything 100 per cent right, or moving as fast as possible? Will you create synergy target setting top-down or bottom up? How will you achieve both?

At each phase of the merger process there are specific activities involving a range of people. The framework for this book broadly follows the merger timeline through from run-up to transition then integration, while pausing to look in more detail at some of the aspects of mergers which run throughout the process, such as communications and the role of HR. Let's look in a little more detail at who and what is typically involved in the phases of the merger timeline (Figure 1.1).

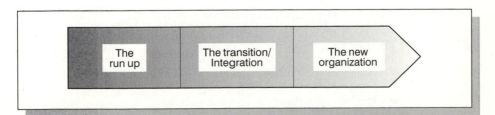

Figure 1.1 Phases of a merger

The run up • • •

Likely timeframe	*Activities*	*Who's involved*
< 6–12 months → Day One	Prospecting for a partner Due diligence Deal making Closure Creating transition plan	Dealmakers – finance, legal chief executive, analysts, HR, transition team, planners, operating director, competition's commission, shareholders board

The run-up period is relatively ambiguous to define. For some members of the Roffey Park/EFMD research group, this was the period of deal-making up to the announcement of the merger. In this period, the people generally involved are the deal-makers – typically chief executives, financial and legal experts and a range of advisors. Activities focus around assessing the value of the deal and various kinds of 'hard' due diligence are carried out. Usually the main area of interest is financial 'fit' which includes availability, price, potential economies of scale, dividend yield, projected earnings ratios, debt to equity ratios and valuation methodologies. The deal-makers disappear for days on end into the data room. Key aspects of risk assessment are carried out. All too often the forms of risk assessment with regard to people are limited. Usually HR and many general managers are excluded from this process.

For other research group members the run-up phase included the closure of the deal and 'day one' of the new organization. This phase usually involves a wider range of people in gathering data, carrying out a variety of forms of due diligence and developing business plans and integration plans, often referred to as '100-day' plans. Management attention often focuses on one or other type of plan, while both need to be developed and implemented if the deal is to realize the predicted value. Key business leaders need to develop an integration plan which will accelerate the business strategy.

During this period it is important that critical success criteria are developed which will provide guidance for all concerned. These should typically include:

- Management commitment
- Open communication
- Carrying out changes quickly
- Acting as fairly as possible

UBS[5] has successfully acquired a number of businesses in the last decade. Their experience suggests that addressing both strategic business issues and people issues through the transition period is vital to success in post-merger development. They uphold seven key success factors which help them to assess whether they are winning or losing:

1 Board level structure must be defined at announcement
2 Publish an integration communications plan
3 Have very clear business and financial targets
4 Keep integration time as short as possible
5 Make decisions swiftly – speed is critical
6 Involve as many employees as possible
7 Make selection process transparent

The transition • • •

Likely timeframe	Activities	Who's involved
+0–9 months	Integration	Transition team, HR, operating director, senior line managers, sponsor: chief executive, management team

The main focus of the post-deal period is to build the market value of the combined organization. To achieve this, some level of integration is usually required. The danger is that, if badly handled, the people and organizational issues relating to the merger will cause managers to take their eye off the ball. A transition period should be the time when the business aims to enhance revenue through some form of integration of product and service offerings. (This may not always be the case – the Bank of Ireland acquired the UK-based Bristol and West Building Society and left product offerings entirely separate, with great business benefit[7].) Typically, managers aim to achieve cost reductions and look for economies of scale by rationalizing business and product lines, central functions etc. The other key business focus should be on developing and exploiting product/service offerings and exploiting brand values. Anticipated financial performance should then start to come through.

These business objectives have to be managed alongside the creation of an organization capable of achieving them. In that sense business and organizational objectives are so intimately entwined as to be inseparable. They are reflected in the key success factors for this stage:

- We maintain or enhance our service/products to customers
- We manage critical integration issues effectively
- We achieve a range of valuable synergies
- People are motivated to deliver high performance
- Key stakeholders, including employees, maintain their commitment.

Communication to all stakeholders is vital in maintaining momentum for change, clarity about business direction and to create a sense of purpose.

Integration • • •

Likely timeframe	Activities	Who's involved
+9 months–2 years	Running the new 'business as usual', completing integration	Line managers, HR sponsor: chief executive, management team, staff teams

The period of integration is largely determined by how much integration is required and how much of the organization is involved. According to research by Roffey Park, this phase is characterized by:

- Pressure to deliver with performance under scrutiny
- New work processes and teams
- Cultural sensitivity
- Reassessment of values.

Managers should be:

- Supporting teams
- Feeding upwards communication from employees
- Identifying gaps in training and development
- Demonstrating · cultural understanding and facilitating integration.

Typically, successful integration strategies focus on three or four key themes which represent the core of integration and reflect a shared image of how the organization will look on completion of the change. They create a sense of ownership for the change in the acquired business, especially at middle and first line management levels. They reflect a clear direction from the purchaser and a gap analysis of where the organizations are now and how the combined organization is intended to be. Conflict resolution should be based on market need, rather than internal politics and should focus on cultural and operational practices.

The end-game of a successful integration is an organization that is capable of achieving more ambitious business targets in the changing marketplace. This means that the integrated organization needs to be capable of further change, be staffed by skilled and motivated individuals who are flexible and committed. Few mergers achieve this higher order of success, largely because top management have taken their eye off the ball and failed to supply the type of leadership needed.

The role of top management in leading mergers

Top managers have a key role to play in achieving merger success, but this involves far more than pulling off a useful deal then moving on to the next project. It involves leading the organization consistently towards developing the business potential of the combined organization. Executives need to take the longer-term end-game into account from the very start of the process, during negotiations with potential partners. To be able really to gauge the bigger potential of a possible merger, it is very helpful if management teams are able to get to know each other and understand each other's position, preferably before news of talks leaks to the press. From these early discussions, the business logic will arise.

Then it is important for top managers to find out the important issues in managing the merger – where there are similarities and differences of approach which could cause friction. Top managers then have to identify who will carry out the research work involved in assessing the opportunity. They then need to assign responsibilities for carrying out transition planning of the key building blocks which will move the organization to where it will want to be. This requires top management to be very clear what the end point (success) looks like, rather than simply seeking to integrate business systems in the shortest time possible.

However, once the deal is done, top managers have both a structural role (i.e. sponsoring work streams and ensuring that the change projects are going to plan) and a cultural role (i.e. using their symbolic influence to reinforce the new cultural practices which will underpin the business strategy). Lack of unity in the senior management team will cause divisions to occur in the new organization before it has even formed as an entity. Top managers must therefore walk the talk on the agreed new values if they expect other people to follow their example. Managers should also be rigorous in policing new systems and practices to ensure that they reflect the desired culture. Reward processes in particular carry special significance as they reinforce what an organization really values more powerfully than a manager's words.

What needs to be managed to build the new organization – from planning to end year one?

To realize the business potential of a merger, it is helpful to operate according to some tried and tested principles for integration success:

Guiding principles

- Set high aspirations – go for realizing the full potential of the merger
- Focus on value creation, not just integration
- Identify possible synergies and build commitment to capture them
- Protect current business momentum and customer service
- Capitalize on the change opportunity to achieve a high performing new company
- Identify the cultural/organizational challenges up-front and design a process to address them
- Involve top performers in leading the integration, with a bias toward line managers
- Aim for excellence, even at the expense of equity
- Go for the speedy solution, not just the 100 per cent solution
- You cannot over-communicate.

Key activities

Pulling together the key areas of activity which will be considered in more detail in later chapters of this book, it is important to focus on:

- Business strategy integration
  - Build relations
  - Understand the potential for synergy
  - Develop a strategy for enhancing business value from the merger

- Develop success criteria
- Clarify the non-negotiables, expectations and differences
- Identify problems caused by non-negotiables and expectations
- Identify how these problems can be resolved
- Feed problem resolution into project plans for integration
- Develop measurement and feedback processes, such as an integration scorecard to track and report key operational, financial, customer and organizational issues most subject to merger-related disruption and risk
- Clarify executive leadership roles and responsibilities, including carrying out initial strategic planning and ensuring that integration issues are considered during initial deal making
- Carry out due diligence
- Do the deal
- Develop the overall communications strategy and ensure fast two-way flow of facts and perceptions
- Keep business going as usual

- Managing the planning and implementation process

  - Create transition management teams, task force roles and responsibilities
  - Integration planning and implementation – develop transition management goals, structure and plan
  - Project management; consolidate the project plan and link all efforts to specific milestones and accountabilities to ensure continued focus on timely completion of tasks
  - Gain top management leadership and sponsorship of plan
  - Gain line management implementation and commitment
  - Create communication strategies for specific stakeholders, especially customers and employees
  - Establish and coordinate a consistent process for all functions
  - Monitor and report progress
  - Create review processes which spread the learning

- Building a culture which supports the business strategy

  - Audit current cultural practices in both organizations
  - Decide how people need to operate to achieve business aims
  - Focus on building a high performing organization
  - Identify appropriate values and behaviours
  - Align all people policies and processes to support more directly the new organization's business objectives and to

reinforce quickly the new organization's culture by driving employee behaviour toward key objectives
- Develop effective performance management
- Develop a structured approach to clarify key management processes that establish how we will choose and reinforce appropriate practices
- Maintain top level commitment to new cultural practices

- Structuring the organization

  - Design the organization to enable appropriate high perform-ance work processes. Develop process for appointments and exits which is as transparent as possible
  - Communicate structure and staffing
  - Re-recruit; develop a specific policy and process to identify key talent and gain their commitment to stay
  - Clarify roles and responsibilities
  - Provide training as required

- Making sure you have the right people in the right jobs and retaining them

  - Carry out people skills and attitude audits
  - Identify key employees and developing specific retention tactics
  - Match jobs and individuals appropriately in the shortest time possible
  - Build the employee value proposition

- Integrating systems effectively

  - Analyse systems to cover all critical areas including manage-ment information and people management systems
  - Identify which approaches are most appropriate or whether new approaches are needed
  - Evaluate success according to scorecard measures
    Embed learning in the organization.

Setting sail for the Golden Fleece

Why is it that with the equivalent of satellite guidance systems, modern-day Jasons on the acquisition trail tend to end up using the equivalent of a compass and a sextant to help them lead their merger to success? The real issue is one of having a fixed recipe for success on the one hand and inexperience on the other. Fixed recipes occur when managers become blinded to the specific nature of any one acquisition and focus on their own approach, such as getting the 100-day plan completed in 60 days, regardless of whether this is the most appropriate route. Managers need to be sensitive to the issues they encounter and flexible up to a point.

Inexperience is an issue because mergers are not a regular occurrence for most managers and they therefore have little chance to learn from their mistakes. Typically, only a small number of people are involved in the early stages and their learning is usually kept within the group. To make matters worse, the people involved in deal-making or managing the transition period usually increase their own market value to the point that they are head-hunted by other companies. Their knowledge and experience is then lost.

What helps is when organizations learn from their own experience – what works and what does not. CGNU is one organization that has attempted to do this by having its transition decision-making documented as well as the impact of those decisions on the people affected. They aim to take this learning into account in the future. Similarly, UBS Warburg, Whitbread plc and others who learn from their experience concentrate on making sure that their own formula for success is constantly refined and that learning is shared beyond a small core team.

The rest of this book explores different aspects of the mechanics of a merger, but also focuses on how you can build the intangibles which will ensure that your merger is a success. Happy sailing!

Checklist

What needs to be managed to achieve a successful merger?

Strategy – understand the potential for synergy • • •

1 Market area – what do we see as our market area, e.g. customer service and what is theirs? What behaviours support these areas, e.g. teamwork, collaboration, win-win?
2 Product orientation – what are our different approaches to product, e.g. emphasis on unique products, price premiums? What behaviours are relevant, e.g. innovation, knowledge, problem-solving?
3 Cost orientation – how do we and they approach this, e.g. low operational costs, cash flow? What behaviours are useful, e.g. stability, accuracy?

4 Volume orientation, e.g. bigger market share, better unit costs? What behaviours support these, e.g. growth, control, speed, aggressiveness, competition?

5 Market – how do we let them keep team-work and win-win and get them to grow more?

6 Product – how do we let them sustain innovation and creativity?

7 Cost – how do we protect their cost structure and get them to take more risks?

8 Volume – how do we let them be aggressive and competitive and be part of our team?

Acquisition integration – the process • • •

1 Do we understand the market environment of the purchaser and the acquired company?

2 Do we understand our own cultural norms and those of the other company?

3 Have we identified inconsistencies and opportunities?

4 Have we identified key issues for accelerating the integration?

5 Have we developed a plan for change?

6 Have we identified stakeholders in leadership and functional positions to champion the plan?

References

1 Pretzlik, C. and Lewis, W. (2000): Cross-Atlantic consolidation gains pace, *Financial Times,* June 30

2 New Frontiers for the mega-deal; *Investment Dealers Digest, Sept–Oct,* (1995): no. 2, p. 69

3 Rivlin, R. (2000): The UK mergers and acquisitions market. In *Managing mergers and acquisitions,* IBM Global Services and CBI Guide

4 Hall, P. and Norburn, D. (1987): The management factor in acquisition performance, *Leadership and Organisation Development Journal,* no. 8

5 SKF, Monsanto and UBS Warburg processes featured in Garrow, V. and Holbeche, L. (2001): *Effective mergers and acquisitions,* Roffey Park Institute

6 Shrivastava, P. (1986): Postmerger integration, *Journal of Business Strategy,* no. 7, pp. 65–76

7 Devine, M., Hirsh, W., Garrow, V. and Holbeche, L. (1999): *Mergers and acquisitions: getting the people bit right,* Roffey Park Institute

CHAPTER 2

The human and organizational aspects of change

The night after their departure, Jason and the Argonauts were driven back by a storm again on the coast of Cyzicum, and the inhabitants, supposing them to be enemies, furiously attacked them

In the first chapter we looked at some of the strategic reasons why mergers fail. This is well-trodden ground for many researchers. However, economic factors alone do not explain or help predict why some mergers will succeed while others will fail. In this chapter we will look at the much less well-explored factors – the human aspects of mergers. The four essential organizational components are the people, systems, organization and culture. We shall be looking in later chapters at how to integrate systems, organization and culture. In this chapter we will look at typical employee reactions during mergers and at what you might expect to happen when two organizational cultures meet.

Given that the human aspects of mergers are increasingly considered as the main cause of merger failure, it is perhaps surprising that executives generally put a great deal more interest and energy into pursuing the deal than into managing the transition towards the new organization. Management teams often fail to carry out any form of pre-planning for human resource issues. Yet, important though the pre-acquisition phase is, 'the real value potentially realized through the acquisition is created by management of the newly emerging organization after the act of buying it'.[1]

Mergers and acquisitions are often highly stressful for all concerned. Why should this be so when surely by now people are used to change? After all, some sort of change has become part of the background noise of working life. Though seemingly momentous at the time, restructurings, 'rightsizings' and new working practices, have all been absorbed by employees who have been in the workplace during the past decade. After a while, they just become the new 'way we do things around here'.

Yet mergers represent something different. They feel more like a step change rather than just a variation on a theme. Just as people who have experienced a mild earthquake do not take the earth's solidity for granted any more, so people who have experienced mergers, or anticipate doing so, expect what is familiar to disappear, only to be replaced by uncertainty.

Indeed, perhaps the only thing you can guarantee in a merger is uncertainty. While some people cope well with this, others don't.

Takeovers, and takeover rumours, have an effect on job satisfaction and security. Changes in ownership usually lead to a decrease in the number of employees as departments are consolidated. Analysts usually expect the results of savings on jobs to be percolating through to the share price within the first quarter, increasing the pressure on executives to 'slash and burn' with regard to jobs. Staff know, or fear this. Some people are not prepared to wait and see and managers can experience real difficulties in persuading key staff to stay.

The unpredictability of mergers

Mergers are inherently unpredictable. That does not mean that they cannot be managed, but that the range of issues that has to be managed is vast and the sheer scale of the task is often underestimated. Here are a few of the factors which make mergers the joker in the pack.

Every merger is different

Mergers vary on a number of factors, ranging from the business rationale behind them to the people involved in making them happen. Strategies refined over time may suddenly backfire if market conditions change or if the two organizations' cultures are difficult to integrate. Even employees who have experienced many mergers find it difficult to predict how things will turn out. Partly because of this, they will look back to previous mergers, especially those that have gone wrong and fear the worst. More to the point, they will share their scare stories with their colleagues. This happens when the earliest news about the merger leaks out, often unintentionally. Even when people understand the company's strategy and the intention behind the merger, the fact that there is typically little formal communication coming from top management allows the gossip factory to work overtime.

Relative sizes of partners

While it is generally assumed that larger, more successful companies acquire smaller, less successful companies, this is not always the case. When one large UK DIY chain was acquired by a smaller, relative newcomer to the field, the first thing many employees of the acquired company knew about it was when staff from the acquiring company turned up to measure the shelves prior to rebadging. Staff in the large chain had a great deal of difficulty coming to terms with the fact that their seemingly successful company had been swallowed up by an inexperienced minnow, as they saw it.

For staff in smaller companies that are taken over by larger ones there are upsides and downsides. A typical complaint is that staff feel less involved in the new company than in the old. In the world of publishing for instance, global consolidation means that small publishing companies are acquired by major corporations whose CEO may have no interest in, or knowledge of, the publishing business. Employees cease to feel that they have a stake in their company and turnover of staff usually increases. Conversely, many employees of small companies welcome the opportunities that being taken over by a larger company offers. Assuming that they survive the job cull, individuals may have more career routes and developmental experiences available to them than would otherwise have been the case.

Whether the merger is hostile or sought

While it might be expected that staff in the acquired company would expect the worst if the merger is hostile, this is not always the case. In a number of recently acquired organizations we studied in the late 1990s, staff were relieved that their own management would probably soon be replaced by what they considered to be more successful managers. Even when a company puts itself up for acquisition, staff may understand the rationale but still not welcome being merged with another company.

Similarly, staff in the acquiring company may consider that life will go on much as before, since their company is in control. In practice, most employees in both companies are likely to be affected sooner or later by the integration and staff may not always be prepared for the change.

Staff views

Another unpredictable element of mergers is the way in which individual employees will react. In one merger in a remote corner of south-east England, rationalization of clerical functions meant that large numbers of employees from an acquired company were made redundant. The company recognized that other employment opportunities were thin on the ground in the locality and made generous redundancy payments. While employees were not pleased initially to be losing their jobs, they were delighted when, by happy coincidence, another major company was opening a new facility in the same location and employed almost all of the redundant staff within three months on better terms than their previous employer.

But some features are common. . .

While mergers are inherently unpredictable, there are a number of features that are common to all mergers. Mergers are both structural/mechanical and personal/cultural. The structural elements include business strategies, communication strategies, the organizational structure, managing appointments and exits, integrating terms and conditions and managing performance. These are the aspects of mergers which tend to receive management attention. The personal/cultural aspects involve assessing the psychological and cultural impact of the structural shifts. These aspects usually receive relatively little management attention yet both aspects of any merger need to be taken into account if the merger is to be a success.

Stress

Stress is a characteristic of all mergers because of the sheer volume and pace of change involved. Research by Angwin[2] shows that 40 per cent of all change takes place in the first two months of an M&A. Over half of this change is immediate. Thereafter, change continues at a high but rapidly declining level for the remainder of the first six months. By the end of the third quarter of the first year, over 80 per cent of all changes have taken place. Stress among executives during negotiations can adversely affect negotiating and decision making.

While many employees cope badly with stress, others seem to cope well. These are very often the more mobile managers who are aware of having options. Having experienced major change elsewhere also seems to equip people to cope well with the potential role ambiguity and confusion, which are typical of the early stages of mergers.

Mergers are also considered to be stressful because they upset in a fairly fundamental way the so-called 'psychological contract', or unwritten expectations and reactions which develop over time between organizations and their members. Since key tenets of this contract include job security in exchange for loyalty and promotion in exchange for high performance, mergers can cause strong feelings of dissatisfaction and disenchantment among employees since the basis of this unspoken agreement is up in the air. Even 'high flyers' are left wondering how their career will progress when they have to prove their worth again in the new organizational context.

There are few models or diagnostic tools available to help predict when and how employees will react. Ivancevich and his colleagues[3] suggest that individuals will classify an event as stressful if it seems to have the potential to be personally harmful. The degree of stress experienced will also be affected by three factors:

- The degree of uncertainty over when an event will occur
- The duration of the stressful event
- The imminence of the event.

Typically people are concerned first and foremost about their own job security, relocation and the potential family repercussions, then about possible changes in role and status and the way in which their colleagues and the organizational culture will be affected. Concerns change over time. Senior managers, for instance, are usually the first to know whether or not they will have a job. They then start to be concerned about what working in the new organization will be like. Marks[4], one of the leading researchers in the field, shows how employees in M&As often pass through four distinct stages:

- Disbelief and denial
- Anger
- Emotional bargaining, ending in depression
- Acceptance.

Marks and Mirvis[5] urge companies to be on the alert for 'survivor sickness', where survivors settle into three different types of mindsets which can become counter-productive. For example, some employees are the 'ready'; they have achieved the hoped for job change or promotion and are full of energy and enthusiasm. They can however be overly aggressive and act superior. The 'wanting' are the survivors who did not receive the job they wanted or were demoted. They may adjust, or they might become angry and depressed. The 'wrung out' have the same job, but their work environment has changed. Some may work through their frustration at the similarities and differences of their work life; others may become demotivated and lack purpose and direction.

Psychological shockwaves

Mergers offer another layer of complexity in understanding what people might be experiencing. Mergers have clear and distinct phases (the run-up, transition and longer-term integration). Each phase has specific requirements and usually involves different groups of people. Like other forms of major change, mergers have a large number of interdependent components to them. However, these components affect different people at different times, triggering multiple waves of change for the organization and for individuals (Figure 2.1).

These psychological shock waves run through the organization, resulting in a climate of ambiguity, weakening trust levels and provoking greater efforts towards self-preservation. They begin pre-acquisition when speculation starts in the absence of hard fact. People fantasize about worst case scenarios and start seeing themselves as potential 'victors' or 'victims' in the period of meltdown which is about to begin.

As previously stated, mergers provide unprecedented opportunities to bring about change because people are expecting it. What tends to happen is that the opportunity to build on people's readiness for change is not seized. Long gaps occur between events. Executives in both companies tend to put off final

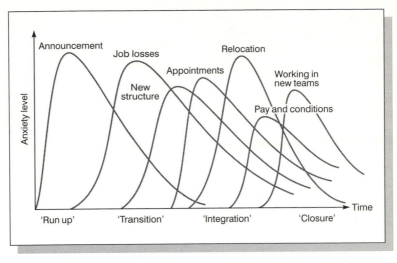

Figure 2.1 Typical emotional waves

decisions because they are so difficult and painful, causing greater uncertainty and stress for everyone concerned. While for some people change is almost immediate, for others there can be a gap of months or even years before they are affected by the merger. Typically, head office jobs are affected much earlier than those of people working in the field. Other staff get bored with waiting and revert to some form of 'business as usual'. By the time field staff are affected, managers have moved on in their thinking and often fail to connect with staff in the most effective way.

The waiting period between announcement and completion can be extremely stressful and, if unmanaged, can adversely affect employee reactions to the event. Marks argues that many deals go astray during this period because the people issues are ignored. This waiting period is the 'Achilles heel' because employee attitudes can surge, depressing productivity and motivation and causing lasting damage to the emerging business. Marks supplies the following warning signs:

- Preoccupation and worthless speculation about the changeover
- Stress reactions, including fear and aggressiveness
- Crisis management
- Constricted communication
- Superior versus inferior – with the acquired company asserting that they are superior

- Winners versus losers – with employees deciding who, including themselves, is in each camp.

Post-acquisition, the psychological shock waves relate to practical concerns, such as securing a job and the resources to do it. People often focus on self-preservation and there can be power struggles as people try to position themselves in the new company. The atmosphere of distrust and deteriorating communications leads to poor productivity, dissatisfied customers and staff turnover as people 'bail out'. If this climate is allowed to run unchecked, a dangerous combination of increased parochialism, less team play and reduced commitment to corporate goals can damage business performance.

Managers who may be under severe stress themselves may not be able to deal with the people issues. There is typically a high rate of turnover among managers, particularly from the acquired company. The combination of uncertainty, the perception that they are 'losers' and culture shock are all contributory factors. The problem is that employees' concerns rise rather than fall when managers are unable to handle implementation issues because of their own stress levels.

What increases uncertainty

Lack of communication

What makes matters worse is the absence of any meaningful information. Usually there are the inevitable rumours, counter-rumours and secret management meetings. Then comes the news: the logic of the deal is outlined, with assurances over the future. In the messages to staff, the terminology used describes the 'what', 'why' and the benefits of the merger. What typical communications fail to address are the things people really want to know, such as, 'Will I have a job? Will I lose out in the career stakes? Who will I be working with? Will I have to move house? What will the terms and conditions look like?'

While it is a truism that you cannot over-communicate, finding something meaningful to communicate before things have been agreed is difficult. As one MD put it, 'Staff wanted information from me the whole time, but I had to find a balance, because it's not worth building up people's hopes and dashing them again every day'. Some attempt must be made to address these so-called 'me factors' early in the game if staff morale is not to be unduly damaged.

However, false promises can be lethal. One MD carried out the usual roadshow, meeting staff in both companies on the day of the announcement. He assured them that the merger was bringing together two companies well-known for different forms of excellence and that the future for the new company looked bright. He implied that there would be great opportunities ahead for staff of the new company. When asked directly whether jobs would go he avoided the mistake of saying 'no', but did say that he would get back to people within six weeks with news of the new structure. Employees were prepared to go along with this. As things turned out, the process of creating the new structure took a lot longer than intended. Underestimating the importance that staff attached to the six week announcement deadline, the MD remained silent, assuming that he had bought time through his presentation. When the silence continued, many key staff decided that the time had come to find a job working elsewhere for someone whose word could be relied on.

Communication strategies are explored in Chapter 8.

Degree and speed of real integration

The degree of integration usually reflects the philosophy and practice of the acquirer, rather than any logical process of identifying what is required to achieve the business strategy. So, if you are a fast food retailer with several different brands competing on the high street, you would logically prefer each brand to operate as a separate company, with integration only being necessary at management level and in the management information and financial reporting systems. Conversely, if you are aiming to acquire market share by taking over a competitor, you may prefer to assimilate the other company at all levels so that a new brand identity is developed consistently across the entire operation. Even this may not be the most appropriate approach. Received wisdom generally dictates that the less integration is required the better, unless there is a genuine attempt to build to the strengths of both companies.

There are four commonly recognized approaches to integration:

- Limited integration, where both companies are integrated only at the level of the holding company. This tends to have little effect on the staff in both companies apart from senior management. There is usually little interaction between the companies for practical business or organizational purposes, such as staff deployment.

- Assimilation by the dominant company, where the acquired company all but disappears and where the acquiring company controls all significant decision-making. This tends to have significant impact on acquired employees, especially senior managers who are usually among the first to lose their jobs. Where the company has been acquired for its plant, manufacturing or other capability which does not rely exclusively on the human asset, assimilation can be a means of ensuring consistency.

- Mutual 'Best of Both', where there is a genuine attempt to forge an integrated new company on the basis of a fair allocation of jobs, working practices etc. While laudable in many ways, the attempt at fairness can lead to odd choices being made at a critical time for the new business. Such an approach can backfire if staff see apparently incompetent colleagues being rewarded with jobs purely to make up equal numbers.

- Integrated new company, where a more strategic approach has been taken to creating the new combined business. In this case, the aim is to build in the best practices of both companies, alongside external good practice, in an attempt to design an organization capable of delivering the company's business plan. This approach tends to be the most productive if the business plan is clear and employees are involved in identifying the practices best suited to the new organization.

The speed with which integration takes place can also cause uncertainty to increase. Companies that have developed skills in M&As generally recommend integrating all the relevant structures, systems and processes in the shortest time possible so as to get the new organization up and running, to refocus staff on the business and to reduce uncertainty. During mergers, people are expecting change. When decisions are slow to materialize, people's willingness to change may be lessened.

Process of deployment

Speed is an important element of the process of making appointments. If people are left guessing about which job, if any, will be theirs, they are likely to adopt 'pleasing' behaviours if they want to stay, or look elsewhere while remaining on the payroll for the time it takes them to find a job. On the other hand, too much speed can backfire. If structures are announced 'out of the blue', before people feel that they have been able to influence the process, people who feel they have missed out on a key opportunity generally nurse a sense of grievance.

Of course, the process of deployment is never perfect. Typically, senior managers in the acquired company are offered packages, while those who remain are used to steady the nerves of the 'troops' before they too are moved sideways or out. Staff watch the appointment process very carefully, studying who gets which job as a means of calculating their own chances. When few senior managers in the acquired company survive, other employees tend to draw the worst conclusions about their own chances.

Deployment is usually damaged by two main factors – politics and lack of information. Typically, the process is never 'fair' but must be seen to be equitable and as transparent as possible. Policies vary, ranging from keeping people in 'guaranteed' positions, slotting people into vacant positions, having all or most people apply for any position, including their own. None of these is a panacea.

When managers are making deployment decisions, there is usually a chronic shortage of relevant information about individuals. This is generally because records have not been kept, or are not available or trusted. HR managers from the acquired company are rarely involved in the process and are often considered to be part of the problem. Consequently, more often than not decisions are taken on the grounds of expediency. Some companies use external consultants to carry out assessments of staff. While this can appear to increase the integrity of the process, the failure to take into account people's work record to date causes resentment among those who have been doing a perfectly satisfactory job for years but who fail the assessor's numeracy test.

The cost of uncertainty

Why should any of this matter? The reality is that takeover rumours, whether substantiated or not, can be damaging to both employees and companies. Productivity slumps as people spend time worrying about how things will develop and whether or not they will have a job. Resources promised for projects prior to merger talks are suspended pending the outcome of the transaction. Empty posts do not get filled as they will be needed for incoming staff from the acquired company. Everyone becomes overloaded. Perception of staff is everything. If the incoming organization does not have a good reputation, anxiety will be that much greater.

Burying our babies

Ongoing uncertainty can also damage the very asset that the acquirer is buying. When one major pharmaceutical company acquired another in the early 1990s, a great asset of the acquired company to the purchaser was the range and innovation of products being researched. When the takeover took place, staff in the acquired company had to wait several months in some cases before they knew whether or not they would have a job and what sort of job. The acquiring company's managers were puzzled why, during this period, many of the promised projects failed to materialize. Acquired staff described this as 'burying our babies' – keeping their best projects to themselves in case they jumped ship and needed something to offer to new employers.

Similarly, when publisher Dorling Kindersley stated that it would consider takeover offers in the aftermath of a major commercial disaster, the atmosphere at the publisher became tense and nervous. 'Everyone, especially the management, was worried about being merged with another publisher and losing their jobs' said a DK editorial employee. 'A lot of people spent their time speculating about what was going to happen and writing their CVs. Books were being pulled everywhere'. As Richard Carr, former managing director of Letts Educational put it, 'there's a danger that large organizations, in buying these businesses, will lose the very thing that keeps them going, which is the flair and imaginative approach to creating products. Contrary to expectations, you don't necessarily end up with the thing you thought you were originally buying'.[6]

So what can be done to manage the psychological aspects of mergers?

First and foremost, managers need to recognize and acknowledge the potentially traumatic nature of M&As. This leads on to finding ways to manage uncertainty and help employees develop realistic expectations of the changes in store. Monitoring employee reactions through various forms of employee survey can help pinpoint areas where specific support will be needed.

Marks[4] argues that companies must devise a detailed communication programme for this interim period to help alleviate the 'merger shock'. This can include detailed and widespread communication to managers and a consistent approach to announcing the details of the deal to employees; regular and simultaneous updates; honest communication; CEO roadshows; group meetings and 'merger rap' sessions where employees can meet together to discuss questions and concerns. Real communication is needed and for much longer than is usually thought necessary. We shall be looking at communication plans in Chapter 8 and how line managers can help manage the people issues, despite their own stress, in Chapter 12.

Mergers need to be managed as a project with clear responsibilities, planning and timeframes step by step. Their multiple strands – structural/mechanical and personal/cultural – and their interconnections need to be understood and well coordinated. This means not only handling the short-term transition and integration issues (Chapters 5, 6 and 7) but the longer-term development of an organization capable of delivering the new business strategy (Chapter 13). Plans need to encompass:

- Creating a new organization
- Skill transfer and teamworking
- Leading others through change.

The appointments process should be as transparent and fair as possible. What is usually not taken fully into account when resourcing an organization is the future direction of the new business. Posts should be filled on the basis of what the new organization needs rather than who is available. People who are high performers should be rewarded with exciting opportunities and given recognition when they start to produce the behaviours and outputs required. Good quality appointments do matter and they are hard to undo.

Individual transitions need to be well handled and staff need to be allowed to deal with their sense of bereavement – for departing colleagues and the changing organization. Watch out for serious casualties, providing employee counselling if necessary. Every aspect of how people are treated during a merger is noted by employees and has consequences for what will follow. The way the people issues are handled will determine whether trust is destroyed, or built anew.

From the acquired perspective

Most writing about merger management is written from the perspective of the acquirer. Relatively little has been written about maximizing the value of the merger from the standpoint of being acquired. Yet for the merger to work effectively, the integration of the two organizations should not be carried out as if one organization simply imposes its will and its ways on another. The most successful mergers are where both companies move beyond aggressive/passive modes and proactively seek to shape a common future, even if one company is being assimilated by the other. This calls for special skills and attitudes in those being acquired.

First, it is important for employees and managers in the acquired company not to let hurt feelings and bruised egos sour their relationship with the acquirer. Of course this can be very hard to achieve if the acquirer acts arrogantly and ineptly and appears to ignore all attempts to share information and influence the process. For the top management group in particular, this can be challenging as they will have been exposed to the acquirer team for longer than the rest of the organization. They are also likely to be most vulnerable to job loss. They should ensure as much as possible that they are handing on a legacy of success and avoid letting their own feelings depress colleagues. Senior managers more than others need to be generous in accepting the power shift and recognize that a new process of power distribution will take place. They may need to perfect the art of compromise and prove themselves in the new organization before regaining some of the power which they may have lost.

Top managers will be watched by the rest of the acquired organization for clues about how they should feel about being acquired. They therefore should embrace the acquisition, focus on the positive, on what can be achieved and on the potential synergies and benefits of the merger. Managers need to embrace new cultural practices, management styles and systems. While this can add to their burdens, learning to work in new ways can be a springboard to further development and increase an individual's ability to cope with change and lead others through change. Ideally, then, requirements for change should be seen as an opportunity to develop flexibility and to enhance personal development.

Managers will need to appreciate what the acquirer is trying to achieve and help the rest of the organization to adjust. They will need to be willing and able to take on additional workloads, particularly during the transition period, to help the new organization to start functioning as a combined entity while keeping business operating as usual from the point of view of customers and suppliers.

As the Roffey Park studies of effective mergers found, the position of 'winners' and 'losers' in the merger stakes is not fixed permanently and can change. Mergers often provide many opportunities for development. For some people who may have felt blocked in their old organization, mergers can enable them to reposition themselves in the new company. The challenge for people working in the acquired company is to ensure that they find ways to survive and thrive in the new environment. Some people are astute at quickly working out who are the real levers of influence in the new organization and they seek to build relationships and visibility with these people. Volunteering for task forces and other cross-functional activity is a good way to learn how things are evolving in the new organization and to have a part in shaping the future while building relationships with counterparts from the other organization. To some extent, the 'who dares, wins' approach carries the day.

Cultural issues

An organization's corporate culture consists of its management style and the underlying values and beliefs that guide the behaviours of managers and people within an organization. Mergers bring together organizations whose cultures are inevitably different. This is known to produce stress in employees but in itself may not seem serious. Interest in corporate culture has grown rapidly over the years for a variety of reasons. The link between culture and performance was brought to the forefront in the 1980s by well-known writers such as Peters and Waterman.[7] Their main contention was that culture – the values, assumptions and customary ways of doing things in an organization – has a major impact on business performance.

The question of why many M&As fail and others succeed has led researchers to scrutinize the role of culture and its ability to help give meaning and stability to organizations. This ability to give stability can, they suggest, become a problem during mergers. Effective cultures normally preserve relationships and behavioural patterns. They act as a well-insulated defence against uncertainty and ambiguity by providing a set of assumptions and expectations about the working world. Culture becomes an organizational glue, helping to integrate and socialize many different individuals. This means that organizational cultures are often notoriously resistant to change. A merger or acquisition may therefore lead to two organizations fiercely protecting their traditions and way of doing things.

Understanding cultures

Business leaders need to make sense of their own cultures before they can begin the task of integration. There are many different models for diagnosing cultures. Culture can be manifested at a variety of levels. Differences in approach can be audited through checklists such as the following by Mark Thomas[8] which focuses on people management systems:

Consider the classic functional areas:

- Management development
- Training
- Appraisal
- Reward
- Recruitment
- Manpower planning
- Communications
- Organization development

Then analyse how each organization approaches each of these functional areas along the following dimensions:

Fragmented	Integrated
Organization led	Business led
Rigid	Flexible
Punitive	Supportive
Feedback	No feedback
Early warning	Reactive
Short-term	Long-term
Closed procedures	Open procedures
Personnel owned	Line owned
Complex	Simple
Communicated	Secret
Challenged	Inviolate
Common schedule	Segmented approach

Finding out how the corporate cultures differ allows you to identify potential 'hot spots' which must be managed in order to avoid unhelpful culture clashes.

Culture clash

To many observers, one of the main causes of merger failure is thought to be the cultural clashes between the two former organizations. Even the most optimistic estimate (by Walter[9]) suggests that cultural disturbances account for up to 30 per cent in lost performance.

While it is often thought that cultures that are similar will combine more easily, it seems that collaborative, complementary cultures are easier to combine. This is where the merging companies have different shared meanings but these meanings provide each firm with something valuable that was missing previously, such as know-how or direction. Symptoms of culture clash include a 'them versus us' attitude, glorifying the former organization, 'hanging on' to the old company name, rubbishing the newcomers. Other symptoms include political in-fighting and a failure to achieve synergy in any part of the organization.

If the merger is intended to produce a new organization with its own culture, there are a number of common errors which can seriously set the process back and should be avoided. The first is to kill off one culture by imposing one culture over another, with no attempt to incorporate some of the practices of the acquired company. This approach usually triggers a wave of departures, mostly of the best people. The next major error is to go too slowly because of over-sensitivity to differences. There is a desire to do things 100 per cent right, which is not always possible in a merger context. (Jack Welch suggests that the 70:30 rule applies to M&As.) The usual consequence is that issues are avoided, things are done too little, too late and frustration can trigger other departures. The third major error is to allow differences to persist with no real attempt to achieve synergy where this is possible. This usually reflects lack of top management team unity and corporate responsibility, as well as 'silo' mentality. The process of creating a new organizational culture will be explored in Chapter 10.

Towards the brave new world

In moving the new organization towards achieving its business and cultural goals, managers will need to stop relying exclusively on formal mechanisms for organizational integration – structures, hierarchies, systems – and focus equally on the lateral integrating mechanisms – teams, project groups, networks – which promote appropriate attitudes and behaviour. They will need to address the following key operational and people issues:

- Planning the post-acquisition implementation
- Communicating intentions
- Integrating management and systems (formal and informal)
- Managing morale issues
- Retaining key individuals
- Resourcing the new organization
- Rationalizing the old organizations(s)
- Reward and incentives
- Managing the corporate culture
- Developing the corporate identity
- Ensuring that customers are happy.

In doing so, it is useful to develop a set of operating principles. Some of the most helpful are as follows:

- Plan for what you can predict on the culture/people front, as early as possible
- Identify synergies and build energy and momentum to make them happen
- Set high aspirations for the new company and strive for excellence
- Fill key posts with top performers who will act as role models
- You cannot over-communicate
- Make and implement the best decisions you can in the time available.

Our studies of a wide range of mergers, both UK-based and international, suggest that the people issues are generally the key determinant of success or failure. The need for rapid short-term decision making when forging two organizations together is understandable, but so often this is used as an excuse for a lack of foresight about how to avoid the potential loss of key talent. The way the people issues are handled to some extent teaches people what to expect in the new organization. Getting round to dealing well with people once the dust has settled is almost always too late. Yes, tough decisions have to be made, but people need at least to understand why and to be treated fairly. This is where visible leadership is called for, so that people have at least the chance to share their views. If people sense your good intentions, they will often give you the benefit of the doubt for a time before you are able to deliver something which gives them a positive feel for the future.

References

1 Deiser, R. (1994): Post-acquisition management: a process of strategic and organisational learning. In Von Krogh, G., Sinatra, A., Singh, A (eds): *Management of Corporate Acquisitions*, Macmillan Press
2 Angwin, D. (1996): *The dynamics of post-acquisition management*, Warwick Business School, January
3 Ivancevich, J., Schweiger, D. and Power, F. (1987): Strategies for managing human resources during mergers and acquisitions, *Human Resource Planning*, **10**, no. 1
4 Marks, M. (1991): Combating merger shock before the deal is closed, *Mergers and Acquisitions*, Jan/Feb

5 Marks, M. and Mirvis, P. (1992): Re-building after the merger: dealing with survivor sickness, *Organisational Dynamics*, Autumn

6 Ricketts, J. (2000): Mere pawns in the game, *The Bookseller*, 25 Feb

7 Peters, T. and Waterman, R. (1982): *Corporate cultures*, Addison-Wesley, Reading, Mass

8 Thomas, M. (1994): *Mergers and Acquisitions – Confronting the Organisation and People Issues*, Hawksmere

9 Walter, G. (1985): Culture collisions in mergers and acquisitions. In Frost P. *et al.* (eds), *Organisational Culture*, Sage Publications, California

Part Two

Starting the search – prospecting and evaluation

This famous expedition has been celebrated in the ancient ages of the world

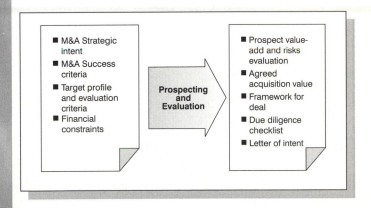

Introduction

If mergers and acquisitions can be thought of as marriages, then the prospecting and evaluation phase is the courtship period of the relationship. During the courtship, both parties need to get to know each other and to evaluate each other against their own needs and expectations. This chapter looks at the important considerations in seeking out a partner and evaluating them as a future M&A partner.

Clarifying the acquisition strategy

A successful courtship will depend on the acquirer having a clear view of their acquisition strategy and intent. The acquisition strategy must provide a context for focused prospecting and for sound evaluation of any prospects that emerge. The important elements of the acquisition strategy to support effective prospecting and evaluation are:

The business intent of any acquisition

The expected strategic business benefits of any acquisition must be quantified as precisely as possible. This may be in terms of improving market position, improved operating performance or entry into new markets. Once the business benefits are clear, criteria can be defined to determine overall success of the acquisition strategy.

The business returns expected from any acquisition

The acquisition needs to be justified on a straightforward return on investment basis. The acquisition costs, including the purchase costs, administrative costs and the integration costs, need to be looked at in relation to the return that is expected. It is a good discipline to go through the exercise, to quantify how any acquisition will be measured in terms of increased shareholder value and over what timeframe.

Target profile and evaluation criteria

Once the rationale for any acquisition is clear and the success criteria agreed, it is possible to determine the likely profile of any prospect. This may cover areas such as marketplace, offerings, customer profile, market position, sales growth and profitability. It may also include an organizational profile covering management style and competency, number of employees and their competencies, or organization culture. This profile will focus in on the key business and organization aspects that underpin the acquisition intent and expected returns. Establishing the criteria by which each acquisition will be evaluated will provide a practical and objective framework for evaluation.

Investment funding amounts and sources

The other influence on the prospecting and evaluation activities is the funding available for investments in mergers and acquisitions and their associated administration and integration costs. There will be some constraints on the amount and types of funds available, whether in the form of cash or shares.

In practice, the timing and initiation of contact with prospects is not always under the control of the acquirer. It may be that the initial contact is led by a company seeking to be acquired or that it simply emerges from other chance or trading encounters. In such situations, it is wise to take time out to flush out the basic strategic plan elements, prior to progressing too far down the merger or acquisition road.

Support from the board for the acquisition strategy needs to be secured at an early stage. Once the pressure and momentum of working with prospects gets under way, there may be little time or opportunity to backtrack to clarify or regain consensus on such fundamental issues. The up front involvement and commitment of key board members is essential. The nature of their involvement will vary depending on the scope and impact of the prospective acquisition on the current business. The board members who are most likely to have an important say are:

- Acquisitions director: responsible for company acquisition and business strategy (where this role does not exist separately it may be a responsibility taken on by the CEO or business development director)
- Finance director: responsible for financial assessment and risk management of any acquisition
- Operations director: responsible for the operations impacted by any acquisition, this person would be responsible for the eventual integration of the acquisition into the company and for realizing the business returns.

If the appropriate board level support is not secured in the early stages then the risk of disagreement or misunderstanding emerging at a later stage, is increased. Once expectations have been set in the minds of managers of both acquirer and acquired, it could prove to be extremely costly and disruptive, if not impossible, to attempt to renegotiate the basis of the deal.

Business drivers of mergers and acquisitions

The business intent of M&As may vary greatly but is likely to fall into a number of categories:

- Entering new geographic markets
- Increasing market share
- Extending product/service portfolio
- Gaining benefits of critical mass in the form of improved utilization of assets or infrastructure
- Acquiring technology or other intellectual property
- Gaining management control of the acquired company to improve business performance
- Diversifying the company's business interests.

During 2000, Roffey Park collaborated with the European Foundation for Management Development (EFMD) in researching M&As in the European context. Companies represented in the learning group included Citycorp, Deutsche Bank, Monsanto, BP Amoco, Siemens, Sonera, SKF and TXU. Group members shared their company's experience, including the reasons why they were on the acquisition trail. Typical drivers included:

- Market share
- Economies of scale
- Government policy
- Deregulation
- Economies of scope
- Imitation
- Buying out competitors
- Potential business synergies, e.g. expanding product lines
- Globalization/market access
- Access to closed markets
- Access to distribution channels.

As these drivers suggest, M&As allow organizations to exploit market opportunities if they choose the right targets. Interestingly, there were also some business drivers that highlight the increasing value placed on a company's intangible assets, especially its people:

- Having a succession pool
- Acquiring specific competence and talent.

Such business needs are less easily fulfilled through M&As. The human asset is far less controllable than others are and individuals can, and do, exercise their options if they are unhappy with the way a merger affects them.

There are clear advantages to adopting a merger or acquisition strategy for growth rather than relying on a purely organic approach. If the business assets are in some way complementary to one's own, then M&A approaches can be much faster. They also tend to entail greater risk in that the very act of integration may diminish or even destroy the value that has been acquired. This is especially true where that value is embedded in a few employees rather than in fixed assets or distributed widely across the organization.

Starting the search

So far the search for prospective partners has been restricted to planning activities, getting clarity and consensus across the key senior managers about the purpose, benefits and funding for acquisitions. The conversations, so far, are likely to have been primarily internal with limited involvement of external advisors. Consequently they will have incurred little expenditure and little, if any, exposure to commercial risks.

The start of the prospecting and evaluation activities will bring with them increasing expenditure and risk exposure, resulting from the involvement of prospective partners and advisors. There is also some exposure to commercial risks arising from contact with prospective partners and the disclosure of commercially sensitive information to people who may be operating, and perhaps competing, in one's own market. There is also potential risk of destabilizing shareholders or employees through untimely leakage of information. In the case of major partnership deals, there can be risk to one's own business through the inevitable distraction of senior managers as a result of their involvement in the deal. It is important to balance the potential benefits and risks in any merger or acquisition strategy and to ensure the risks are effectively managed.

Identifying prospects

Information to help search out a potential partner may come from a wide variety of sources. Some of these are:

- Partners who have an existing trading relationship
- Partners identified through executive networks either directly or through third parties
- Partners who make contact with the intention of being acquired or wishing to acquire or merge
- Introductions through market advisors or merchant banks.

Senior management contact

In most acquisitions the initial contact is between senior managers. The nature of these relationships plays an important role in the eventual success of any partnership. It is dangerous to assume companies are stable entities that can be acquired without disrupting their operation. The dilemma for the acquirer is that, more often than not, the operational performance of the company depends on the senior managers who run it. The acquirer is therefore doubly dependent on the senior managers of the prospect. They are the prime source of information about the business and its operation as well as potentially underpinning its future performance. It is therefore hardly surprising that the relationship and trust between the two management teams is a major influence on acquisition success.

There are some situations where the relationship between the two management teams cannot be that close. An obvious example of this would be a hostile takeover bid where the intent is to replace the senior management team. In the case of acquiring a manager-owned company, where the management team is looking to be bought out, there still remains a high degree of dependency on the out-going managers. Whatever the situation, the inherent risk of a poor, or non-existent relationship between the two teams, needs to be factored into the risk evaluation.

The first meeting

Often the initial contact, in the case of acquirer-led initiatives, is a very informal meeting and perhaps arranged under the pretext of some other business issue. The meeting may be an exploratory process between a single senior representative from each company. The intention of the meeting will be to test out the interest in any possible partnership, in such a way that both parties can walk away without feeling compromised.

The nature of the initial contact will depend on the stance and intent of both acquirer and acquired. In cases where there is limited need to establish effective relationships across the two management teams, the initial contacts will inevitably be more formal and impersonal and may be through third parties. In vendor-led transactions, for example, where the owners are simply looking for the best bidder to acquire their company, a more formal and structured approach may be appropriate. There is, however, a strong body of anecdotal evidence that acquisitions built on a friendly, open and honest relationship between key players of both parties are far more likely to succeed than those built on clinical negotiation or incomplete disclosure of intentions.

A recent case of an acquisition of a software production company by a public company in the same market shows how important the level of openness and honesty between both parties can be to a successful deal. The acquired company had an excellent track record of success with a strong and distinctive leadership style that was heavily centred around people. It was a software development company that had built some innovative and market-leading products. Its managers saw its informal, open and fun culture as core to their business success. In the early discussions these 'soft' issues and any potential conflicts of culture were not openly discussed.

The deal went ahead and, as the companies began to integrate, it became apparent that the management style of the parent company was far more hierarchical, oriented towards short-term results and centrally controlled. This cultural disparity became more and more visible and a source of conflict between the two parties. As a result, three of the four senior directors of the acquired company left within six months of the deal. This in turn put the stability of the acquired business at risk. This is one of numerous examples of how 'soft' and intangible issues can have a very real and significant impact on the potential value of an acquisition and the importance of identifying and discussing 'soft' issues in an open and honest way.

Most successful acquisitions have a high degree of synergy providing benefits to both parties that can only be gained by the partnership. In these cases, having the active support of both parties' managers and employees is often essential in realizing those benefits. The importance of such initial meetings between the two parties cannot be over-stressed, as they tend to set the tone for the future relationship and negotiations. Developing a spirit of openness, honesty and trust from the start is likely to lead to a more productive and mutually beneficial partnership and reduce the risk of costly discoveries later in the process.

Vendor-led acquisitions

In the case of vendor-led acquisitions, where the current owners are seeking to sell the company, it may be that the nature of contact and information flow is more formal and perhaps controlled through a formal bid/purchase process driven by a third party. In such cases the process may require up-front signing of a non-disclosure agreement (NDA). The purchase process may involve the supply of information packs providing the outline information about the prospect and the requirement to respond with an 'early indicative offer' based on the summary information. The early stages of such acquisitions are therefore formal in nature and more competitive with only 'acceptable bidders' becoming involved in detailed follow-on discussions. Once the early indicative bidding phase is over, there will be the same need for informal, open and honest discussions between both parties.

Establishing a shared intent

If the initial contact has led both parties to want to explore the partnership possibilities further, it is likely that meetings involving more representatives from the two companies will need to take place. They are still likely to remain fairly restricted in attendance and informal in nature. The agenda for the meetings may cover:

- Level of shared interest in some form of collaboration
- Needs and goals of individual owner/managers
- Form and benefits of any collaboration
- The potential risks of any collaboration
- Chemistry and ability of managers to work together.

In the Articon-Integralis case, this last factor of chemistry between the two boards was seen by all those involved in the early discussions as the most important factor in deciding to proceed. It therefore played an important part in the eventual success of the merger.

The outcome of the initial meetings may be an agreement that there is an opportunity of sufficient interest and benefit to the two companies and their shareholders that it is worth investing the effort to thrash out the nature of the deal. If a non-disclosure agreement has not already been signed then it is desirable that it happens at this stage to protect the commercially sensitive information that will need to be shared.

Determining company value

Determining the 'true' value of a company is more of an art than a science. It is, especially in today's world, more based on people's beliefs about the future than on facts about today. This section is intended to lay out the fundamental principles of company valuation rather than offer explicit recommendations on the valuation methods to be used.

The approaches to company valuation can be thought of as a spectrum of differing approaches or perspectives depending on the purpose of the valuation or the situation the company is operating in. Usually the final valuation uses a combination of all these approaches.

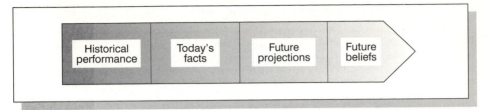

Figure 3.1 Basis for company valuation

Figure 3.1 represents the differing perspectives and factors that influence the valuation of a company. Which perspective more accurately represents the 'true value' of a company will depend on the intentions of the person doing the evaluation. Their interest may be solely in the value of the company as it is now, with no interest or confidence in the company's future potential. This may be the view of a receiver brought in to wind up an insolvent company. In such cases, they may wish to look only at those assets that can be quickly turned into cash today.

In most company acquisitions it is important to take into account the value of the company's potential future trade. For a company in an established position and in a relatively stable marketplace, the best way of doing that may be to project the company's current trading position forward into the future.

The alternative perspective is often the position adopted by the stock market looking at the longer-term trading value of a company. This perspective is especially relevant for companies trading in more volatile or emerging marketplaces. This is a much more subjective valuation based more on beliefs and judgements about the future nature of the marketplace and that company's position in it than with the company's current performance. These three approaches to company valuation can all contribute to establishing the 'true value' of a prospective acquisition. The key elements of the three approaches are described below.

1. Net worth or net asset value

This is the most conservative view and may be the one adopted by accountants. It looks at the tangible net assets of a company in terms of its total assets and liabilities. These include:

- Fixed assets such as plant, equipment, machinery and buildings
- Current assets such as stock, cash and debtors.

These are offset by the company liabilities of:

- Long-term liabilities such as loans
- Current liabilities such as overdrafts and creditors.

This traditional approach to evaluating a company's net worth has most relevance in capital intensive industries such as manufacturing or engineering. Such businesses are heavily dependent on the investment of capital in plant and machinery and therefore their net worth is a significant factor in their true value.

Many of today's new businesses do not have that same dependency on fixed assets. They are more dependent on intangible assets such as knowledge and expertise, which are difficult to value in the same way, even though they are equally critical to a company's future success. Companies that fit this profile are the knowledge-based businesses and service businesses that have represented the highest growth sectors over the last 25 years. This includes companies such as consultancies, software development companies and many of the emerging e-business companies.

In addition to new start-ups, many traditional industries such as banking and insurance are transforming into service businesses, a process that has been accelerated by the use of information technology. This process has shifted the companies' core assets away from physical assets such as buildings to intangible assets such as knowledge and information. In many marketing and service companies, the key asset is the knowledge they have of a particular process or product, or simply their knowledge about their customers. In this case, the valuation of their assets is more difficult to quantify and their value is determined, instead, by valuing the future business they are able to generate.

Goodwill, recognizing the value of future trade • • •

The net assets of any business do not fully represent the total value of that business. There is clearly value in a business's future trade potential and its ability, through that trade, to generate future profits. In putting a value on the flow of future profit over time, the profits have to be discounted somewhat relative to current or shorter-term profits. Today's profits have more value as they can be invested immediately to generate further future profits. Goodwill can be thought of as today's value of the company's potential to generate future profits over and above its net assets value. This value represents the amount of money, required to be invested today, to generate that same set of profits.

In this way, the 'true' value of a company can be estimated as:

'True Value' = Net worth + Goodwill

Conversely, goodwill can be seen as the difference between the net asset value of a company and the price actually paid for a company or its current market value.

2. Projected future trade value

One method of determining the future trade potential of the company is to project its historical trading position into the future. This approach would be appropriate for companies operating in established positions in relatively stable markets. The future trade position is derived from current operating performance and looks at future revenue growth rates and expected future profits. The risks to that future trade are evaluated by building up a risk profile of the company. The profile looks at:

- Spread of customer base; a small number of large customers may increase the risks to future trade
- Any critical dependency on major suppliers
- Any major dependencies from the product mix of the business, i.e. products generating disproportionate volume or profit
- Risks due to the mix of products and services; a service business tends to be viewed as being more sustainable as it builds stronger customer loyalty or dependency
- Risks due to the mix of contract type; ongoing renewable contracts are seen as more sustainable than one-off contracts
- Risks due to the mix of contract size; large contracts with a disproportionate impact on the business could be seen as higher risk
- Customer retention rates; low retention rates may reduce overall sustainability of the business.

This approach to estimating future business has the benefit that it is based on the facts about current company performance with judgements applied to determine future performance. This method is less helpful when attempting to value small, high growth companies in emerging markets, as there are few relevant data available about historical performance on which to base these judgements.

3. 'Future belief' based trade value

This is an approach to estimating a company's future trade position that is based primarily on views of the future rather than looking at current performance or assets. This, if you like, is the entrepreneur's view of a company's value. This view is more heavily based on beliefs about the future opportunities and returns that the company can realize. The factors that influence this view are:

- Beliefs about future size and growth rate of marketplace
- Beliefs about future dominance or competitive strength of the company in that market
- Level of faith in the competence of management to lead the company.

These factors are much more subjective, based on beliefs about the future and less dependent on current company position or performance. In this world, a company's growth performance or its leadership in terms of new product releases will be more important than its current profit performance. The trading value of the company is heavily weighted towards its future capacity to generate profits.

Bursting bubbles! • • •

When company valuations are based on future beliefs about a market or a company's potential in that market, they are likely to be much more volatile and more influenced by perceptions of the marketplace rather than a company's actual performance. The e-business marketplace has exhibited all these volatile character-istics in recent times. The value of e-business companies was greatly inflated by the 'dot-com' bubble, a bubble driven by the belief that this was an exciting, high growth and high potential market. This resulted in some dot-com companies having valuations of hundreds of millions of pounds, yet these were companies with few assets, few customers and had probably not generated any operating profit in their short history. The inflated value of such companies serves to support the organization's ability to invest and therefore its growth potential.

Bubbles built on beliefs about the future of a market can only be sustained by a continued belief in that future and anything that dents that belief can cause the bubble to burst. In the case of the 'dot-com' bubble, news of young companies going under or chief executives' talk of 'resetting expectations of future growth' had a traumatic impact, resulting in reduced market confidence and reduced company valuations. In a sense, this volatile marketplace is self-fulfilling, since the act of reducing the valuation of a company or marketplace reduces the investment potential of that market and, in turn, reduces its future growth potential.

Using ratios to determine value (peer company comparisons)

One approach to determining company value in these circumstances is to use ratios that compare their market capitalization or value to their current operating performance. These ratios can be used in a particular market sector to evaluate and compare values of companies operating in the same sector. The commonly used ratios are:

1 Price–earning (P–E) ratio. This is the ratio of a company's current market value to its earnings or profit. This ratio will be higher the more the market inflates a company's value based on projected future profit earnings or market potential. This ratio could be used to establish a company's value where it is generating operating profits in a more mature or established marketplace.
2 Price–sales ratio. This ratio is on revenues rather than profits and used for evaluating companies operating in high growth or emerging markets. The company's growth and future market position is seen as more important than the current operating profit. In the case of start-up companies, they may be investing heavily in growing very quickly and may not be generating operating profits.

Both of these ratios can be calculated based on current performance or, particularly for companies losing money today, the ratios can be calculated on future expected performance.

Future perceived value

The key factors underpinning organizations valued on future belief, are perceptions of the market in which the company operates and perceptions of the company's position in that market. The factors that influence each of these areas are:

Market trends

- Current market size and growth rates
- Analyst projections of market futures
- Technology drivers in the market and projected innovations that will stimulate the market

- Economic drivers of the market, i.e. the likely impact of the overall economy on the market
- Commercial drivers of the market, potential customers for market, price trends etc.

Company's market position

- Current market leadership and competitive position
- Uniqueness of current offerings
- Uniqueness or market-related knowledge or intellectual properties
- Company vision and investments in future
- Company growth record and plans
- Current competitive strengths and threats
- Barriers to new entrants in market
- Management leadership of company.

Evaluating a potential merger or acquisition

1. Acquisition risks

The focus in mergers and acquisitions is primarily on the synergies of the two potential partners, but there are other aspects of the two companies that may represent some form of risk to the partnership. These risks are a result of the potential reaction to the partnership from the key stakeholders of the two companies. These could be:

- Customers: major customers with high dependency on the trading relationship may see a threat if the partner has one of its main competitors as a key customer
- Suppliers: integration may result in the new company having competitive or conflicting product offerings that may be seen as a threat or unacceptable to some suppliers
- Selling channels: integration may result in third party selling channel overlap and therefore conflict, e.g. two channels now selling into the same market or geography
- Shareholders: the reaction of existing shareholders, whether informed and rational or purely emotional, can have a direct impact on the viability of any deal
- Management: the integration may be seen as a threat because of a perceived loss of power or opportunity for some managers, and therefore an increased likelihood of them leaving
- Employees: the integration and any perceived shift in company values or management style may reduce employee loyalty and increase turnover.

2. Integration or transition risks

This is often the greatest risk of any deal and reflects the risk that the integration of the two companies represents in terms of its disruption to current operations. There is also risk related to realizing the synergies or expected added value from the partnership. The higher the level of integration that is required to realize the benefits, the higher this risk is likely to be. This area is discussed in greater detail in later chapters.

Agreeing the deal price

The final deal price is driven by a number of factors. The first of these is the perceptions of value of the deal by vendor and purchaser, specifically:

- Vendor perception of value of their company
- Purchaser's perception of value of the company
- Purchaser's perception of added value to both companies from integration synergies.

The value and nature of the deal will depend on these valuations, as well as the relative negotiating power of purchaser and vendor. The level of interest the vendor may have in maintaining a stake in the new integrated company will also impact the nature of the deal.

Quantifying acquisition costs

The other consideration in evaluating any deal and its viability are the costs associated with the deal. The deal costs are:

- Settlement costs: this is the purchase price paid to the vendor in the form of cash or shares
- Acquisition costs: these are the administrative costs associated with the deal. They would cover external cost of advisors and the internal costs of management involvement
- Integration costs: these are the one-off costs of the post-acquisition integration or transition activities
- Development costs: these are the ongoing business development costs related to realizing the business benefits and improved earnings arising from the acquisition.

Overall viability of deal

The final go/no-go decision on the deal will be based around a straight return on acquisition investment decision. The balance of the costs required to finance the deal and the projected improvements in future earnings resulting from the deal, determines the viability of the deal. The balance of these two must be great enough to generate an acceptable rate of return. The financing costs of the deal are:

- Interest costs of any cash invested to cover settlement costs or external acquisition costs
- Cost of maintaining the original earnings per share forecast if any new shares were issued as part of the deal.

The settlement and acquisition costs (the cost of purchase) are compared with the net assets acquired and the difference in value (the goodwill) is capitalized as an asset which, over a period of time, is then written off to the profit and loss account as 'goodwill amortization'.

Interest, integration and development costs are carried into the profit and loss account and therefore need to be covered by increased operating revenues to maintain earnings. If new shares have also been issued, additional profits will also be required to maintain the earnings per share.

Once these costs have been taken into account the likely net impact of the deal on the new company's projected earnings can be calculated. The final go/no-go decision would be taken based on a judgement on the likely net return of the deal and its associated risks.

Shaping the deal

Once both parties have reached an agreement on the nature of any deal, the form of a letter of intent (LOI) will need to be agreed that will establish a clear and comprehensive basis for the final contract. The final stages of discussion will need to cover:

- Nature and benefits of the partnership
- Valuation of the business to be acquired
- Financial structure of deal
- Potential synergies and added value of partnership
- Level of integration required to realize benefits
- People and organizational profile of two organizations, including any possible conflict areas
- Perceived costs and risks of integration
- Timescales and process to finalize a deal.

The level of involvement of external advisors up to this point will depend on the degree of expertise in both companies and on the legal and financial issues being discussed. It is likely that the bulk of the work will still be done by the senior managers of the two companies, supported by specialist advisors. This work forms the basic shape and framework for any deal. The discussions will start to set expectations and build a momentum for the deal, making it increasingly difficult to pull out without some risk to relationships, or even to the business itself. However, taking the decision to pull out, for whatever reason, tangible or simply a sense that it will not work, is preferable to proceeding with a deal that becomes a sink of effort and money and does not realize the hoped for benefits.

It is now that the basic framework of the strategic plan should guide the discussions. The goal is to establish an agreed form of deal that will satisfy both parties' business and personal goals and satisfy the strategic requirements agreed up front in the strategic plan.

The legal structure of the partnership

The scope of the partnership needs to be clarified early on. Is this a partnership involving the whole company or does it merely involve specific trading assets, departments or divisions, e.g. a manufacturing plant or the intellectual property rights (IPR) relating to some process or product? If the purchaser's interest is limited, then the contract may be restricted to acquiring some named 'trade assets'. More commonly, the contract is based around purchasing all the shares in the company and therefore all of its assets and liabilities.

The interests of purchaser and vendor in the new entity also need to be agreed. This could be a straightforward acquisition or takeover where the vendor gives up all interests in the acquired company. Alternatively, it could take the form of a merger where both parties jointly own the new entity.

The preferred form of partnership may be a looser form of alliance with both parties maintaining their existing interests in their companies but agreeing a form of collaborative venture where they both contribute and benefit from the arrangement. In such cases, it may be that both parties take an interest or stake in each other's company to underpin the alliance. Whatever structure is chosen, it should be the one that best supports the agreed partnership intent and helps realize the expected benefits and returns.

Financial structure of partnership

This is likely to be determined by the needs and expectations of individual shareholders as well as the intended legal structure of the partnership. In the case of privately owned companies where the managers are also key shareholders, shareholder needs and top management needs are intertwined.

Cash or shares

The deal may take the form of a straight cash or share deal or will more likely be a mixture of both. The mix of the offer can be driven by a number of factors such as the ability of the acquirer to raise the cash, the desire of the existing owners of the acquired company to maintain an interest in the new entity or the personal preferences of the owners. A share deal has the benefit of not requiring the acquirer to raise the same levels of cash, but may also result in a dilution of existing shareholdings. In the case of acquiring a manager/employee-owned company a share deal will tend to motivate the managers and employees to work for the longer-term success of the new partnership. There may also be personal tax benefits to considering a share deal rather than cash, which is liable to income tax.

In contrast a cash deal may seem attractive to manager-owners especially if they are not expected to play any ongoing role in the partnership or if they simply look to realize some, or all, of their stake in the company. In general a cash deal will have the effect of buying out the interests of the shareholder of the acquired company in the new venture. In the case of the acquisition of private companies, the structure of the deal offers an opportunity to encourage managers and employees to maintain operational performance through the transition and also support the integration process itself.

Finalizing the deal

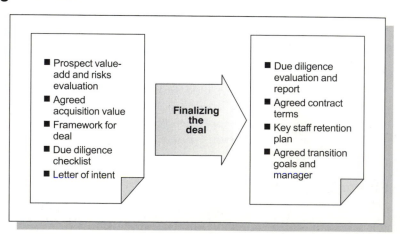

The end result of all these discussions and negotiations is normally the letter of intent (LOI) to purchase. The LOI outlines the basic elements of the agreement and the process and timescales for finalizing the purchase contract. In the case of more complex deals, the letter of intent may be replaced by a more complete heads of agreement, which details the scope and nature of the acquisition, structure of the deal and the process and constraints under which it will be implemented. Normally the LOI will have been drawn up with minimal, if any, use of external financial and legal advisors. In the case of complex multinational deals it may already be necessary to seek advice from experts in local law and financial practices. It may also be prudent for private owners to seek such advice if they have limited knowledge or experience of these matters or could be deemed in law to be 'inexperienced owners'. In such cases there may even be a legal requirement that the existing owners take such advice for the eventual contract to be legally binding.

The time to go from initial contact to LOI can be as short as a few months but this will be much longer in deals that involve complex shareholder structures and complex business operations. The purpose of an LOI is to commit both parties to an agreed deal subject to further substantiation of the information on which the deal has been struck. The substantiation of this information is done through a due diligence exercise.

The LOI is not normally a legally binding contract on either party and usually contains the wording of 'draft' and 'subject to contract'. The LOI usually covers:

- Overall company valuation
- Structure of agreed offer and description of what is to be purchased
- Assumptions on which the valuation is based (e.g. audited accounts or management accounts)
- Some form of non-competition agreement
- A confidentiality agreement
- Notice of a requirement for warranties and indemnities
- Offer dependency on due diligence exercise and agreed scope of exercise
- The intended nature and level of integration
- Period of exclusivity of purchase and liability for breach
- The law under which the contract will be governed (usually the acquirer's).

Purpose of due diligence

The legal essence of any acquisition is still *caveat emptor* or buyer beware. It is the responsibility of the purchaser to take appropriate steps to evaluate fully what they are buying. The due diligence phase should form the vital link between the negotiation phase and the eventual integration phase. It is the point where the assumptions made in the previous negotiation are substantiated and any further obstacles to the successful integration quantified. The basic framework of the agreement should be in place with the due diligence process merely confirming or clarifying the details. In addition to confirming the details contained in the LOI, the exercise should also establish a firm basis for the future operation of the acquired entity. This is done by establishing an 'opening balance sheet' for the acquired company that identifies all assets and liabilities and an 'opening operating plan' for the acquired business operation.

The other important purpose of the exercise is to substantiate the organizational aspects that are seen as key to the successful integration of the company. These may be because they are potential areas of synergy, such as current customer profiles or product portfolios, or because they are seen as potential obstacles or risks to integration such as management style, business process, or key staff and skills dependencies. In summary the purpose of the due diligence exercise should be:

- To identify potential risks or liabilities embedded in the business
- To confirm the financial status of the business and its performance
- To evaluate future business projections and possible risks
- To validate assumptions made in the previous negotiations
- To gather data to evaluate risks and assist the planning of the integration.

The scope of the due diligence exercise is discussed in more detail in Chapter 4.

Managing the due diligence process

The due diligence process is often a point where the accountability for the acquisition starts to move from the 'strategic' or acquisitions management to operational management. It is important that the due diligence management structure reflects that shift. The accountability at the highest level may be shared between the acquisition and operations directors during this phase with the operational director having the final go/no-go decision on the acquisition. Following this decision, the operating director takes full responsibility for the opening balance sheet and achievement of the opening operating plan. They also take on responsibility for the effective integration of the acquisition and so will have an interest in ensuring that there are clear integration goals agreed between both management teams prior to giving the final go-ahead.

The due diligence exercise almost always involves the use of external specialists and advisors to conduct the legal and financial aspects of the exercise. It is important to maintain a broad view of the purpose of the due diligence exercise and set up the appropriate management team to control the process ensuring it covers its full remit. It is valuable to appoint a manager with overall responsibility for the due diligence project and its progress. This same individual could also take charge of the subsequent integration project and so provide a smooth transition from the acquisition phase to the transition phase. The key members of the due diligence management team are likely to be:

- Operating director, responsible for the acquired operation
- Legal advisors to undertake legal due diligence
- Financial advisors/accountants involved in financial due diligence
- The due diligence project manager
- HR manager responsible for organizational due diligence
- Appropriate acquirer and/or acquired line managers involved in commercial and organizational due diligence
- Integration project manager.

Use of external advisors

We have already identified the likely use of external advisors and the value they can bring. This is not an area where it is wise to cut costs by use of unproven or little known advisors. Money spent in securing top quality advisors will bring a breadth of experience that may prove invaluable. Equally important, they can also bring credibility to the whole proposition in the eyes of shareholders.

Use of data rooms

The volume of information involved in a due diligence exercise can be extensive even for a relatively small company and an order of magnitude greater for larger, more complex deals. There is a need normally to structure and manage access to such data for a variety of reasons:

- Efficiency of access especially in multiple bidder situations
- Better control over information access

- Enables more streamlined due diligence process through indexing information relative to agreed checklists
- Reduces wastage of key managers' time by duplicate requests
- Enables more efficient maintenance of data
- Makes it easier to demonstrate what information was made available in case of dispute.

The use of data rooms dedicated to the storage of structured information required to support a company's due diligence can facilitate a more structured and potentially more effective approach.

Agreeing transition goals

Once the due diligence findings are available it is important that both parties agree the goals for the transition project. These will identify the priorities for the transition to ensure that the business value add is realized, that any organizational integrations goals are met and that any other issues arising from the due diligence are addressed.

The sale and purchase agreement

At the appropriate point, where both parties feel they have sufficient substantiation of the purchase deal, the agreement is translated into a legally binding purchase contract. The agreement will detail all aspects of the purchase and any obligations or constraints on either party. The content of the agreement will vary depending on the nature of the deal but is likely to cover:

- Terms and conditions of sale
- Any agreement completion conditions (e.g. satisfactory completion of due diligence)
- Any restrictions and obligations on either party pending completion
- Rights to terminate agreement
- Any warranties and indemnities.

The announcement

Often the initial announcement is time critical, with a need to announce both externally and internally as soon as possible after the purchase agreement is signed. The planning of what is to be announced, to whom, by whom and when, needs to be agreed prior to signing the contract.

Case study

Introduction to case study

Articon-Integralis AG is today the leading supplier of IT security solutions and services in Europe with ambitions to become the leading supplier worldwide. The security technologies and services supplied include applications such as security gateways or firewalls, mail and Internet content filtering, message encryption and intrusion/hacker detection. The supply of network security technology is a fast growing market fuelled by the boom in use of the Internet and e-business. Articon-Integralis currently has 22 offices in Europe and the USA and over 650 employees. The company offers a wide range of services to its customers ranging from the design, supply and maintenance of security solutions to the provision of managed services that enable customers to outsource the management of the security of their computer network. The company has among its customers a majority of the FTSE 100 and DAX 30 companies.

Acquisition has played a key role in the rapid growth of this company over the last ten years. A combination of organic growth and selective acquisitions has grown the company today to a capitalization of over 400 million Euro. At the peak of the 'dot-com' share market boom it was valued at four times that amount!

Articon-Integralis grew to its strong position today from humble beginnings. The company took on its current name and form in late 1999 through the merger of Articon Information Systems AG, a German based company and Integralis Limited, a UK based company. Both these companies had previously been established as private companies during the late 1980s and early 1990s. They both independently recognized the huge opportunity represented by the IT security market.

As the explosion of the internet and e-business marketplace have taken place world-wide, companies have become more and more dependent on electronic trading and electronic communication and so have moved more and more of their business operations onto public networks. This in turn has exposed them to a host of commercial risks resulting from sensitive business information being accessible from the Internet. To minimize this exposure companies have needed to invest in the appropriate business and information security solutions. It was this opportunity that both companies recognized during the last ten years and each committed itself to exploit.

Both Articon Information Systems AG and Integralis Limited were formed by entrepreneurs who had previously been employed in the IT industry. They chose to leave the relative comfort and security of employment to set up on their own.

Throughout this book we have used the Articon-Integralis merger as a case study to demonstrate how M&A can result in real benefits for all parties concerned. As with all mergers and acquisitions there was no shortage of things that did not go quite to plan or which could have been managed better. Yet there were undoubtedly some key elements of the approach taken that contributed directly to the successful outcomes that were realized. The Articon-Integralis merger eventually took place in February 2000, after over six months of discussion and negotiation. To help you better appreciate the opportunities, risks and the learning from the merger, a short history of the two companies prior to their merger is included here.

Articon Information Systems AG

The company was originally formed in 1993 by two founding members, both of whom played an active role in the company. They specialized in security products and solutions with the aim of becoming the No. 1 solution supplier in Europe. The company grew through a combination of organic growth and acquisition to the point where the company was floated on the Neuermarkt exchange in 1998. The founding members used the monies raised to invest in the company infrastructure to support future growth.

The effects of their sustained success were beginning to show in terms of the pressures they were facing as a management team. They saw their strategy for continued success was to:

- Continue to grow through acquisition
- Strengthen their management team to cope with business and organizational complexity
- Strengthen their cashflow position to fund future continued growth.

In early 1999 the founding members were in discussions with a potential acquisition in Germany, a privately owned company called Centaur GmbH. They soon discovered that they were in a competitive bid situation. The other bidder was a UK company they had come across on a number of previous occasions. This company was based in the UK, but had operations in Germany and was looking to expand its German operation. The name of this company was Integralis. The relationship between the two was mixed. They had a trading relationship with Integralis's German subsidiary, supplying a number of security products to Articon and its customers. They were also seen as a competitor by Articon, offering a competitive range of security services to German customers. In January 1999 Integralis successfully acquired Centaur. The effect of this acquisition was to increase Integralis's service capability in Germany to the point where Articon now saw them as a serious competitive threat in their home marketplace. Articon consequently terminated their product supply agreement with the Integralis subsidiary in Germany.

Integralis Ltd

The company was formed in 1988 by five founding members, all of whom played an active day-to-day role in the company's formation and growth. Their initial focus was on computer network interconnection solutions. However, as use of the Internet grew, so their ambition, like that of their future partners, shifted to becoming the No. 1 supplier to the European IT security marketplace. They grew initially through seeding relatively autonomous business ventures, with individual managers responsible for their successful development. With the decision to focus on security solutions they were very effective in shedding ventures that did not form part of that core focus.

Central to their success was a strong business culture that ran throughout the company. This culture encouraged individual enterprise, hard work, freedom and a spirit of fun! This approach served them well but was not delivering the rate of growth they were looking for to achieve a European leadership position. They therefore adopted a strategy of complementing their organic growth by acquisition and also of increasingly focusing their resources on the European security services marketplace.

They also looked to strengthen their service business capability and therefore increase the value they added to their customers. During 1998 and into 1999, they underwent a total of five mergers/de-mergers to realize this. One of those companies was a potential German acquisition that would enable them to strengthen their operation in Germany and help them to compete more effectively in the German market. The potential acquisition was a company named Centaur GmbH. The German marketplace was seen as a priority; increasing their operation in Germany would enable them to compete more effectively in that market and strengthen their position against the market leader Articon.

By early 1999 Integralis saw their priorities as:

1 Establish a stronger European operation
2 Float the company in order to :

- Establish company profile for future global growth
- Generate investment funds for investing in the company infrastructure
- Realize monies for the company stakeholders, who by now consisted of the founding owners, 3I plc, the venture capital company and the employees who had a sizeable stake through a recently introduced Employee Share Scheme.

In January 1999 Integralis acquired the German company despite competition from Articon. The termination of the trading agreement between Integralis and Articon seemed a clear signal that the fight for the German marketplace was about to commence. Potentially the stage was set for the two leading IT security service companies in Europe to battle it out.

Prospecting selection and contracting

The scene was set for war and the natural course of action for both parties was to fight. There were, however, others who saw the situation differently. They could see the opportunity for collaboration rather than the inevitable battle. In May 1999 the chairman of Articon struck up a meeting with the CEO of Integralis. They agreed to meet informally to explore the scope for collaboration. This meeting went well, with an agreement that it was worth pursuing the opportunity further. The two boards met a few weeks later in the informal setting of a beer garden to test out further the opportunities to collaborate. When asked about these initial meetings and what really influenced their decision to proceed, the same single factor emerged from all board members.

Perhaps surprisingly the key factor that influenced their decision to proceed was the chemistry of the two management teams. They felt that they could work together and enjoyed each other's company!

At this and further meetings of their top management teams they came to a joint agreement in a number of areas:

- Both boards shared a common vision of the future
- They saw both market and financial benefits in collaboration
- Created market leadership position
- Better geographical coverage

- Less effort wasted on competing
- Complementary skills, products and services
- Opportunities to cross sell
- Strengthened management team/capacity
- Integralis brought stronger cash position
- Articon was already listed on the stock market so providing an easier route for Integralis flotation
- The basic legal and financial structure of deal
- Articon would acquire all shares in Integralis
- The offer would comprise a mix of cash and Articon shares
- The launch of a Secondary Public Offering (SPO) scheduled for April 2000 following the acquisition (this would require the integration of the two companies to proceed smoothly to ensure a successful SPO)
- The appointment of a merchant bank, legal advisors and auditors to support the due diligence and SPO process.

A letter of intent was issued at this point.

Over the coming weeks issues emerged about the viability of raising the amount of cash required to fund the original deal. As a result, the mix of cash to shares in the offer was changed, reducing the amount of cash offered and increasing the share mix. Despite the fact that this only changed one element of the deal, it had the impact of shifting the management balance in the merger, as now the Integralis managers had a much stronger interest in ensuring the longer-term success of the merged companies. The deal now took on a new dimension. From a legal point of view the deal was a straightforward acquisition of Integralis by Articon. However, from a management perspective it now looked more like a merger with both management teams looking to play an active part in ensuring the success of the new company. The third perspective was the relative sizes of the two companies. With Integralis twice as large as Articon, it could even be argued that this was a reverse takeover.

These changes required them to establish a clear position on how the new joint management structure would work. They set up a management meeting of all their top managers and thrashed out the approach:

1 The high-level business structure and management structure for the joint business was agreed. This included an unconventional approach to restructuring the board. The key positions of chief executive officer (CEO) and chief operating officer (COO) were to be joint roles with representation from each company, taking on responsibility for a specific area. The resulting board structure comprised:

Joint CEO:

- Articon director with responsibility for market/product strategy
- Integralis director with responsibility for acquisitions

Joint COO:

- Integralis director with responsibility for USA and North-west Europe
- Articon director with responsibility for Central and East Europe.

And a chief financial officer (CFO).

This structure was the source of concern for a number of external advisors who were looking for a more conventional and accountable structure. Despite this external pressure, the board stayed with a joint structure at CEO level but split the COO into COO and vice-COO. This proved to serve the company well through the integration.

2 The remaining management structure was agreed between the two COOs including business unit structure, geographic structure and corporate structures.
3 The new company name and logo were also agreed.

Over the coming months the due diligence proceeded and threw up a number of issues that were addressed and eventually resolved. Many of these issues resulted from the different accounting practices and policies across the two companies. The differences stemmed from:

- Their public vs private company accounting standards
- Differences in local country financial and legal standards and practices
- Different company business models
- Different company policies especially regarding matters such as deferred tax and revenue recognition on maintenance contracts and projects.

These issues may appear small in hindsight but, at the time, could have become showstoppers because of their impact on the structure of the deal itself or, equally important, their impact on the perceived level of risk in the deal. The sensitivity of deals of this nature to unexpected financial liabilities is high as they can impact the whole cashflow in a deal.

The quality and expertise of the legal and financial advice throughout the period of the merger and SPO proved to be fundamental in maintaining clarity and trust. A quote from the then CFO emphasizes the importance he attached to the role they played.

'It's always worth paying the premium for the best external advisors in these situations. They bring you both quality advice and, equally important, their own credibility and reputation' (*Martyn Webster, ex-CFO, Articon-Integralis*).

All parties emerged from the challenges of the due diligence exercise with the deal structure agreed and, even more importantly, with their trust in each other still intact.

The original shared vision of collaboration was now tempered with the practical problems of merging two companies and all that that entailed. The situation was no longer seen as a clear win-win with few risks, but as an opportunity to work together to develop a strong market position which they could not have achieved separately. They also now had a more realistic view of the demands the integration activities would place on their management capabilities and time.

The Integralis CFO just prior to the final go/no-go decision produced the pros and cons checklist shown in Table 3.1. It highlights the dilemma as he saw it:

These kinds of reservations were also felt on the Articon side. The joint COO Gunter Fuhrmann felt that the company's past success was already stretching the management team and that this deal might take their management capability to the limit. All these issues were openly discussed in the new team prior to them taking the final go/no-go decision.

There were certainly enough issues and risks for the more prudent board members to have doubts about the wisdom of proceeding. There was, however, practical and emotional momentum that made saying no at this point very difficult.

The deal was still seen as the best way forward for both parties and the Share Purchase contract was signed in November 1999 subject to completion of due diligence and the necessary shareholder approvals.

Finalizing the deal

The period from November to February was taken up with a number of key activities including:

- Initial external/internal announcement
- Completion of due diligence
- Formal offer and acceptance of share swap deal by Integralis

Table 3.1 Pros and cons checklist

Pros	Cons
• Management team chemistry • Trust, honesty and faith between board members • Clear European market leaders together • Avoids expensive competitive battle • Good news story for investors • Good synergies from market and product perspective • Potentially a one-off opportunity to realize their ambitions	• Five months hard work to realize the benefits through the SPO • Up to £1M in advisors' fees • Are we locked in already . . . emotional cost of pulling out now? • From financial perspective deal now less attractive (more risks) as it is now an all-share deal • Depends totally on successful SPO in April 2000 • If it goes wrong could destroy both our businesses • Short-term cash flow critical as combined cash burn • No cash to shareholders till April 2000 • Very different accounting practices, part business model differences, part culture • Eleven years of hard work by founding owners at risk • Still some further financial liabilities until due diligence is complete

employee shareholders (circa 20 per cent of Integralis shares were owned by employees)

• Articon shareholder acceptance at an Extraordinary General Meeting (EGM).

The value of the deal

Prior to the deal going unconditional, significant effort was put into running an investor road show to potential institutional shareholders to inform them about the deal and promote the business benefits of the merger and the intended SPO due in April.

• When the deal was first announced in November 1999, the Articon share price was about 30 Euro. The positive benefits of the deal were communicated via an investor roadshow. This activity combined with the dot.com and technology boom saw the share price rise to over 150 Euro when the deal went unconditional in February 2000. With eight million shares in issue, this valued the combined company at 240M Euro when the deal was announced and 1.2 billion Euro when the deal went unconditional!

Learning points: prospecting and contracting

- Importance of chemistry between top managers
- The value of seeing the opportunity to collaborate rather than only the competitive threat
- Most M&As are a mix of takeover, merger and reverse takeover
- The value of acquiring the best legal and financial advice available
- Impact of accounting practice differences (stemming from legal, financial and cultural differences)
- The need to identify the inevitable risks and ensure they are effectively managed

---

Summary

The prospecting and evaluation phase sets the destination and route map for the journey of any successful merger or acquisition. It will form the basis for success or failure for any deal and must consider all financial, legal commercial and organizational aspects of the deal. The outcome of this phase will be a sound and complete contractual basis for the deal and a shared understanding of the opportunity and risks that it represents as well as an outline plan to realize the benefits. The key considerations in this phase are:

- An acquisition strategy approved at board level
- The chemistry and collaboration between top management teams
- Clear and common view of opportunities and risks
- A clear and common view of the integration priorities and risks
- A sound valuation of the acquired company
- An agreed view of the added value that can be realized by the deal
- An agreed and committed opening operating plan for the acquired company
- An agreed outline integration or transition plan.

Further reading

1 Rankine, D. (1998): *A Practical Guide to Acquisitions*, Wiley
2 Galpin, T. J. and Herndon, M. (2000): *The Complete Guide to Mergers & Acquisitions*, Jossey-Bass

Legal aspects of mergers

A number of the Argonauts were specialist at some skill, such as Argus the shipbuilder, Tiphys the pilot, Lynceus with his marvellous eyesight. . .

Introduction

This chapter aims to provide an overview for the layperson of some of the legal issues arising during a merger. It is not intended to offer advice but to flag up areas of legal concern and activity. It first looks at some of the external legislation affecting mergers and acquisitions and then at some of the internal processes that take place in order to do a deal.

The broader legal context: antitrust legislation

Antitrust legislation has been in force in the UK since the Monopolies and Mergers Act in 1965 and the establishment of the Monopolies and Mergers Commission (MMC), now known as the Competition Commission. Additionally, in 1990, legislation was introduced for EU mergers which aims to provide a 'one stop shop' for clearance of European mergers. Bids for companies outside the EU are subject to antitrust laws in the target country. Antitrust legislation is designed to maintain effective competition.

The process at present is that a proposed merger goes through a preliminary screening by the Office of Fair Trading (OFT). The OFT is an independent watchdog set up in 1973 and screens all merger proposals. Each proposal is judged on its own merit, but the following factors are taken into account:

- Competition in the UK
- Efficiency of the merging organizations
- Regional employment and industry distribution
- National strategic interest and current government policy
- The viability of financing the merger
- The future prospects of the acquired company.

The proposal may then be referred to the President of the Board of Trade for a detailed investigation by the Competition Commission. The President has to accept the finding that the merger is not against public interest but may overrule an adverse conclusion.

The Competition Commission is an independent advisory body whose role is to establish whether the proposed merger is against the public interest. Again there are no hard and fast rules but the Commission takes into account:

1 The maintenance of effective competition in the UK
2 The promotion of consumer interests
3 The promotion of cost reduction, new techniques and products and new competitors
4 Balanced UK distribution of industry and employment
5 UK companies' international competitiveness.

The 'public interest test' tends to be subject to the prevailing political climate and has in the past furthered various economic policies, although there are now moves to de-politicize the process.

Takeover regulation in the UK

In the UK, bids for private companies are regulated by the UK Companies Act 1989. However, if the target is a public company, the bid is regulated by the City Panel on Takeovers and Mergers (the Panel) with reference to the City Code (Blue Book). The Panel exists to combat market 'rigging' and manipulation and is a self-regulatory, non-statutory authority. Its members include nominees from the Bank of England, banks, investment institutions, accountancy and industry. It aims to facilitate the transfer of ownership of listed companies and is recognized by the government and other regulatory bodies under the Financial Services Act of 1986. The City Code represents good practice in ensuring the fair treatment of all shareholders and a balanced approach to the interests of the acquirer and the target. The Code also provides a timetable during which time the bid process should be complete.

In addition to the Code, the Panel administers the Substantial Acquisition Rules (SARs) which were introduced to make voting rights more transparent and to prevent potential bidders acquiring substantial stakes in the target before announcing their intention to bid.

The London Stock Exchange Rules (LSE)

These rules apply to:

- The announcement of bids
- A requirement for shareholder approval for large transactions
- Offer documents and notification to the LSE
- The content of listing particulars when securities are issued in consideration.

Mergers, acquisitions and takeovers are dealt with according to size in financial terms. The bigger the class size, the more obligations there are which will include:

- Notifying the Company Announcements Office (CAO) at the LSE
- Advising the bidder's shareholders of the details of the offer and gaining approval at a general meeting.

Cross-border issues

Regulatory processes in Europe continue to be complex as more countries adopt their own competition laws and time taken to work through these should be built into merger planning. The various jurisdictions have different criteria for merger control, e.g. turnover, asset values or market share. Local legal expertise is therefore essential in any transaction. In some cases completion will be subject to local regulatory processes while in others an indemnity may be needed to cover regulatory risk after a transaction where notification is not essential before the close of transaction.

In most cases detailed business information will have to be supplied to regulators, sometimes simultaneously, which can add significant workload to the process. Alternatively, there may be cooperation between jurisdictions or clearance by one authority may assist clearance in another. Merger control regimes present an important consideration when a variety of bidders are involved. Occasionally non-binding confidential guidance may be available to assist bidders. For example, in the UK, the Secretary of State for Trade and Industry may provide an initial assessment of the likelihood of public interest concerns.

It is still difficult to say whether the future of regulation lies in more cooperation or a tougher stance on national interests.

Internal processes

The structure of mergers and acquisitions will rarely be driven by HR considerations but it is important for HR managers to have some understanding and early involvement in the process to identify people implications.

According to Rankine (1997), the acquirer's lawyers' brief can be split into three main areas:

1 Spotting problems that are yet to arise and solving them in advance of the deal being signed
2 Seeking protection in areas of uncertainty that could impact the value of the business by using warranties and indemnities
3 Assessing the cost and feasibility of potentially contentious post-acquisition actions.

Spotting problems early is an essential task for the law team as post-merger litigation is complex and costly. The legal representatives of the team should not work in isolation and ensuring excellent communication between each facet of the merger team is important. Information received by any one of the team may, for example, constitute deemed knowledge of disclosure information for legal purposes, whether or not it has been shared with other members.

Confidentiality agreement

A confidentiality agreement is normally required by the seller from a prospective buyer before information about the target company is released. The potential buyer must:

- Not disclose the information to any other party
- Not use the information other than for the proposed acquisition
- Return the information on request
- Keep confidential the negotiations and discussions taking place
- Not make copies of information
- Keep the information at a particular location
- Not store or transmit information electronically
- Ensure that all employees receiving the information sign confidentiality agreements
- Not compete with the seller or solicit the seller's customers, suppliers or employees for a period during and after the breakdown of negotiations.

Information requests and disclosure

The onus is on the purchaser to ask for the information needed to make an accurate assessment of the purchase price. Requests for information are more effective when tailored to the specific situation rather than produced as a standard form. A checklist of information should include adequate questions to cover particular areas of concern. Disclosure of information assists in establishing an appropriate price against warranties. Decisions to be made include:

- Who will be responsible for verifying the accuracy of the information?
- How extensive will disclosure be and what will it include? The fuller the disclosure, the less requirement there will be for warranties.

Disclosure of particularly commercially sensitive information may be phased as negotiations progress in order to protect the target should the deal fall through. It is important at each stage to document exactly what has been disclosed particularly in view of the volume of information involved. This will become part of the disclosure bundle that will be cross-checked by both parties' lawyers. A disclosure letter will cross-index the range of information supplied and the extent of the warranties. There may be further enquiries generated for some time.

Offer letter

Should the acquirer wish to proceed after reviewing the key information or information memorandum, it will issue an offer letter. This constitutes an offer to buy the target 'subject to contract'. The purchase will be subject to such matters as:

- Due diligence
- Completion of legal documentation
- Key named staff remaining with the business
- Structural issues
- Financial assumptions
- Other conditions such as pension liability, ownership of intellectual property
- Restrictive covenants.

The purchaser may also negotiate an exclusivity or 'lock out' agreement to prevent the target from entertaining approaches from third parties while the investigations proceed and a firm contract is negotiated.

Due diligence

Due diligence is the fairly rigorous process by which the purchaser gets to know as much as possible about its target for legal, financial and commercial reasons. A shopping list of key information is normally drawn up by the acquirer's legal team and this results in the production of several reports which should facilitate an accurate assessment of the value of the target. In addition it will provide information for the running of the company post-transfer. Areas generally covered include:

1. Financial DD

A review of the performance and value of the business. The objective is to ascertain that the financial information and assumptions used when valuing the business are valid. Financial information will be provided by the finance director with external support from accountants or auditors and is likely to cover:

- Copies of audited accounts
- Copies of management accounts
- Current period results and forecasts
- Cashflow statements
- Details of bank, leasing, HP and other borrowings
- Accounting policies and practices
- Analysis of sales by product/service and customer
- Analysis of gross margin by product/service and customer
- Overhead expenditure analysis
- Current business plans and forecasts

- Analysis of fixed assets
- Analysis of stock and work in progress
- Creditors and age profile
- Analysis of inter-company loans and balances
- Corporation tax liabilities.

2. Operational DD

A review of the commercial potential of the business. The objective is to ascertain that the commercial assumptions used during the valuation phase are valid.

- Corporate business plans
- Market and competitive positioning
- Internal and external branding standards
- Key performance indicators used by senior management
- Existing customers' profile and retention
- Customer satisfaction trends
- Product and service sales history and forecasts volumes and gross margins
- Pricing, credit terms, discount structures financing terms
- Existing and potential suppliers and volumes.

3. Technical DD

A review of the technical base and framework of the business. The objective is to evaluate the threats to and future potential of the technology used. For example, the costs of maintaining the system, compatibility with the purchaser's system and quality of management and customer information.

- Company owned computer hardware and software assets
- Details of data and voice networks
- Computer and telecommunications service suppliers
- Company owned telecommunications equipment
- Details of corporate office, mail, intranet and website systems and standards
- Company personal mobile phone and laptop/PC policies and assets
- Infrastructure contingency cover (disaster back-up facilities)
- Any software licensing liabilities.

4. Human resource DD

A review of the employment conditions and working climate of the business. The objective is to assess liabilities relating to the employees and information required will include:

- Director and board structure
- Management structure and responsibilities
- Profile of senior managers
- Management succession plans
- Organization charts
- Numbers and profile of employees
- Employee turnover statistics
- Employee satisfaction survey statistics
- Company mission, vision, culture and values statements
- Employee communications policies and practices
- Pay policies and schemes
- Bonus, profit share and performance management policies and practices
- Pensions and benefit policies and practices
- Key management and staff on which business depends
- Details of employee stock schemes
- Details of any trade union agreements
- Details of any employees subject to TUPE.

5. Legal DD

A review of the legal situation of the business. The objective is to identify and value the legal risks to the business. Pending liabilities may include employee claims, industrial tribunals, environmental damage or other lawsuits. Information required will be:

- Articles of association
- Holding companies and shareholders
- History of acquisitions and divestments
- Details of share capital issued and authorized
- Recent board meeting minutes
- Customer terms of trade
- Product licence terms
- Suppliers' terms of trade
- Premises leases and service agreements
- Schedule of any contingent liabilities
- Details of any litigation underway
- Summary of environmental liabilities and provisions
- Employee standards terms and conditions
- Director/senior manager employment contracts.

6. Tax DD

A review of the tax situation of the business. The objective is to identify and value the tax risks not already accounted for in the financial records.

7. Insurance DD

A review of the insurance situation of the business. The objective is to identify the current insurance coverage and potential insurable risks.

8. Environmental DD

A review of the environmental situation of the business. The objective is to identify any environmental risks that could have an impact on costs or operations, both currently and in the future. This is carried out through a review of documents, if needed supplemented by physical tests of emissions, soil, water, etc.

This may not be an exhaustive list and due diligence is tailored to the particular circumstances of the acquisition. In addition, many organizations are beginning to extend the human resource aspect of due diligence from purely contractual liabilities to cultural issues which might impact on subsequent integration.

Cultural due diligence

Where the purchaser has access to the target's employees, valuable information of a cultural nature may be forthcoming. The purchaser may get a real insight into employees' views on their organization and aspirations for the merger.

Useful information may be gleaned on:

- Management styles and compatibility with the purchaser's management team
- Hierarchical relationships and balance of power
- Decision-making styles
- Acceptance of accountability
- How people are motivated
- Working styles, e.g. teamworking, project oriented, directive
- Role clarity and standards of performance
- Customer service orientation
- Employee views on management effectiveness
- Investment in training and development and attitudes to learning and adaptability
- Skill areas of weakness and strength
- Flexibility and willingness to change.

Information that is already in the public domain should not be overlooked. This can be particularly useful when the acquisition is hostile and full cooperation not forthcoming. News on industrial disputes or past litigation may be important.

On the other hand, much of the employment data will be in the form of computer records which will be covered by the Data Protection Act 1984. It is a criminal offence to hold data without being registered on the Data Protection Register. Any party wishing to transfer data must ensure that it is registered. Penalties for not doing so may be financial or the restricted ability to hold data in the future.

Warranties and indemnities

Since the 1970s warranties and indemnities have played a major part in contract agreements. Their role is to limit liabilities which arise under the principle of *caveat emptor* – buyer beware – which applies to all business acquisitions. In effect it puts the onus on the purchaser to reduce, where possible, the risks in the transaction. The scope of the warranties and indemnities required will be negotiated between buyer and seller and to a large extent relates to the adequacy of the disclosure letter. In general unlisted companies provide wider ranging warranties and indemnities than do listed companies.

A *warranty* guarantees that the information disclosed is accurate. Details will be provided in a schedule and should cover all areas of concern and are referred to in the sale and purchase agreement. A time limit will normally be imposed and the value may be limited.

An *indemnity* is a guaranteed financial solution against a specific liability. The seller promises to meet such liabilities should they arise. There will, however, normally be a stated ceiling of liability.

In spite of detailed warranties and indemnities, it is often not worth the time and cost of litigation to settle disputes and their real benefit probably lies in drawing attention to areas of doubt at the negotiation stage.

Escrow accounts

These are accounts set up to cover liabilities potentially arising from indemnity agreements and consist of accounts held by a third party into which is deposited an agreed amount of cash or shares. The accounts exist for an agreed time period and provide a guaranteed fund to cover liabilities up to an agreed maximum amount.

Employment contracts and TUPE

Transferring employees from one employer to another and the responsibilities and liabilities involved can have far-reaching effects when planning a merger or acquisition. It is an issue that can eat into the time of HR professionals so that they are unable to give time to the vital interpersonal work needed to make integration successful.

Legislation has made it increasingly difficult to ride roughshod over employees during a merger or acquisition and the courts tend to take a hard line on such attempts. There is also a good deal of room for argument by lawyers as to when TUPE regulations apply. The question will usually arise from the first draft of the heads of agreement.

The nature of the transaction

The transaction will invariably fall into the category of:

- A share sale – where the acquired retains its legal identity and relationships but is taken over lock, stock and barrel. Employees of the target remain on existing contracts with existing benefits.
- An asset sale – where the acquirer chooses selected assets. The business is extracted from the legal entity so that legal relationships are affected. This category may include the sale of a division, outsourcing an activity or forming a joint venture. Employer/employee relationships are 'broken' but TUPE may apply.

The business rationale

The significance of employment law will depend on the strategic objective of the merger. Some key questions are likely to be:

- Are employees an asset or a liability?
- Will the merger focus on economies of scale, e.g. reducing duplication in head offices or in operational areas?
- Is the value of the acquisition dependent on retaining customers and key employees?
- Must employment costs be reduced and how can this be achieved?

For example, an acquisition whose value lies in the technical know-how of its employees will have a different legal focus to one where the key task is to assess the liabilities of severance costs and potential impact on the local community. In the former case the purchaser may link the payment of part of the consideration to the continued employment of such employees. Once the strategy is clear, employment law and human resource management can be put into context.

What is TUPE?

During the due diligence phase, personnel or HR departments are often preoccupied by assessing the implications for the deal of TUPE transfers. TUPE or the Transfer of Undertakings (Protection of Employment) Regulations 1981, applies when there is relevant transfer of an undertaking. If the merger or acquisition is solely a share purchase then the relevant legislation is that of standard employment protection. If it is an asset sale TUPE usually applies. Amendments are currently in progress to clarify when a 'relevant transfer' occurs but the situation is by no means clear. Factors that are taken into account include:

- The type of undertaking or business concerned
- Whether tangible assets such as buildings and moveable property are transferred
- The value of intangible assets which are transferred
- Whether a major part of the workforce is taken over by the new employer
- Whether customers are transferred
- The degree of similarity between the activities carried on before and after the alleged transfer
- The period, if any, the activities are suspended.

The Acquired Rights Directive (ARD) is designed to 'provide for the protection of employees in the event of a change of employer ... in particular to ensure that their rights are safeguarded'. A TUPE transfer therefore takes place when a business or 'economic activity' or part of a business is acquired and where the 'economic activity maintains its identity both before and after the transfer'.

The implications for the purchasers of a TUPE transfer are that they step into the previous employer's shoes and automatically take over the contracts of existing employees with associated rights and liabilities including those that arose before the transfer. Clarification may be required as to who is included in the transaction, particularly on high value employees or managers. Apart from occupational pensions (at the time of writing, but this is likely to change), all other terms, conditions and benefits, collective bargaining agreements and consultation agreements transfer to the transferee. Pension benefits remain with the seller but can no longer accrue funds and therefore the purchaser will normally try to offer an equivalent pension benefit. Any benefit which cannot be transferred such as profit sharing, must be matched with a similar scheme. Where terms are not upheld, employees can claim constructive dismissal.

Trade union involvement

It can be difficult to assess the union membership profile of a target as individuals will often have direct debit arrangements with a union which is not known to the employer. Collective agreements with unions transfer to the purchaser. However, the purchaser can bring this collective agreement to an end but may find that trade union recognition comes in through the back door as the employee's contract will still be effective.

In general, large organizations may find union consultation a beneficial aid to employee communication. It is often helpful to use the union infrastructure for important information and union officials can be astute in spotting potential problems before they arise, particularly where they are involved throughout the process. Good union relations are reassuring to employees that their interests are being looked after.

Consultation

There is no legal obligation in the UK to inform or consult on a share sale, but companies have an obligation to inform and consult on a collective basis under TUPE. This must be either with recognized trade union representatives or elected representatives of employees where there is no trade union membership.

Consultation must take place before the transfer and information supplied regarding the transfer: when it is to take place; the reasons for it; the legal, economic and social implications for employees; the measures to be taken regarding employees by the organizations involved. The consultation itself must aim to seek agreement, consider and reply to representations and give reasons for rejecting any.

This can prove difficult where time is of the essence in a merger context. Nevertheless, a failure to consult may result in a claim for up to 13 weeks' pay for each employee affected. Employees have the right to object and terminate the employment contract.

Where an employer is proposing to make 100 or more employees redundant at one establishment within 90 days or less, the consultation must begin at least 90 days before the first dismissal takes effect. This is a minimum timeframe and if the decision is made earlier, consultation should not be delayed in order simply to comply with the statutory period. Consultation should begin at the earliest opportunity.

If employers do not comply with consultation regulations, the employee may take the case to an Employment Tribunal. Price sensitivity is not accepted as a reason to withhold information.

Effecting change

In the case of a share acquisition, changes of terms and conditions can be done by normal means, i.e. by giving notice or by mutual agreement. TUPE transfers, however, make it very difficult to effect change which can be said to be 'in connection with the transfer'. Dismissals may only be achieved for reasonable economic, technical or organizational reason (an 'ETO' reason). In this case they are required to be reasonable and conducted fairly. It must also be shown that there are 'changes in the workforce'.

Changes in terms and conditions relating to a transfer will be invalid and even consensual change may turn out to be unlawful. Nor is there a particular time after the transfer which enables change to be distanced from the transfer. A fundamental change to T&Cs relating to a transfer may constitute unfair dismissal irrespective of length of service. A business case unrelated to the transfer would be needed for any attempt to harmonize terms and conditions.

Nevertheless, gaining consensus from each employee for the variation of terms and conditions is a good place to start and some organizations choose to risk a consensual agreement knowing that they risk future objections. Increased pay may provide an incentive.

It is difficult to persuade a tribunal that there is a true business need for variations of contract, particularly when things are going well.

Redundancy

The announcement of redundancies has an impact on several areas of the business:

- Legal procedures
- Public relations
- Employee relations.

As well as conforming to employment law, it is also therefore essential that the process is seen to be handled professionally and equitably. Criteria for the selection of employees for redundancy should be clarified as well as the reasons for the need for staff reduction. Options for voluntary redundancy may be considered.

Under TUPE, dismissal will be unfair unless it can be shown to be for an ETO reason. This will also apply to pre-transfer dismissals that are seen to be transfer-related. In the case of more than 20 redundancies in one location, whether by share or asset transfer, the company will have obligations under the Trade Union and Labour Relations (Consolidation) Act 1992. This involves an obligation to consult union or elected representatives and to notify the Department of Trade and Industry within 90 days.

Time must be allowed for consultation and the provision of information. Employees must be given due notice of redundancy or offered severance payment in lieu of notice. A good employer will offer comprehensive details of a severance package together with outplacement help, counselling and full support to the employee while looking for other positions. For employees in sensitive roles their immediate departure may be required for commercial reasons. 'Garden leave' (where employees are paid to stay at home for a period) or other restrictive deals may be offered to those who may benefit a competitor.

The sale and purchase agreement

The sale and purchase agreement is the central document in the acquisition process and governs all aspects of the transaction. When this is agreed and disclosure accepted the contract can be signed. If completion is not effected immediately, the parties will need to reach agreement on the management of the interim period. Should the purchaser wish to take immediate control, TUPE will operate before completion and warranties and indemnities will need to be adjusted.

As already suggested in this chapter, fulfilling the letter of the law is necessary but not sufficient for a successful merger and acquisition. Purchasers may need to go well beyond the contractual agreements to release the value of the merger and gain the full value from their new employees. Much goodwill can be forfeited in difficult negotiations and attitudes to legal transactions can be a powerful symbol of organizational culture which may have an impact on subsequent performance. Other chapters in the book will examine these issues more closely.

Appendix

Due diligence – draft TUPE transfer plan – analysis of employment issues

NB This is by way of guidance only and is not exhaustive and no liability is accepted for any reliance on this document: legal advice should be sought before taking any action.

Would you provide us with the following information, including copies of all personnel policies and procedures.

1. Transferring senior employees

a. Name, date of birth, starting date, job title, periods of notice, salary and bonus arrangements not detailed elsewhere in this checklist

b. Fixed term contracts/expiry dates

c. Vacancies to fill or 'frozen'/recruitment policy

d. Non-competition/restrictive covenant undertakings

e. Senior employees and those who may have left and have/or may have claims pending

f. Specimen employment contracts

2. Redundancy

a. Consultations procedures

a. Contractual arrangements with agencies/agency staff/consultants

b. Mobility clause/redeployment arrangements

d. Planned/proposed redundancies

3. Unions

a. Which are currently recognized

b. Relevant National and local (substantive and procedural) Agreements – termination period expiry date(s)

c. Negotiating timetables/groups/unions

d. Arrangements for consultation and participation

e. Levels of membership/to day activities

f. Deduction of union dues/administration fee

g. Outstanding recorded warnings/ET claims/litigation/threatened claims

h. Lay-off agreement? Guaranteed week/payments

i. Current or threatened industrial disputes

j. European W/Councils – constitution/composition

k. Information/consultation with Trades Unions or employee representatives re the proposed sale

4. Wages/salaries

a. Settlement date(s)

b. Minimum wage, rate scales, regional variations including casuals/agency staff

c. Performance related bonus payment/values

d. Grading structure

e. Hours worked – contractual/non-contractual, maximum/minimum

f. Supplementary payments, e.g. Xmas bonus, service

g. Overtime/shift premiums – rules and rates/hours worked/shift rotas

h. Deductions from wages including loans

i. Payment method: bank, building society, cash

j. Frequency paid: weekly, four weekly, monthly

k. Allowances: travel, laundry, lunch and telephone

l. Paid/unpaid breaks special function rate

m. Profit share scheme – or similar arrangement

n. Save as you earn stock option scheme – or similar arrangement

o. Share ownership by employees scheme

p. Free meals or subsidized transport

q. Weeks unpaid/retainer costs

r. Comparability with competitors/alternative employers

s. Any TUPE consensual variations within the defence of a comprehensive agreement

5. Sickness benefit scheme

a. Eligibility/entitlement/ payments/penalties

b. Records of absenteeism/long-term sickness/injuries

c. Private medical insurance – entitlement/cost

d. Permanent health insurance – entitlement/cost

e. If (c) or (d) are self-insured detail the basis of the accrual

f. Contractual/SSP sickness costs

g. Registered disabled/statutory compliance or non-compliance

6. Holidays

a. Eligibility/entitlement/records

b. Current or accruals/value of accrued at time of transfer

7. Pensions (see separate schedule)

a. Scheme(s) – booklets – rules – trustees

a. Eligibility/benefits – employer/employee contribution levels

b. Actual membership

c. Contracted in/out of state schemes

e. Life assurance level of cover

8. Retirement

a. Normal retirement age/exceptions

b. Severance/long service awards and payments

9. Maternity/paternity

a. Maternity/paternity pay/leave/enhancements to statutory provisions

b. Career breaks, child care facilities etc.

c. Names of those on maternity leave and expected date of return/names of temporary replacements

d. Creche facilities/child care vouchers

10. Future employment

a. Confirm who is staying with you/joining us

11. Other

a. Learning/training/development plans and costs

b. Staff turnover and industry comparisons

c. Company credit/charge card details for employees

d. Agreements with suppliers for payroll/pension/permanent health/HR/training services

e. How does the company communicate with its employees

a. Staff discount club

Reproduced by kind permission of Mike Spiller, from a DLA Advance Conference

Further reading

Rankine, D. (1997): *A Practical Guide to Acquisitions: how to increase your chances of success*, John Wiley and Sons

Ryley, M. (1997): *Employment law aspects of mergers and acquisitions – a practical guide*, A Hawksmere Report, London

Smith, M. and Hadden, M. (2000): Legal issues in a cross-border context. *Managing Mergers & Acquisitions*, CBI Business Guide. Caspian Publishing Ltd, London

Preparing to set sail – transition planning

In preparing to set sail, Jason was joined by a band of the noblest heroes in Greece. A number of the Argonauts, a name given to those ancient heroes who went with Jason on board the ship the Argo, to Colchis, forthwith made preparations for the expedition. . .

Introduction

Jason's quest to return with the Golden Fleece was clear enough in its intent, less clear to him were the challenges and obstacles he would face on his journey. The strength of his vessel served him well. It had to withstand the rough seas and the Clashing Rocks that threatened to crush the Argo. It was also the courage and skills of his Argonauts that contributed to his success.

The transition manager needs to be equally well equipped and prepared. The preparation for a successful transition needs to be done in these early days prior to the transition launch. This critical transition planning period is outlined in Figure 5.1.

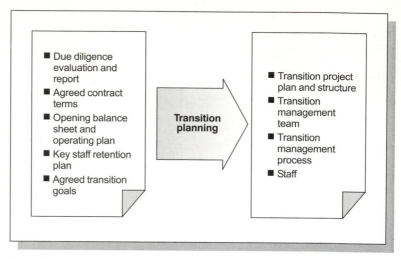

Figure 5.1 Transition planning

The transition manager's involvement in the earlier due diligence phase will help to provide the essential continuity between the due diligence phase and transition planning. In particular, the plan must reflect:

- The original purpose, intentions and success criteria for the acquisition as defined in the strategic plan
- The findings of the due diligence report in terms of areas of identified synergy or misalignment
- The opening balance sheet and operating plan for the acquired company
- The key staff retention plan that identifies who the key staff are and mechanisms to retain them
- The agreed goals for the transition project.

Perhaps the first activity of this planning phase is to test out the clarity, realism and strength of sponsorship for the transition goals. The goals are agreed as part of negotiating the deal to establish a focus and approach for the integration process. Testing out the interpretation and likely impact of these goals at this early point can have real value and help in building a strong sense of purpose, direction and practical understanding for the members of the transition management team. The transition is normally challenging enough without having crew members who are either confused or reluctant travellers.

The transition manager's equivalent of Jason's ship, the Argo, takes the form of a well-designed and well-structured transition plan and management process. This will ensure they maintain a clear sense of purpose and progress throughout the transition. The third element, as with Jason, is the skills and leadership capabilities of his crew. This team may need to be drawn from far and wide in an attempt to pull together the right leadership and business capabilities, the right cultural perspectives and, importantly, the right balance of representation across acquirer and acquired organizations.

From possibilities to practicalities

The focus of transition management swings from the concepts and possibilities of the earlier phases to focus on the practicalities of how to engage people in the transition. The high level picture of direction will play an important role in instilling a sense of clarity of purpose and help to reduce the level of uncertainty likely to be felt by staff at this stage. The attitude and actions of senior managers have a large bearing on the mood of employees. Management energy, clarity, honesty, openness and consistency are important in painting an enticing picture of the future. In particular a trusting and positive relationship between acquirer and acquired senior managers helps to build a more positive mood among staff.

In the earlier due diligence phase, the emphasis is on identifying the legal and financial implications of the partnership and the 'soft' due diligence will have identified the organizations' partnership synergies, risks and obstacles.

The transition plan has to respond to these needs by turning high level statements of purpose into pragmatic and practical plans. These plans help deliver the business value-add expected of the integration and help staff to understand how they will be affected. The focus on the added value to be achieved can sometimes get lost in the single-minded drive to integrate the two operations. The integration of the two organizations and management structures can become a purpose in its own right, with insufficient regard for the value that it delivers. In these circumstances, the whole transition is more likely to dissolve into a political battle with no more laudable an aim than the maintenance or assumption of power by individual managers.

In one example of an acquisition of a large public services operation, acquired as part of an outsourcing deal, the focus of the integration was primarily one of structural integration. Insufficient attention was paid to the fundamental issues around lack of commercial and selling skills in the acquired organization and the fundamental cultural differences between the two organizations. The approach resulted in an expensive and drawn-out integration process that failed to realize the full business potential of the acquisition and left staff feeling under-valued.

Defining the scope for the transition project

The scope for the transition project needs to be centred on the business value-add to be realized and the necessary realignment of people, skills and business processes. In the early days, the project must also address issues such as sustaining the current business operation and the retention of the key staff in whom the current business value is embedded or on whom the operation critically depends. The project must also specifically look at the short-term needs of staff in both acquired and acquirer organizations, helping them to settle into the new organization as soon as possible. Addressing some of their needs for further clarity and reassurance can create a climate in which staff are more likely play a positive and active role in the integration activities.

The scope of the transition project can be summarized as:

- Creating the business added value for the future
- Securing current business operations
- Retaining and engaging the key staff
- Creating a climate for staff support for the integration.

Each of these areas is dealt with later in this chapter.

Finding time to plan

The pressure on transition management to move directly to implementation in these early days is great and often difficult to resist. The frenzied activities of due diligence, coupled with the sense of achievement in striking the deal, plus a groundswell of uncertainty in staff, often leads to an irresistible pressure for immediate action. Yet there is an even stronger need for considered plans and actions; rushing into announcing incomplete plans or ill-considered actions will most likely backfire. Starting to plan the transition as early as possible in the acquisition cycle can ease these apparently conflicting time pressures. It is often possible for transition planning to take place in parallel with due diligence, so allowing for more detailed and considered communication soon after the initial announcement. This has the benefit of creating a sense of open and purposeful leadership from the earliest point.

An example of this is the approach adopted by SKF, the engineering company, in having joint top management meetings to discuss the transition at the earliest possible stage of the acquisition process[1]. This is intended to establish a clear and common framework to support a successful transition. The normal SKF approach is designed for acquisitions that involve the full assimilation of the acquired company into the SKF organization. The intent of the SKF foundation plan is to surface and resolve at the earliest possible point any issues that could arise and to get joint management understanding and support to resolve them.

SKF Foundation: meet, greet and plan

Acquired/acquiree management teams meet to:

- socialize and exchange information
- discuss acquired company needs, expectations, fears and reactions
- discuss acquired company markets, products, organization, people and plans
- discuss acquired company strengths and factors that have led to their success
- discuss acquiree's values, responsibilities, rewards, policies and practices
- discuss acquiree's business strategies and markets
- communicate, discuss and decide required changes to management structure, reporting, restructuring and potential layoffs
- communicate and clarify the non-negotiable elements
- draft the short-term transition plan.

Although this approach is designed for use where the intention is fully to integrate the acquired company, it does touch on some important aspects of early planning discussions between senior management that are potentially applicable to all acquisitions. Discussions at this stage can help to establish a solid base for transition success, by avoiding 'showstoppers' emerging later on in the project when announcements have been made or even in the midst of implementation.

The early meetings are likely to cover issues such as:

- Opportunities for senior managers to get to know and start to trust each other
- Open sharing of information between managers
- Raising concerns or fears about the partnership
- Putting the hard decisions on the table and getting them taken quickly

- Deciding/reviewing senior management restructuring
- Getting clear about the issues which are non-negotiable
- Clarifying the transition goals that define the added value to be achieved
- Agreeing the focus and scope of the transition project
- Agreeing any business or financial constraints on the transition project
- Agreeing how to set up two-way communication channels between the management teams.

Until these areas have been addressed and successfully concluded there is always a risk of future disruption, delay or even failure of the transition project caused by fundamental issues or conflicts emerging at a later point.

Sustaining the business operation

The history of acquisitions consistently shows the potential short-term disruption that they can have on the business. Historical data suggest that *operational productivity can fall by as much as 50 per cent in the first few months of a merger.* This does not have to be the case if a practical and sensitive approach is taken to the transition and sufficient time is spent in ensuring business continuity. The factors leading to such disruption include:

- Staff and management uncertainty leading to a loss of motivation and reluctance to put forward ideas and to contribute fully
- Less focus on the business due to involvement in the transition project
- Unclear accountabilities for business performance
- Unclear decision-making authorities
- Lack of linkage between the opening operating plan from due diligence and the goaling or commitment of managers in the new operating structure.

Taking the necessary steps to stabilize the business at the earliest possible time will help to minimize the disruption. One of these steps should be to establish clear management accountabilities for the immediate operation either through taking the high level restructuring decisions up front, or if this is not possible at this stage, by creating an interim management structure. It is also important to agree with these managers operational goals that support the 'opening operating plan' emerging from due diligence. Previously agreed earn-out deals or performance bonuses may be used to underpin these goals.

The high-level management restructure involved in many major deals is likely to disrupt long-established management accountabilities and decision-making processes. Each area of disruption needs to be addressed and alternative practices agreed and then communicated to all those affected. This work ideally involves members of the existing staff to help surface the issues and secure their commitment to the solutions.

In the case of the Articon-Integralis merger one of the early integration projects was the definition of common business authority levels across the company. These were driven by the needs of the new joint business and decided and communicated by senior management.

Another important area of stabilization is that of management reporting. It is essential that standards and processes of reporting are established and implemented from day one. This may involve the content, format or frequency of reporting and often will also include implementation of standard revenue and cost accounting methods.

The business disruption resulting from the drain on time and resources caused by the transition project activities is not easily avoided, but its impact can be managed by ensuring this issue is considered when structuring and phasing the transition plan. To attempt to achieve too much too quickly in the project is likely to increase dramatically the impact on the business and therefore the level of disruption.

The timing of these decisions is critical, as any confusion over management of day-to-day operations will be very visible to employees and potentially to customers. Such disruption is likely to leave both customers and employees with a diminished view of the value of the deal. Any sustained disruption may even put the financial viability of the deal at risk.

Getting the people bit right from the start

The very nature of mergers and acquisitions is likely to disrupt many aspects of an organization and consequently eat away at each employee's sense of belonging and motivation. This in turn can lead to uncertainty and often a level of cynicism or withdrawal. In these early days after the announcement of the deal, senior managers will have been involved in the deal for some time and may well feel a sense of excitement about the future possibilities, feeling as though they are now in control of events. By contrast, employees are likely to feel uncertain about the nature of the deal and anxious about the impact it may have on them. In this state they will not necessarily be able to share the enthusiasm and excitement of their managers. Any early announcements or contact with staff should be sensitive to these differences.

The actions and attitudes of managers can either heighten staff anxieties by their insensitivity to these issues, or can start to reassure staff of their future value in the new regime. In most companies, especially knowledge-based or service companies, the current and future value of the business is heavily dependent on having a knowledgeable and motivated workforce. The transition itself depends on the participation and support of that workforce to realize the necessary changes. Value can be disrupted or even destroyed by an ineffective transition or a poorly communicated one.

In these early days of uncertainty, employees are likely to gain some reassurance from managers' empathy. Their reassurance helps to create an environment where staff will be more inclined to open their minds to a new future and, at least in part, to share the enthusiasm of their senior managers.

The case of a recent acquisition of a very successful software company demonstrates how insufficient focus on these people issues in the early days can put the whole deal at risk. The acquired company had built a strong position with a number of leading products in a rapidly growing marketplace. The business was heavily dependent on the energy and values of a small number of key employees and owners and had a distinctive culture that encouraged creativity and risk taking. The new owners paid a premium for this company based on its leadership position and future potential.

Once the deal was struck, the acquirer adopted a structured and business-like approach to the transition, with the emphasis on structural integration and business control. There was little time spent with staff or managers listening to their views or discussing the cultural differences. This left many staff in the acquired organization with a sense of not being valued and an anxiety that the company values were shifting away from ones they had held dear. All the actions of the acquirer appeared to emphasize values of business control and accountability and an apparent lack of value for the people they had acquired.

In the first few months of the transition, the turnover of senior staff increased dramatically; the same staff in which the company's business value was embedded. This resulted in an acquisition where the new owners had paid for the significant value they recognized in the company but had unintentionally put that value at risk as a result of the early transition approach they adopted. The CEO of the acquired company later observed: 'I always sensed there were some cultural differences between us but somehow we never really put them on the table until it was too late'.

In the early stages of any transition the actions and attitudes of managers will be seen by anxious employees as representing the values of the new organization and a measure of how the acquired organization is valued by its new owners.

Often the early visible actions of managers are associated with either management restructuring or the launch of the transition plan itself. These activities are an opportunity to be seen to be treating people with respect and fairness and in a way that demonstrates the value with which the acquired company is regarded. These early activities will be for some the first face-to-face contacts between the two parties. It is important to ensure they are conducted in a way that will have a positive impact on those involved. Such initial encounters will have more impact on forming new relationships and attitudes than a thousand words about company values or an exciting vision of a bright new future together! This doesn't mean putting off tough decisions or holding back bad news, but it does mean adopting an approach to the decisions and their implementation that is sensitive to the needs and feelings of staff.

In summary some of the key factors in getting the people bit right are:

- Spending time understanding employee needs, views and concerns and factoring them into the plan
- Being sensitive to and acknowledging employee uncertainty
- Ensuring any restructuring or redundancy decisions are taken and implemented in a fair and balanced manner
- Informing people of the impact of the transition on them as soon as possible
- Supporting line managers in their essential role of helping their staff through the changes
- Demonstrating the value with which staff (especially acquired) are regarded through management words and deeds
- Helping people to understand what is expected of them in the transition
- Helping people find out about their new partners and their business
- Early involvement of staff from both acquired and acquirer organizations
- Creating opportunities for cross-boundary working
- Giving people the opportunity to meet senior managers in the new organization
- Establishing immediate and on-going two-way communication with staff.

Core values and principles of the transition

In an atmosphere of staff uncertainty and with the possible differences in cultures between the new partners, it is often helpful to declare some values and principles to steer the transition project. These principles should guide the way decisions are made, staff are treated, changes are initiated and the project and its progress communicated. The senior managers of the two companies should explicitly agree these as part of their early planning discussions. It may be dangerous to assume that the values and approaches that have been applied by either company in the past will still be appropriate in this transition period. It is also important in developing the new organization to have these values explicitly stated. The values that are applied during the transition are likely to be seen by the acquired employees as those of their new owners.

In addition, declaring these principles can reinforce the importance that managers attach to people and their contribution to both the business and the transition project. There is also value for the new senior management team in sharing their views on this topic as it is likely to surface any issues about the integration approach and any possible cultural differences between the companies. Any issues arising will more likely be resolved at this early point rather than later on when they can become symbols of and rallying points for resistance to proposed changes.

Mere declarations of principles and values serve little practical purpose. All managers involved in the transition need to demonstrate their meaning through their actions. The transition principles and values need to reflect the culture and values of the two organizations and the needs of the transition project. They may cover areas such as:

- Senior management involvement and accountability for success
- Empowerment and make-up of transition management team
- Desired values of the new organization
- Level of openness and honesty of communication during the transition
- Importance of and channels for two-way communication
- Role of line managers in the transition
- Involvement of impacted people in decision making
- The principles and processes to be used for restructuring, redundancy and appointment
- The value of the acquired people, practices and business
- How transition success will be measured.

Defining the transition plan

We have already talked about the need for the transition project to address issues beyond that of integrating the organizations; it requires a broader focus covering:

- Creating the business added value for the future
- Securing current business operations
- Retaining and engaging the key staff
- Creating a climate of staff support for the integration.

These high level intentions need to be translated into a comprehensive and well-structured transition plan developed by the transition management team. They will need to establish common views of the factors that will influence the make-up of the plan, before the plan itself is developed. Some of these factors are:

- Their interpretation of transition project goals. These could be business goals relating to improvements in areas such as market share, sales penetration, revenue, gross margins or operating costs as a result of the transition. They may also include organizational goals covering integration of key policy practice or capability areas or of specific groups.
- The key measures that are to be used to measure transition success. For example, in the case of a transition goal, say, to integrate product portfolios, the measure of success adopted may be the trends in the level of 'cross-selling' of specific products or changes in product mix. In the case of organizational goals the measures may be softer ones, looking for shifts in attitudes or practices. Agreeing these measures up front will help to keep the transition project focused on the expected outcomes.
- The actions that need to be taken to establish a common level of staff understanding of the integration purpose and plans and address their concerns.
- The likely different starting points and needs of staff and managers from acquired and acquirer organizations.
- The values and principles to be used to guide the transition project and the methods it uses.

The transition management team will need to take all these factors into account in building a transition plan that is focused on the expected business benefits and also sensitive to the needs of people in the organization.

Structuring the transition plan

The complex nature of most integration projects is such that they involve many activities spread widely across the organizations and often involving different time horizons. Attempting to manage or communicate a project of such complexity may prove unwieldy. The situation is often further complicated by the fact that the clarity required for some aspects of the transition is not yet available and further data gathering and design work are required in these areas. A common solution to this complexity is to split the project into two separate phases (Figure 5.2). The two phases being:

1 A short-term phase often referred to as the *100-day plan*. This comprises the integration quick wins, the immediate actions related to sustaining business operations and staff retention and the planning and design activities for the longer-term initiatives.

2 A subsequent phase or *integration phase* that includes the more complex longer-term initiatives. It is often these initiatives that will deliver the business benefits of the integration. The initiatives probably require more time to plan and design and also are likely to have implementation times in the order of six to twelve months.

The transition plan can be thought of as an iceberg with the tip consisting of the quick wins. These tend to be the more visible initiatives that can create an early sense of urgency and progress. They also create the opportunity for people to gain knowledge

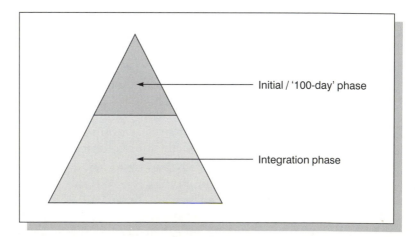

Figure 5.2 Transition plan structure

and experience of working with their new colleagues. The activities of the 100-day phase help to build a greater level of understanding and trust to support the more challenging initiatives of the integration phase. The 100-day plan also allows for quality planning and design of the more complex integration initiatives.

The integration phase lies beneath the water line, covering the more complex and longer-term integration projects. It is these longer-term and potentially more costly and disruptive initiatives that are likely to deliver the lasting business benefits.

Defining the 100-day plan

The 100-day plan needs to be developed as part of the overall transition project. All the potential activities of the full transition project will need to be identified, then those that can be practically implemented within the first 100 days flagged up. The full set of transition project activities needs to be teased out by the transition management team in a structured manner to ensure no critical activities are overlooked and that the interdependencies between the initiatives are understood. One possible approach to defining the plan is:

1 Brainstorm of the initiatives and activities to realize the transition goals
2 Brainstorm the activities necessary to sustain business operations
3 Brainstorm the activities necessary to ensure key staff retention
4 Identify any other activities to address other issues arising from due diligence
5 Identify any activities to prepare for and deliver the transition launch

Then:

6 Group the activities into possible change initiatives that are relatively autonomous and have clear and measurable outcomes
7 Prioritize the initiatives according to the business benefit they will deliver
8 Prioritize the initiatives according to their impact on staff retention or support the change process
9 Scope each initiative in terms of likely complexity, resources required, elapse time and disruptive impact
10 Developing an outline transition plan looking at practical time horizons

11 Review the plan based on any affordability constraints on the integration project, i.e. slipping costly initiatives such as new systems to fit budget constraints

12 Finally, review the plan to smooth out the disruptive impact on the business operation and its staff.

This process can prove to be a valuable investment in defining a realistic transition project in that it brings home the true nature of the transition. It may bring a practical insight into the likely time and effort required to implement the changes. Without this up-front investment, the transition project is more likely to be subject to on-going slippage or redesign.

One approach to the review and categorization of the initiatives described above is to categorize them according to timespan of a project and the project's cost or disruptive impact. Project timing will likely be driven by the urgency of the project or the time it will take to implement the change. The project impact reflects the human or financial resource requirements to execute the project and the operational or organizational disruption of implementing it.

The initiatives can then be thought of on the impact matrix shown in Figure 5.3.

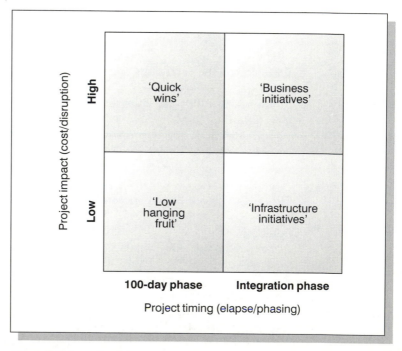

Figure 5.3 Impact matrix

The matrix highlights four types of initiatives, the first two making up the 100-day plan.

The 'quick wins'

These are the initiatives that bring real short-term business or organizational benefit and are affordable in terms of their implementation costs or level of disruption. Typical examples of 'quick wins' include integrating product portfolios, removal of duplicate resources or wasteful practices, asset sharing and on the people side, implementing a key staff retention plan.

The 'low hanging fruit'

These are activities with a low level of disruption or implementation costs. Their business or organizational benefit may be less direct but still important. They may be more symbolic in nature or deliver value over the longer term. Examples of these would be: changes to employee ID badges, office signage, establishing communication mechanisms, cross-boundary meetings or updating employee mail lists.

The remaining initiatives are of a longer-term nature and make up the integration phase.

The 'business initiatives'

These are the initiatives that bring the longer-term business benefits expected of the acquisition. They will require higher levels of investment of time and effort and potentially be quite disruptive to the business; they may perhaps involve significant restructuring or adoption of new working practices. Some of these projects may have been potential quick wins deferred due to lack of short-term investment funds or to spread their disruption on the business.

The 'infrastructure initiatives'

This final group of initiatives has a lower direct business or organizational benefit and may be driven by the need to integrate the companies more broadly. They could be focused on integration of company business infrastructures, such as corporate information infrastructure, IT systems or HR policy and practices.

Laying the transition plan initiatives on a matrix of this sort can help to prioritize and phase the initiatives and so develop a plan that has a better balance and a more realistic set of time horizons. A typical plan is shown in Figure 5.4.

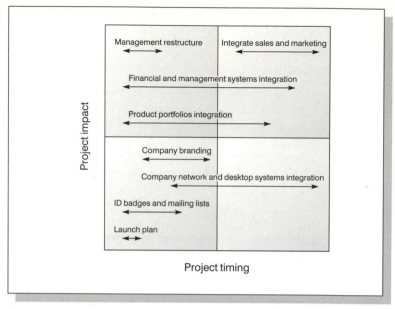

Figure 5.4 Transition plan initiatives matrix

100-day plan checklist

The 100-day plan initiatives will vary greatly from case to case. Below is a checklist of the issues that will usually need addressing during the 100-day phase:

1 IT infrastructure

- E-mail and telephone directories update
- Company network inter-connection (voice and data)
- Intranet updating and linking
- Internet update and linking

2 Management

- Senior management restructure appointment and announcements
- Operational management restructure and accountability and authorities (even if interim)
- Management reporting and escalation procedures
- Management briefing sessions

3 Employees

- Group briefing sessions on transition
- One-to-one briefing and data gathering session
- Employee database update
- Employee corporate ID badge and business card update/re-branding
- Key staff retention plan

4 Transition management

- Define and document transition plan and projects
- Appointment of transition project teams
- Set up transition plan web page on intranet
- Announce transition management teams
- Launch transition plan and introduce players
- Transition progress reporting formats and schedule
- Transition query/suggestion hotline

5 Communication

- Internal/external communication manager appointment
- Set up internal communication distribution list for transition
- Internal communication plan
- Shareholder/investor community communication plan
- Customer communication plan
- Supplier/partner communication plan
- Building signage re-branding
- Corporate marketing communication and branding standards (internal and external).

The transition plan launch

This event is likely to be the most visible and formative event of the transition project. The timing and content of the event must paint a picture for employees of a well-planned and managed transition project. If the launch is to establish a solid platform for a successful transition, it will need to be well planned, professionally presented and supported by a quality transition plan. The transition launch will need to:

- Confirm and clarify the original goals of the merger/acquisition

- Clarify the scope and goals of the transition project
- Announce/confirm the new management structure and any interim management structures
- Emphasize the value of the acquired company and its people
- State the underlying principles and values of the company that will guide the transition plan
- Outline the possible impact on people and provide any reassurance about how and when these issues will be managed
- Clarify what is expected of individuals in the interim
- Announce/confirm any decisions already taken
- Introduce the transition project structure and timing
- Introduce the transition management team
- Commit to on-going two-way communication process and explain mechanisms
- Acknowledge and set expectations related to specific local issues
- Outline the next steps in the transition
- Open question and answer session.

To ensure the launch events are well received and effective there will need to be a consistency of content across all the launch sessions. This will probably require the events to be fronted by members of the transition senior management team and based on an agreed set of standard presentation materials. Getting the right mix of management representation at these events is important: there should be a mix of managers from the acquirer and acquired organizations and a mix of corporate and local managers. The presence and participation of senior managers from acquired and acquirer organizations will help to create a sense of strong leadership and support for the initiative. If local managers have had little or no previous involvement in the acquisition, it is important to brief them in advance of the session so they feel better able to handle questions and concerns from their staff about the plan.

These sessions can be more powerful if they are face-to-face meetings between transition management and staff. The size of group attending each launch session needs to be considered if they are intended to be interactive. Groups greater than 30 attendees are less likely to be interactive and therefore will not provide an opportunity for people to air their concerns. On occasions, the only practical way of reaching those impacted in an acceptable timeframe is to increase the number of attendees at each session. These larger sessions can then be complemented by smaller follow-on question and answer sessions to allow more open debate to take place.

A typical agenda for the launch would be:

- Acquisition history and intent
- Outline of the two companies and their managers
- Immediate decisions and appointments
- Introduction of new managers
- The transition goals and plan
- Company/transition principles and values
- Introduction of the transition management team
- Managing the impact on individuals
- Two-way communication plan
- The 100-day plan and players
- Question and answer

Whatever the content of the launch, it is wise to adopt a conservative approach and to ensure that commitments made in these sessions can be and are delivered. In this way clarity and confidence is gradually built around the transition. It is also important to pick up on any actions that are committed at the sessions and ensure they are followed through and the outcomes effectively communicated.

Getting employee reaction

The gathering of attendee reaction to the transition launch either through structured feedback forms or informally, is an important part of the on-going two-way communication process. The feedback itself will form invaluable commentary on the plan and help highlight any omissions or sensitive areas.

The stage should now be set for a successful transition project.

Case study

The Articon-Integralis case study – Part II

Board accountabilities

At an early stage the Articon-Integralis board agreed responsibilities for the key activities related to the merger. The joint CEOs and the CFO took responsibility for managing investor relations and the joint COOs and the CFO took responsibility for managing the merger itself.

Initial announcement

On the day the deal went unconditional, a series of external and internal announcements took place. The external announcement covered the nature and intent of the deal. The internal announcement was in the form of a common presentation given at all offices by board members. The presentation covered the following:

- What had happened: acquisition of Integralis by Articon
- Outline of the two companies
- Benefits anticipated
- Shared values
- Shared mission
- Nature of the acquisition (financial takeover, management merger and reverse takeover in terms of relative size of the two companies)
- Impact on employee shareholders
- Restructuring of the board
- Framework for other management restructuring
- What happens next
- Question and answer session

These initial announcements were well received, although there was clearly uncertainty over the impact of the deal on individual careers and shareholdings. The situation was greatly helped by the open approach of the announcement which put all the issues on the table. A direct reference was made to the nature of the deal. It referred to the various aspects of the deal in terms of:

- An Articon *acquisition* of Integralis shares
- A *merger* of the management boards
- A *reverse takeover* in terms of Integralis' relative size

This totally open approach, together with the joint roles on the board, had the effect of defusing some of the anxieties about who was really in control. There was an acceptance of a collaborative approach. Managers were also in a position to state clearly that there would be no redundancies as a result of the deal, although clearly a number of managers' jobs would change and the structure in which most people operated would clearly change over time.

Perhaps not surprisingly the biggest topic of conversation in the Integralis Q&A sessions was on the employee share scheme.

This was a good news story in that employees stood to make an excellent return on their investment, subject to a successful SPO. It therefore served to provide employees and managers with a common interest in a successful integration and SPO.

The internal announcements were well received and provided a good basis for starting to integrate the organizations.

Transition planning

Prior to the offer going unconditional, the COOs had developed some outline plans for the integration exercise. This work served to highlight the volume of work involved in integrating the two companies. They concluded that the integration project would inevitably be complex with a high impact and demand on employees' and management time. This was particularly true for the board members who were already stretched from apparently endless demands from all quarters! They felt that they needed a project manager to design and manage the whole integration and provide the necessary focus. They concluded that this resource did not exist internally and that there were potential benefits of bringing in outside expertise. They were looking for someone with:

- Experience of previous integration projects
- Strong project management disciplines
- A dedicated resource that could focus on the integration activities and not be distracted by other business pressures
- Someone who would have credibility with their managers.

The integration project manager was appointed from outside in March 2000.

Developing the 100-day plan

The integration project manager worked with the COOs and the finance director to develop the plan. In developing the plan the basic background information and key principles for managing the integration project were agreed. These covered:

- The business intent of the merger
- Joint company mission and vision
- Joint company values
- Medium term business objectives
- New management structure and accountabilities.

A management team was also set up to manage all aspects of the integration transition project. The team met fortnightly to approve plans and to review progress. The team comprised:

- The COOs
- The CFO
- The IT director
- The transition project manager.

The meeting discipline was strong with agendas agreed in advance, thorough progress reviews and all decisions and actions minuted and progressed.

The immediate priorities for the transition project were agreed by the team and included a mixture of planning and short-term integration activities. These were developed into a phase one transition plan. The selection of these activities was driven by the following priorities:

- The need for quick wins to emphasize the urgency of the integration
- The need to clarify the scope and approach to be adopted for the longer-term more complex issues
- The need to get some short-term visible activities completed quickly for both internal and external impact
- The need to ensure that the transition proceeded smoothly without any crises or apparent loss of control to support a successful SPO
- The need to establish the most effective processes and procedures to plan, monitor and communicate progress.

As a result, the initial plan was focused on those activities that could be completed in the first 100 days and had most impact on the above priorities. The 100-day plan included:

- Set up of a communication forum for all employees that relied on cascading information two ways through the line management structure
- Set up of an integration project page on the intranets
- Updating and inter-linking the company internets and intranets
- Updating of company internal and external branding, e.g. promotional materials, business cards, letterheads
- Customer communication plans and campaigns

- Company mailing list updating
- Employee ID and access badge updating
- Employee database updating.

Each of these initiatives, although apparently straightforward was carefully planned up front. It was felt that the best way of establishing credibility for the plan was to ensure that all initiatives were clearly scoped and were sponsored by one of the board members. A champion was then appointed from the existing management to manage each project, who in turn defined the project plan outlining deliverables, milestones, resources required and any perceived risks.

The make-up of these project teams was used as an early opportunity to break down the barriers between the two organizations by working on these projects together. Appointments of staff to the projects demonstrated the principle of picking the most appropriate people, those directly impacted by the intended change while, at the same time attempting to get balanced representation.

Each initiative was also required to report progress against agreed milestones on a regular basis to the overall project manager. These progress reports together with the overall project progress report were widely circulated and placed on the company's intranet.

The role and value of the project champion and sponsor became apparent very quickly as the various projects began to slip. This was caused by the need to get more clarity of the scope and deliverables and by the unavailability of committed resources. There was continuous pressure to assign a higher and higher priority to the transition projects to ensure resources were freed up from the operating business. Despite these problems the initial phase tasks were all completed with little slippage.

Overall it was felt this phase progressed well and gave employees a sense of comfort with the integration. In the post-completion review of the 100-day plan, it became clear that insufficient attention had been given to ensuring that new policy and practice emerging from these early projects was handed over to the appropriate managers for on-going ownership.

The secondary public offering

In March an investor roadshow was run to promote the SPO, and the SPO launch took place in April with the share price now at 70 Euro – a rise of over 100 per cent in five months.

Learning points: Transition planning

- The need to focus initially on a small number of key achievable integration topics and deliver them
- The value of a dedicated and experienced integration project manager who has mandate from the board to maintain focus on the integration
- Importance of clearly scoping what is to be done and the expected outcomes
- Value of translating the transition goals into clear transition projects and plans
- Essential role of senior management sponsors for integration projects
- Value of having champions for each project
- Inevitable conflict of priorities between integration and regular business and need to assign right priority to projects
- The importance of having on-going owners for new policy and practices
- Value of focusing on short-term priorities to ensure short-term action and progress

Summary

The complex nature of most transition projects and their potentially disruptive impact on the business, makes timely transition planning essential. Planning can help to focus on the real business benefits and to reduce the level of disruption of the business.

- A quality transition plan can help to:

- Flush out the true nature of the transition
- Set and manage expectations of what needs to be done and their relative priority and urgency
- Develop a well-structured, balanced and realistic plan
- Gain better senior management understanding of the transition project and therefore stronger sponsorship
- Develop a strong transition management team and shared plan
- Establish a clearer staff understanding of the transition project and its impact on them
- Start to build staff confidence in the transition project and its management team.

References

1. Garrow, V. and Holbeche, L. (2001): *Effective mergers and acquisitions*, Roffey Park Management Institute

Designing in the value – integration initiative design

The conditions under which Jason was to recover the Golden Fleece were so hard the Argonauts would have perished in the attempt. . . The impracticability of such a journey is well known

Introduction

The challenges that Jason faced during his quest to obtain the Golden Fleece were more to do with the obstacles he encountered on his journey, rather than the acquisition of the fleece itself. Jason's experience has

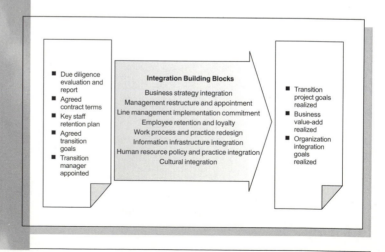

- Due diligence evaluation and report
- Agreed contract terms
- Key staff retention plan
- Agreed transition goals
- Transition manager appointed

Integration Building Blocks

Business strategy integration
Management restructure and appointment
Line management implementation commitment
Employee retention and loyalty
Work process and practice redesign
Information infrastructure integration
Human resource policy and practice integration
Cultural integration

- Transition project goals realized
- Business value-add realized
- Organization integration goals realized

parallels with the challenges often faced by those involved in mergers and acquisitions; challenges that, in the past, have resulted in over half of them failing to achieve their financial objectives. It appears that having clarity of purpose for an acquisition, by itself does not guarantee success. The threat to successful acquisition is more often in the practical problems encountered while attempting to integrate the acquired company.

Major factors in increasing the chances of acquisition success are the appropriate design of the integration and the effectiveness of the methods used to manage it. Integrating organizations in areas that are unlikely to yield any direct business benefit is likely simply to increase integration costs and risks. A key to improving acquisition success involves bounding the scope of integration initiatives to areas that deliver direct business benefits rather than assuming full integration or assimilation is the desired goal.

This chapter looks at some practical steps to achieving the expected business benefits of any acquisition through well-designed and focused integration initiatives. The variety and complexity of mergers and acquisitions makes it impractical to provide a set of golden rules that will lead to success. Instead, this chapter provides a guide to more effective integration design.

Business drivers for integration

A prerequisite to adopting a more focused and business driven approach to integration is having a clear business intent for any merger or acquisition that quantifies the business benefits that are anticipated from the deal.

Buono and Bowditch[1] provide a perspective on the possible business drivers or strategies for mergers. They divide the strategic purpose of an acquisition or merger into five different categories:

1 *A horizontal/related merger:* when two organizations have the same or closely related products in the same geographical market, with approximately the same customers and suppliers
2 *A vertical merger:* when the organizations involved had, or could have had, a buyer–seller relationship prior to the combination and operate in the same industry
3 *A product extension:* where the variety of products increases but the products are not competing directly with one another
4 *Market extension:* where the firm is producing the same products or services but in different market areas
5 *Conglomerate/unrelated acquisition:* where the firms involved are unconnected.

Other M&A classifications include:

Concentric marketing: the target has the same customer types as the buying/dominant company but uses different technology.

Concentric technology: the target company uses the same technology as the buying/dominant company but has different customer types.

What is interesting about these different types of strategic purpose is that they tend to drive different attitudes and behaviours in employees within the acquired company. In addition to having different types of purpose, mergers can be defined by the nature and level of integration they involve. Napier[2] distinguishes three types of mergers: extension; collaborative; and redesign mergers. In extension mergers, the acquired organization is left untouched or only slightly changed with regard to its management or operation. Typically it is important to retain managers in this type of merger. Collaborative mergers occur when two organizations blend operations, assets, technology or cultures. This can take place in a synergistic way, when both organizations make compromises, or when exchanging or transferring knowledge or something else between the organizations. Redesign mergers mean that one organization widely adopts the other organization's policies and practices.

Regardless of the strategic purpose behind the merger, the greatest impact on employees comes from the ways in which integration decisions are made, communicated and implemented. Some types of M&As will require shallow levels of integration while others will call for total absorption or 'assimilation'. Not surprisingly, these different approaches will produce different effects on employees.

In extension mergers, employees remain generally unaffected and, if they are kept informed, they are likely to maintain performance and satisfaction. The situation in redesign or collaborative mergers could be totally different. Changes in management, policies and direction are likely to occur. Decisions are made about which managers are to leave and which are to be retained. Human resource planning involves incorporating the remaining managers of the acquired organization. Employees may suffer from anxiety about job security and adapting to the new situation. Even though uncertainty may only be temporary, our various research projects suggest a cocktail of ingredients, which are potentially lethal to the success of a merger.

Any integration design needs to be mindful of its impact on staff anxiety and it needs to minimize employee anxiety while still making the changes necessary to realize the business benefits.

The scope of integration initiatives

One way of minimizing the disruption of integration is to focus any integration initiative on only the essential business and organizational aspects necessary to realize the benefit. A way of approaching this is to break the business areas down into the key elements of any business. This would lead to a set of business building blocks as summarized below:

- Strategic integration: this includes the integration of strategic direction, investments and associated processes
- Managerial integration: the integration of management structures, styles, business policies and procedures and information systems
- Assets integration: the sharing of financial, physical or intellectual assets
- Market and product integration: the integration of product portfolios, policies, selling channels, marketing standards or operations
- Operational integration: the integration of specific operating functions such as research and development, manufacturing or customer services
- Infrastructure integration: integration of the supporting business infrastructure of the companies including human resource or information or IT policies, standards, procedures, systems or operations
- Financial/legal integration: this is the integration of financial policies, standards, procedures, systems or operations. This could be at a corporate or operational level. It also covers the integration of legal structures, polices and standards.

These integration building blocks can be represented as shown in Figure 6.1.

By way of illustration, the merger categorization of Buono and Bowditch[1] could then be characterized as to their potential integration impact, using these same building blocks (Table 6.1).

The actual levels of integration will, of course, vary according to each specific M&A situation and the areas of potential synergy and targeted return. Even if full integration is seen as the long-term goal, it is important to be realistic about the time and effort that will be involved in achieving this. In cases of full integration, the integration risks are inevitably higher and it may be desirable to break down the transition into separate integration projects, each with their own focus and targeted business benefits.

It is also worth bearing in mind that full integration cannot always be completely realized if the cultural differences between the companies are too diverse. This is highlighted by a leading

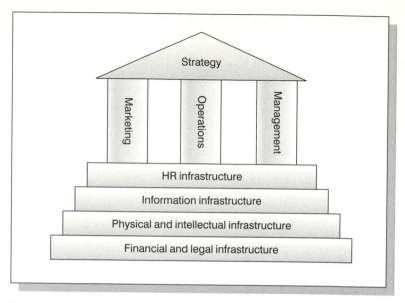

Figure 6.1 Business building blocks of integration

European IT services company that had grown very successfully over the years through acquisition primarily from public sector organizations. Despite a heavy investment in integration transition projects and in cross-company cultural development programmes, the organization maintained a number of powerful subcultures and loyalties that ran throughout the new organization. Loyalties were to events and people in the distant past. The impact of these subcultures was to create a level of fragmentation and internal politics that on occasions distracted both managers and employees from pulling together as effectively as they might otherwise have done.

A good example of the consequences of adopting too broad or ambitious an integration approach is demonstrated by a large international business services company. The organization acquired a 2000 strong IT services group, which was originally part of a large public service organization. The business, organizational and cultural differences between the two were massive in terms of work practices, management culture and commercial acumen and practices. The acquirers adopted an ambitious full integration approach and found themselves engulfed in a large and complex restructuring that impacted the whole company. The scale of the integration was large enough to distract management and disrupt service operations over a period of two years. The transition project had insufficient focus on the integration areas around improving work practices and

Table 6.1 Merger categorization and potential integration impact

M&A type	Likely scope of integration	Integration complexity and risks	Likely integration duration
Horizontal	The broad overlap of the partners is likely to result in a broad integration scope leading to eventual full integration. Likely to be some key areas where integration delivers the largest benefits. Some level of strategic, management and financial essential	High	A year + for full integration
Vertical	More focused integration scope. Focus on strategic, management and some level of financial. Work processes between companies critical	Medium/low	Variable but likely months
Product	Integration likely to be focused on sales and marketing integration especially product portfolios. May involve strategic integration and financial with limited managerial integration	Medium/low	Variable but likely months
Market	Integration likely in operational areas related to manufacturing and service operations. May involve strategic and financial with some managerial integration	High/medium	Months +
Conglomerate	Limited merger, potentially only legal and financial with very limited managerial	Low	Weeks +

reskilling (areas that could have yielded the business benefits). The net effect was to delay realization of some of the expected business benefits and to consume managers and employees in a disruptive and prolonged restructuring.

Even if the end-game plan is full integration, there is value in focusing the integration initially on the areas that deliver direct business benefits. Using these as 'stepping stones' on a longer journey towards full integration is part of the recipe for success.

The depth of organization integration

In addition to limiting the scope of integration through focusing on specific business areas, it can also be limited by the depth of integration that is targeted. Organizations are far more than structured groups of people. They operate, as their name suggests, in a much more organic manner. The organizational elements cover the whole spectrum from the more tangible aspects such as business policy and management structure through to more complex areas such as changes in work practices, skills, cultures and values. In addition, each of these elements operates within an interconnected system, with one change having some impact on the others.

Organizational make-up can be thought of as an iceberg with the visible tip made up of the more tangible and often more easily changed elements (Figure 6.2). The larger part of the iceberg beneath the water line is made up of the less tangible and less visible organizational elements. These elements are often far more resistant to change.

The more an integration initiative can be focused in on one business area, the easier it should be to maintain focus on specific business outcomes. Limiting the depth of the organizational change to that necessary to realize the benefits, will tend to reduce the implementation impact and therefore the risks. Understanding the depth of organization integration required also gives a good indicator of likely implementation timescales. Examples of typical integration initiatives and their likely impact are shown below.

1. Business policy change

This could be a fairly high level change involving the setting of the new policy and gaining the appropriate approvals. This sort of change can be achieved in a matter of weeks. The implementation of the policy is likely to involve some education or reskilling activities to ensure the policy can be implemented. In the case of a policy on management authority levels, for example, it may

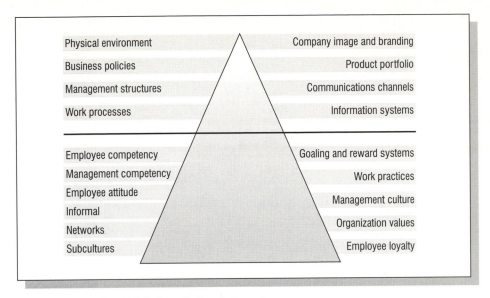

Physical environment	Company image and branding
Business policies	Product portfolio
Management structures	Communications channels
Work processes	Information systems
Employee competency	Goaling and reward systems
Management competency	Work practices
Employee attitude	Management culture
Informal	Organization values
Networks	Employee loyalty
Subcultures	

Figure 6.2 Organizational elements

require managers to have some business or accounting skills to operate the policy effectively. This in turn can be completed in a matter of a few months for a medium-sized organization. It may be felt that other organizational elements deeper in the iceberg, such as organizational culture, would have little impact on the change and therefore could be ignored. This type of assumption is likely to be costly in the long run. Approaches to understanding organizational culture are explored in Chapter 10.

2. Customer services operations

This type of change initiative can be more complex. It may embrace a deeper level of organizational change including policy, structure, reskilling and changes in work practices and systems. At this level, the elapse time is likely to be measured in months rather than weeks. In some cases, even deeper changes such as shifts in attitude, management styles or even cultural shifts may be required and the duration of these interventions may well extend into many months or even years.

Strategies for change

The other value of thinking of organizational change in terms of the 'iceberg' elements is that it also helps to clarify the need for different approaches to engineering the changes depending on the depth of change being attempted. At the higher levels, such as structure and policy change, the approach can be more top down

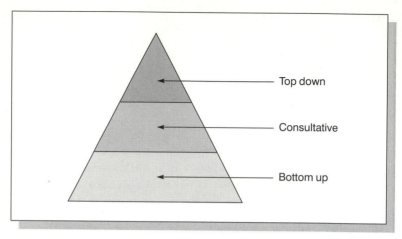

Figure 6.3 Change management strategies

or directive driven by senior managers. At lower levels such as work practices, employee skills and management style changes, the approach would need to be more consultative, with guidance and direction from the top. When deeper changes are intended, involving shifts in employee attitudes or organizational cultures, any lasting change is likely to require a highly participative approach with the momentum needing to come from the bottom up. The strategies for managing change can be thought of as shown in Figure 6.3.

On occasions, high level policy or structure change can realize short-term benefits in their own right. For example, having a more effective business control policy or restructuring to remove duplication, can realize rapid benefits as long as they are implemented in an appropriate way. Where top down changes by themselves can realize the benefits, they become quick-wins and play an important part in creating momentum for the integration and ensuring rapid business paybacks.

It is important to remember that all these layers are in some way connected or interdependent. Actions taken at one layer may result in changes at lower levels of the iceberg. A classic example would be the redundancy programme that is seen by the survivors to have been implemented in an unfair or uncaring manner. This may result in a shift to a more guarded or negative employee attitude towards future change. The impact could be even deeper, heightening a sense of distrust or reduced loyalty to the company.

Table 6.2 summarizes the key organizational elements, the likely organizational impact of change in that area and the possible interdependencies or issues associated with change at that level.

Table 6.2 Key organizational elements, the likely organizational impact of change in that area and the possible interdependencies or issues associated with change at that level

Organizational element	Potential impact	Change issues and interdependencies
Physical environment	Improvements can lead to short-term boost to morale Can support new working practices/culture, e.g. open plan, social areas	Requires sensitive and participative approach to realize full benefits May depend on other competency and culture developments
Company image and branding	Helps to develop sense of identity and belonging in new organization Can act as a symbol of change	Can be negative or positive symbol! Needs to be used widely to be effective
Business and financial policy and standards change	Can support more effective financial and management reporting and control Removes inconsistent practices Can reduce business risks identified in due diligence	Effective communication and feedback on policy change needed to test appropriateness and acceptance Need to manage impact on work practices, systems and skills for effective implementation
Management restructure	Refocus or clarify management accountabilities Improve focus on key areas Can encourage collaboration cross boundaries	Profiling of candidates to fill new positions Perceived fairness and openness of appointment process important Supported by effective goaling and reward to reinforce accountabilities and priorities Only as effective as the quality of people appointed!
Product portfolio changes	Supports cross-selling of both companies' portfolios Identifies areas of duplication or redundancy	Market based rationale for changes required Need for supporting marketing practices Need to manage emotional attachment or symbolism of retired products

Table 6.2 (continued)

Organizational element	Potential impact	Change issues and interdependencies
Product portfolio changes *(continued)*		Need to ensure sales commitment and incentives to sell new portfolio Careful phasing out of old products to avoid negative customer impact
Communication channels	Helps improve customers and employee communication quality and consistency Reinforces commitment to communication	Ensure understanding and use of new channels by managers and employees Identify any human or system bottlenecks Build in two-way/feedback mechanisms
Business process and practice changes	Adoption of best practice across both organizations' practices Enables operational integration Careful implementation required when acquirer's practices are imposed on acquirer	Effective process to identify business best practice Ideally participative; identification and implementation processes Need for investment in selling and education especially where practices are imposed Opportunity to implement on-going improvement mechanisms
Information systems integration	Enables cross-boundary operation and communication Potential savings in infrastructure and support costs	Short-term linking of systems to enable immediate communication/operation Longer-term development of shared infrastructure and standards
Goaling and reward systems changes	Focus organization on business priorities Incentive to key staff to achieve goals Helps retention of key staff Improves uniformity of practices Helps to clarify and strengthen individual accountabilities	Careful design and introduction of changes Need for effective appraisal practices to support changes Consistency and perceived fairness of new scheme

Table 6.2 (continued)

Organizational element	Potential impact	Change issues and interdependencies
Employee training and development	Helps to develop common knowledge base of both companies Support implementation of new practices and skills	Involvement of management in training to demonstrate support for intended changes Opportunity for cross-boundary working to breakdown barriers
Management competency and development	Can help to build shared management culture and identity Cross-boundary training can improve collaboration Can help to identify best practices Addresses identified management competency issues Can become effective way of surfacing key issues and obstacles	Use of interactive group working to encourage experience and values sharing Involvement of senior managers strengthens credibility
Informal networks	Can help accelerate the integration process Can help identify hidden blockages and issues	Identify key players and influencers Involvement of key influencers in change initiatives Tap into network to sense issues Test out and respond to key issues
Organization values	Can be key enablers of business transformation Developing shared culture and breaking down subcultures may improve organizational flexibility and effectiveness	Needs for good research on current culture and clear change goals Sustained senior management leadership Use of interactive workgroups to identify obstacles and ways forward Shift will rely on staff motivation, confidence and support

Table 6.2 (continued)

Organizational element	Potential impact	Change issues and interdependencies
Organization values *(continued)*		Needs to be seen as longer-term change Can help to integrate into management and staff job profiles
Employee loyalty	Improves retention of key staff Improves contribution of staff to company	Attitude surveys or workgroups to test perception Open addressing of issues raised Company demonstration of value of staff Promote/improve company benefits Provide rewarding working environments Improvements will come from actions and experiences rather than promises

Integration project design checklist

Once the key building blocks that deliver the required business benefits have been identified, the specific areas of change need to be identified. Below is a checklist of some of the potential issues that may need to be addressed within each of the integration building blocks.

Business strategy

- Company vision and mission
- Business strategy
- Strategic management processes

Business and financial management

- Business and financial accounting policies
- Business and financial accounting practices
- Management reporting standards
- Business forecasting practices

- Management accountabilities
- Management authority levels
- Management bonus schemes
- Management information systems and procedures
- Accounting systems and procedures
- Finance function integration

General management

- Management structure and accountabilities
- Business culture and style
- People management culture and style
- Market and customer attitudes and expertise
- Goaling and rewards systems
- Performance management systems
- Management information systems

Sales and marketing

- Market strategies and segmentation
- Sales structure and incentives
- Product strategies, portfolios and development plans
- Brands and trademarks
- Marketing communication standards and materials
- Indirect selling channels and incentives
- Customer and product discount structures
- Customer contract terms
- Account management structures
- Customer management systems and procedures
- Market intelligence systems
- Internet based customer communication and trading

Business operations

- Staffing levels and productivity
- Operational policies, systems and tools
- Working practices and procedures
- Employee knowledge and skills
- Customer handling attitudes and skills
- Staff goaling and rewards
- Quality policies and procedures
- Geographic structure

Human resources

- Employee contract terms
- TUPE agreements

- Employee benefits

  - Car policy
  - Mobile phone policy
  - Pension policy
  - Private health policy
  - Maternity/paternity leave
  - Share option scheme
  - Profit sharing scheme

- Employee information and communication systems
- Employee database
- Employee communication policy and practices
- Employee compensation

  - Salaries structures
  - Performance bonus policy
  - Recruitment incentive

- Recruitment policies, practices and agents
- Employee training and development policies and practices
- Employee promotion and appointment policies and procedures

Information infrastructure

- Network architecture and standards
- Corporate computing architecture and standards
- Personal computer policies and standards
- Desktop application platforms and standards
- E-mail systems and distribution lists
- Information security policies procedures and systems
- Group conferencing standards and practices
- Internet and intranet policies, standards and systems
- Internet and intranet content and structure
- Information systems management policies and standards
- Information systems support policies, capabilities and resources

Corporate culture and values

- Openness of information access
- Decision-making styles
- Style of cross-company working
- Market and customer focus
- People management values and practices
- Entrepreneurial attitudes and values
- Quality/improvement culture

- Employee centric culture
- Employee development culture
- Risk culture
- Individual/group autonomy and accountability
- Attitude and approach to non-performance

Sustaining an open culture

Companies may adopt an acquisition approach to business growth for tactical and opportunistic reasons or for more strategic reasons; most of these reasons relate to market or business performance improvement. Yet one common characteristic of many companies that have grown through merger and acquisition over a long period is in the culture of their organization. As a result of the influx of new attitudes and experiences, there tends to be a more open culture, a willingness to recognize good ideas, wherever they come from and an enthusiasm to adopt them for their own benefit. This can be in sharp contrast to more traditional organizations that have developed through internal growth. Here the years of success have reinforced the company's culture and practices and can lead to a more rigid set of attitudes and a more inward-looking perspective. In a turbulent world, rigid or inward looking cultures can prove to be fatal and are very difficult to break down.

Applying an integration philosophy of seeking out best practice whether found in the acquired or acquirer organizations can not only help to realize the full potential value from the partnership but also reinforce an open, outward-looking improvement culture in the company.

Summary

Mergers and acquisitions can offer acquirers great potential benefits and added value if selected carefully. They also bring with them inevitable integration risks. Those risks can be minimized by effective integration design that:

- Focuses the integration efforts into the specific business areas that deliver the expected benefits
- Identifies the minimal depth of integration required to realize the benefits
- Adopts the appropriate change strategy dependent on the nature of the change
- Recognizes the time that full organization integration can take and focuses on identified stepping stones along the way that deliver business value in their own right.

References

1 Buono, A. and Bowditch, J. (1989): *The Human Side of Mergers and Acquisitions: managing collisions between people and organisations*, Jossey-Bass, San Francisco
2 Napier, N. K. (1989): Mergers and acquisitions, human resources issues and outcomes: a review and suggested typology, *Journal of Management Studies* **26**, 3

Related reading

Galpin, T. J. and Herndon, M. (2001): *The Complete Guide to Mergers & Acquisitions*, Jossey Bass, San Francisco

CHAPTER 7

Delivering the value – transition management

Orpheus was another famous Argonaut. A superbly skilled musician, his lyre playing and singing could make stones and trees rise up and follow him. His music calmed the other sailors enough to stop their quarrelling. . .

Introduction

Quality planning and design form the foundations for a successful transition project, but it is only through

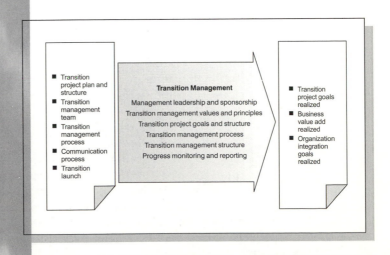

Transition Management

- Transition project plan and structure
- Transition management team
- Transition management process
- Communication process
- Transition launch

Management leadership and sponsorship
Transition management values and principles
Transition project goals and structure
Transition management process
Transition management structure
Progress monitoring and reporting

- Transition project goals realized
- Business value add realized
- Organization integration goals realized

effective transition management that the expected business benefits can actually be delivered. It is through the skills of the transition manager that the project is kept on course and the inevitable distractions overcome. It is through their facilitation that the transition team and the individual projects are kept in harmony. The transition manager also plays a key role in minimizing project slippage by tracking and chasing progress until the end goal is reached. In this chapter we will look at the role of the transition manager and management structure and processes to support them.

Getting off to a good start

The most skilled and experienced transition managers can only hope to succeed if they get off to the best possible start. This requires that the transition planning phase has been successfully concluded prior to proceeding with the transition. The cost of remedying project mistakes may be relatively small at this early stage, but is likely to grow exponentially as the transition progresses. The previous transition planning phase should have delivered a sound base for the transition project in the form of:

- Transition goals that are agreed and documented
- Transition project values and principles that are agreed and documented
- Transition management structure agreed and key appointments already made
- Transition communication plan and processes in place
- 100-day plan initiatives agreed and the scope of each documented
- Transition launch complete and attendee feedback gathered.

Transition management role

The role of the transition manager involves balancing three main elements of responsibility throughout the transition:

1 *A strategic element*: responsible for steering and monitoring transition progress towards the expected business benefits and transition goals. It is a role that requires close working with the senior management team who is sponsoring the transition. The transition manager needs to ensure they are kept informed of progress and help to resolve any strategic obstacles. The role also requires close working with the managers of the individual projects to ensure that any overlaps or interdependencies are managed.

2 *A project management element*: responsible for the structuring of the overall transition into separate transition projects and overseeing the subsequent, design, resourcing, implementation and progress tracking of the projects.

3 *A change agent element*: responsible for monitoring and sustaining the energy for change. This element is focused on people and groups and their emotional responses to the proposed changes. It is in this world that that the transition manager seeks out symbols of progress and exemplars of the required attitudes and behaviours. This role also involves looking out for signs of organizational resistance or cultural impasses and responding to them appropriately. This is a facilitative role rather than a driving role. The energy for change ultimately needs to come from those directly involved in the changes.

The three roles are summarized in Table 7.1.

Table 7.1 The roles of the transition manager

Strategic	Project	Change agent
Sponsorship	Design	Uncertainty/fear
Transition goals	Resourcing	Communication
Maintaining focus	Tasks	Participation
Harmonizing efforts	Milestones	Commitment
Delivering benefits	Progress	Belonging

The profile of the transition manager

The appointment of a competent transition manager early in the process is an essential insurance policy against transition failure. For larger transitions it is likely the role will need to be full-time because of the workload demands. A dedicated transition manager provides the benefit of having a leader who is exclusively committed to achieving the transition goals and not subject to the distraction of having other business goals and responsibilities as most other players will have.

The profile of a transition manager is a demanding one and the relevant skills and experience are not readily available inside many organizations. It demands a good mix of business management and organizational development expertise. There is no real substitute for previous experience as this brings with it an insight and judgement that can prove invaluable. In mergers of any size or complexity, the consequences of appointing an inexperienced transition manager or delaying the appointment can lead to a significantly increased risk of transition failure.

An organization needs to be able to gain access to this scarce resource in a timely manner before embarking on an acquisition of any size. Organizations that see acquisition as a core and on-going part of their business may choose to build this capability into their organization. Organizations with limited expectations of M&A activity need to resource the manager as required, either from their own management team or through external consultancies. In these cases the selection of the right person in terms of their skills and experience and their timely availability must be carefully planned.

The role of the transition manager is a hybrid one, demanding sound business judgement and practical experience of how business works. The profile of a transition manager candidate includes:

- Good business acumen and business management experience
- Knowledge of the company's markets and business
- Many transitions have expected business benefits that are dependent on, or specific to, the marketplace they operate in. The transition manager needs some understanding of that market
- Good organizational development skills and experience
- Good project management skills and experience
- Previous experience of transition management of mergers and acquisitions.

The candidate will also need to have:

- Credibility with the senior management team
- Credibility to lead the team of transition project managers
- Ability to operate at all levels inside the organization
- Good communication and influencing skills
- Understanding of business operations (policy, processes, systems and structures).

The added value of the transition manager

The transition manager brings value to the transition at each stage of the process from the due diligence activities through to transition completion reviews. The value is often through the facilitation of good transition management practices, working with both the senior management team, the transition project management teams and, on occasions, directly with staff groups to ensure an effective transition.

The value they can bring includes:

Due diligence

If involved early enough in the due diligence process, the transition manager can work with senior managers to ensure that the scope of the exercise is wide enough to identify the full range of legal, financial, commercial and organizational risks and opportunities that should be explored. Also the transition manager can coordinate the various parties and activities of the due diligence to implement a structured approach to the exercise. They provide a vital role in ensuring continuity between due diligence and the transition itself.

Senior management sponsorship

In the early definition stages of the transition, the transition manager adds value by ensuring the scope, overall goals and approach are clear and agreed across the senior management team. The transition manager, especially an external one, can facilitate these sessions and check out levels of clarity and consistency, flushing out any undeclared differences or potential sources of future conflict or ambiguity.

Sustaining management commitment

The management of any complex organizational change requires strong leadership and commitment from senior management. This leadership demand is intensified in mergers and acquisitions by the number of people involved and the different backgrounds of acquired and acquirers. Sustaining the level of management commitment can be a challenge, as many of the managers involved in the transition will have a 'day job' to do in addition to their transition role. This often leads to workload pressures and reducing levels of participation and commitment to the project. Managing conflicts of priorities is the responsibility of the transition manager, who has to gain the support from senior managers to resolve them. The right balance must be found between progress of the transition project towards its goals and the acceptable level of disruption to the business.

A quality transition plan

The translation of the transition goals into a comprehensive plan is the distinctive value the transition manager must bring, by producing a well-structured project design and set of project plans. This exercise gives a further opportunity to check out senior management interpretation and support and allows for the effective delegation of some aspects of transition management to individual project managers.

Effective integration project design

This involves the categorization of each project within the plan depending on its urgency and value to the business and its cost or disruptive impact on the business. The design of each project needs to apply sound business judgement and understanding, project management disciplines and be sensitive to how best to gain people's involvement and support for the required changes.

Creating balanced project teams

The transition manager needs to oversee the appointment of project leaders, local implementation managers and other representatives from various groups to ensure the appropriate skills and representation to support each project.

Leadership of the team of individual transition project leaders

This team is made up of the leaders of each transition project and can provide a forum to share issues and address project overlaps and conflicts.

Transition management best practice

In many projects there is limited previous experience of transition management and the transition manager plays a vital role in bringing their personal experience of best practice to the team.

Effective communication progress

This is the lifeblood of any effective transition and has to be effective and in place from the initial deal announcement through to transition completion. The transition manager must ensure the channels exist and are used.

Effective progress management process

Effective progress management must be consistently implemented at all levels in the transition management structure. As the transition project starts to roll, it is easy for managers to become distracted by other business issues and to lose touch with progress made or obstacles encountered. Discipline must not be allowed to wane and mechanisms such as holding regular review meetings with senior managers and project leaders can help to sustain energy and focus. Regular and effective progress reporting is also an essential part of this discipline. When asked what was the value of having an external transition manager, Dan Collins, the COO of Articon-Integralis identified: '. . .the discipline that it brings to busy managers of having to plan and commit to deliverables and then be held to account for those commitments.'

Transition management process

The transition management process needs to operate at two levels: the overall or strategic level and the individual transition project level. The key elements of the strategic management process are:

1 Tracking progress against the overall transition goals
2 Tracking progress in terms of any success criteria that have been agreed
3 Ensuring transition value and principles are adhered to in all transition projects
4 Applying the discipline of effective transition project management
5 Applying effective change management disciplines
6 The definition and progress monitoring of the 100-day plan
7 The definition and progress monitoring of the integration plan
8 Monitoring overlaps, gaps or conflicts between the individual projects
9 Ensuring overall and individual project progress and issues are reported on a regular basis
10 Ensuring effective sponsorship and problem escalation to support the transition
11 Ensuring effective communication throughout the project.

Transition management structure

The transition management structure should result in clear responsibility and authority for all aspects of the transition and

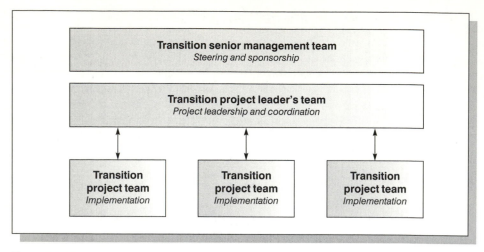

Figure 7.1 Transition management structure

ensure that each team member has a clear role and interfaces to their colleagues. The structure can be thought of as having three layers as shown in Figure 7.1.

The roles, responsibilities and make up of the teams are summarized below.

Transition senior management team

The responsibilities of the team are:

- Transition project leadership
  Agreeing project scope and structure and appointment of key members of the transition management team
- Operational business performance
  The accountability for the new business operation must be clear at the highest level from day one. It is the responsibility of this team to ensure that the management structure and accountabilities for the business are established
- Transition values and principles
  This team is responsible for agreeing these and ensuring they are applied during the transition
- Transition plan approval
  The senior team would approve the transition plans and transition management processes developed by the transition manager and his team
- Ensuring progress towards the transition goals
  The senior managers play a key role in tracking overall

progress against the transition plan and ensuring that the transition goals are realized
- Resolution of escalated issues
The senior team must provide responsive ongoing support to resolve issues escalated from the project teams.

The transition senior management team members may include:

- Operations director: the director with operational responsible for the acquired organization
- Finance director: responsible for ensuring all financial issues emerging from the due diligence are managed effectively during the transition
- HR director: responsible for the organizational aspects of transition and ensuring that any organizational issues emerging from the due diligence are addressed effectively in the transition plan
- Other functional directors with strategic interest in the acquisition: often an acquisition may have specific strategic significance in addition to any operational goals, e.g. new manufacturing capability, new technology, new market entry. The appropriate director with responsibility for that area may be part of the team to ensure the strategic benefits are realized
- General manager of operating entity: general manager with operational responsibility representing the needs of the operating business and the transition project's impact on it
- Transition manager: the transition manager provides the link to the transition project leader's team.

Transition project leader's team

The responsibilities of the team include:

- Transition project plan definition: the team is responsible for defining the overall project plan and the project management processes based on the transition goals, values and principles. The senior management team normally approves the plan
- Transition project overlaps and interdependency: the transition plan comprises a set of individual project plans, each with its distinctive projects, scope and goals. The team manages any project overlaps and interdependencies
- Overall progress tracking and reporting: the team reviews individual project progress and issues, tracks progress towards the transition goals and escalates key issues and obstacles to the transition senior management team.

The transition project leader's team members include:

- Transition manager: the transition manager is responsible for leading the team, coordinating across the projects and supporting the individual transition project managers
- Transition project leaders: the project leader is responsible for the design, resourcing, delivery and successful completion of their project and reports to the transition manager in this role. The project leader role may be a part time or full time one depending on the size of the project.

Transition project team

The responsibilities of each project team include:

1 Planning, design, resourcing and delivery of a specific transition project
2 Achieving agreed goals within project budget and timescales
3 Project reporting and escalation, i.e. reporting of progress and escalating project issues and obstacles to the transition manager.

The project team members will potentially include:

- Transition project leader
- Transition project sponsor: for some major projects that have impact on corporate policy or practices, it may be necessary to have a senior management sponsor with responsibility for that area, e.g. the finance director may sponsor a project that has an impact on corporate financial accounting policy
- Project advisors or experts: specialist contributors to the project with expertise in a key business area or discipline
- Project user representatives: representatives of the groups affected by the project to ensure local expertise, contribution and commitment
- Local implementation managers: representatives of particular groups who have responsibility for project implementation in their local group.

Transition team balance

At all levels in the transition management structure it is important to achieve the right balance and breadth of representation from the acquirer and acquired organizations. Balance or lack of, will be seen as a sign of the balance of power in the new organization. Any lack of representation from the acquired

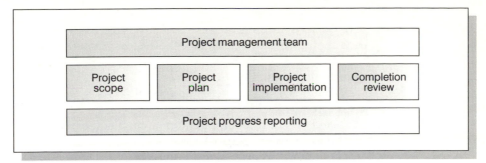

Figure 7.2 Transition project management process

organization may be seen as reflecting a disinterest in the needs and views of that organization.

Transition project management process

Project management process disciplines should be applied to both 100-day and integration projects, although it may be unnecessary to apply them as thoroughly for some of the simpler 100-day projects. There is a risk to dropping these disciplines for apparently simpler and more straightforward projects, in that their true complexity may then only be discovered during implementation. This pitfall can be avoided by ensuring clear project definition and outline design is completed for all projects and, only at that point, agreeing the level of ongoing project management required. Some basic disciplines such as establishing project milestones and regular progress reporting should apply to all projects.

A good example of apparently simple projects would be the typical early initiative of rationalizing letterheads and logos. At face value, this is a straightforward issue but can rapidly become embroiled in corporate marketing standards and conflicting local requirements. In such cases it is preferable to have agreed the ground rules up front rather than in the midst of implementation.

The elements of the project management structure are shown in Figure 7.2.

Project scope

This is a high level definition document produced by the transition manager for each transition project and addresses the following issues:

- Overall project scope
- One of the most important aspects of any project is to establish clarity about what business aspects the project will address, where the project boundaries are and what parts of the organization it will affect
- The expected business benefits and possible risks
- The expected project milestones and timescales
- Anticipated organizational/operational impact (i.e. the level of disruption in various groups)
- Overall success criteria for the project (how the impact/benefits of the project will be monitored)
- Project leader profile and candidates
- Project senior management sponsor (if required)
- Make-up of the project team
- Estimated project costs and resources required
- Recommended implementation approach.

The document should provide just sufficient detail to ensure agreement to the scope for the project between the project leader, the transition manager and the senior management team. Defining the scope of each project helps clarify and manage any project overlaps or interdependencies and ensures the project leader has a clear charter.

Project plan

This is a summary delivery plan developed by the project leader in line with the agreed project scope document. The plan should cover:

- Proposed or interpreted scope
- This is an opportunity to refine the scope as a result of more detailed project planning and design
- Committed project deliverables and timescales
- Proposed implementation approach and accountabilities
- Project resource requirements and costs
- Progress milestones and timescales.

The development of this plan is an opportunity to involve the key influencers, experts and representatives from groups involved. Their early involvement and contribution to the plan will help to build a broader base of support for its successful implementation. It also provides the opportunity for them to influence the shape of the project and so ensure it reflects local needs and views.

Project implementation

Once the project plan is approved, the project leader and team take on full responsibility for its management and for providing regular progress reports. Some key considerations in project implementation will be:

- Involvement of those directly impacted at the earliest possible stage
- Involvement of the key experts or influencers from the organization in project design
- Involvement of line management and gaining commitment for local implementation
- Pilot implementation. If a project involves major changes to operating practices it may be appropriate to test out those practices and the implementation approach in a limited pilot prior to rolling out across the wider business.

Project progress reviews and reporting

The review of progress on a regular basis is essential to the control of a transition project. It provides an opportunity to review project progress against milestones, to discuss any obstacles and issues that have emerged and any conflicts or overlaps with other projects. The impact of the project in terms of business benefits realized can also be reviewed as implementation occurs. Regular progress reports should be concise and focus on the key project issues of:

- Progress versus milestones
- Current issues and obstacles
- Project resources used versus plan
- Future planned activities.

Project completion review

This takes place on successful completion of a project, its purpose is to:

- Review project deliverables vs. plan
- Review project benefits vs. overall success criteria
- Review of project costs vs. plans
- Identify other opportunities or issues that have emerged
- Identify key learning for the future.

This review includes the project leader, transition manager, key project team members and, for larger projects, the senior management sponsor and implementation managers.

Keeping the transition on track

As the transition management phase progresses, the initial turbulent times of uncertainty, doubt and even scepticism should be replaced by a clearer and calmer sense of direction and an increasing level of energy in the organization to participate in the changes. This change in organizational mood is built through carefully planned changes, that have involved the appropriate people and been communicated in a timely and effective manner. As people begin to operate more and more across the old organizational boundaries a new sense of belonging to one organization will slowly develop.

As the transition progresses, so the source of energy for change begins to shift. In the early days it was centred in the senior management sponsors and then transferred in part to the transition manager and the individual project leaders. As the transition begins to gel, so the energy should come increasingly from staff and managers in the newly merged organization.

Sustaining focus and the energy

At this point, the risk of loss of project energy or focus is highest. The immediate hiatus of the transition is over and the apparent threats diminishing, yet the real rewards in terms of sustained business benefits may still be some way off. The transition manager needs to maintain focus and re-double the discipline, reminding people of the end goal and holding them to their committed role in realizing it.

The role of the transition manager is to sustain the energy for change and to ensure the new organization does not 'refreeze' and so begin to resist further change. This can be achieved through a variety of interventions. Some of these are summarized below.

100-day plan completion

This is an opportunity to share the progress achieved in the first 100 days, acknowledge the progress made and promote the success stories.

Integration phase launch

Once the initial scoping and design work of the integration projects is complete, the launch of the integration phase can provide another injection of energy. Again this represents an opportunity for involvement of the senior management team and further management and employee briefing sessions.

Reinforcing the context for the transition

There is often a need to remind people of the overall intent and progress at this middle point. It is easy for everyone to lose sight of the bigger picture as it gets lost in day-to-day activities. Looking at transition progress against overall goals to date, putting the future plans in the context of these goals and also gathering employee data on their perceptions of progress to date can all help to reinforce that context.

Maintaining transition priority

One of the frequent symptoms of 'mid-term blues' is the increasing number of resource conflicts between the transition project and the operating business. It is often at this point that the demand for involvement of local business resources in design and implementation activities increases. If the resources are not forthcoming the integration projects can get delayed and the implementation momentum lost. The pressure for these resources must be maintained to ensure transition success. The freeing up of scarce resources often depends on the active support of the senior transition management team.

Strength of the transition management teams

It is difficult for any one individual to sustain sufficient inner belief, clarity and energy over a long transition project, especially when confronted with increasing resistance from the organization. Strong and supportive transition management teams can be invaluable at this point in helping to share that pressure and provide support to the transition manager.

Overall transition completion review

The sense of release at the end of a successful transition project can result in a lack of enthusiasm for conducting a completion review. Yet there is real value in such reviews. They help to acknowledge what has been achieved and, importantly, help to identify the learning from the acquisition experience. There is an opportunity at the end of the transition phase to conduct a strategic review, evaluating the overall success of the acquisition in terms of achievement of the overall business benefits. At this level the review should be done by the senior transition management team and may look at:

- The business benefits realized by the acquisition
- Other strategic benefits or opportunities that exist
- Organizational and cultural assessment of the integration

- Impact of this acquisition on the business and acquisition strategy
- Improvement opportunities for the acquisition process.

Interim reviews at a more tactical level can be undertaken at the end of the 100-day and integration phases. These reviews might be with the transition project leaders team, looking at:

- Overall effectiveness of transition management process
- Specific improvements to the process for future acquisitions
- Overall effectiveness of the transition project leaders team
- Effectiveness of progress monitoring and chasing
- Effectiveness of employee communication process.

Case study

The Articon-Integralis case study – Part III

The integration phase

This second phase of the transition project in practice overlapped with the initial 100-day phase, with design work and, where possible, some implementation work initiated during the first 100 days. The integration phase projects were more complex than the initial phase projects and, in general, they were more resource intensive. The integration phase projects were, in the main, those that delivered the longer-term synergies and therefore the business benefits of the merger. These projects had a project life cycle of six to nine months and in some cases even longer.

The approach adapted to this phase was similar to the initial phase, with emphasis on project scoping, appointment of senior management sponsors and project champions. In some cases these projects demanded full-time champions and supporting resources. The implementation of these projects had significant impact on operations and therefore needed the early and appropriate involvement of line managers. The role of the senior management sponsor was even more important in this phase as many of these projects were establishing new business policy which impacted on operational business practices. Once again, investing in the planning and design phases proved valuable in establishing the clarity of project scope and purpose and helping to anticipate some of the project risks and obstacles.

To ensure sufficient quality time and effort was invested in the planning and design of these critical projects, the following activities were undertaken prior to going ahead with them:

Strategic planning session with the key board members to scope and evaluate the business impact and benefit of each project.

Scoping document produced for each agreed project by the sponsor covering:

- Initiative boundaries and constraints
- Business benefits
- Anticipated organizational and operational impact
- Anticipated deliverables and timescales
- Likely investment required (money, people, equipment)
- Possible project champion.

These documents were reviewed and approved by the transition management team prior to proceeding or allocating any resources. The projects that formed the integration phase were:

- IT infrastructure standards, tools and support
- Employee communication and feedback
- Financial and management information systems
- Human resource policy and procedures
- Corporate positioning
- Inventory management infrastructure
- M&A integration practices and tools for future acquisitions
- Management team development.

Some twelve months on from the merger announcement five of the eight projects are completed and two due to complete in a further six months. The project that proved to be most problematic was the human resources policies and procedures. This was compounded by the lack of consistent HR management infrastructure throughout the company and the delay in recruiting a corporate HR director.

Learning points: Integration phase

- Essential role of senior management sponsor for these complex/strategic projects to approve policy changes and support implementation
- The value of scoping each project to clarify its purpose, outcomes and impact before proceeding
- The value of quality design and planning to ensure clarity and commitment to project goals, resources, deliverables and benefits
- The timely involvement of operational managers to ensure their support and commitment to implement
- The need to apply project management disciplines to maintain focus and momentum to these critical projects
- The importance of keeping sight of the expected business benefits and whether they are being delivered

Communicating with effect

Effective two-way employee communication was the lifeblood of the whole integration process giving employees the opportunity to hear the latest position directly from top management and their local line manager. The communication channels were numerous depending on the message. They included:

- Board member briefings for high level messages
- Management forum, a communication channel that cascaded information via line management. This was a structured two-way communication process for regular updates and announcements
- E-mail for specialist communication (project team members, line managers etc.)
- An intranet integration page for general browsing of project plans and progress reports.

Throughout the integration there was a strong commitment from top management to be open and honest about plans, problems and progress. This was a key ingredient in assuring employees felt that they were being kept effectively informed.

Case study learning: communication

- The value of open and honest communication throughout (plans, progress and problems)
- Use of appropriate channels for different topics and audiences
- Value of structured two-way communication to gather feedback on employee perceptions
- The importance of face-to-face communication from senior management on high level or sensitive issues
- Need to devote adequate time and resource to communication

Summary

Transition management is the key vehicle for delivering the expected business benefits of a merger or acquisition and therefore delivering the expected returns on the acquisition investment. The key elements of effective transition management are:

- A quality transition plan and effective transition launch
- Early appointment of an experienced transition manager

- Effective sponsorship and support from senior managers
- Transition project structure that establishes clear goals and boundaries for each transition project
- Appointment of credible and competent transition project leaders
- Development of effective transition project management teams to lead and coordinate transition project activities
- Effective progress reporting and chasing
- Effective two-way employee communication processes
- Conducting completion reviews to maximize the learning from the acquisition.

References

Garrow, V. and Holbeche, L. (2000): *Effective mergers & acquisitions* Roffey Park Inst.

Part Three

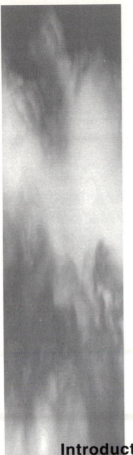

CHAPTER 8

Communicating with effect

They were preserved from the sirens by the eloquence of Orpheus

Introduction

Communication is often hailed as the most important factor in M&A success. A frequently cited rule is that 'you can't over-communicate!' Unfortunately the reality is not quite so simple, as those who face a long scroll of daily e-mails will testify. Employees can be overwhelmed with a surfeit of communication, particularly in a large organization, with daily announcements about new appointments that they feel are of no concern to them. Indeed in one organization, where people were waiting to hear about their own jobs, it was irritating to have to read about successes elsewhere.

In reality, it is the quality of the communication rather than the quantity that is important. Furthermore, where a merger or acquisition has been viewed negatively by employees any 'spin' put on both internal and external communication is likely to generate cynicism. Communication strategy needs therefore to be integral to the deal and planned from the outset to present a coherent message to all stakeholders.

Everything sends a signal in the heightened tension following a merger announcement. Employees read the 'signs' such as which 'side' is getting the key appointments and whose offices or premises are being used. In this sense every management action is part of the communication process. For example, there is little point in having a written set of values on respect for the individual if the reality is clearly otherwise. In order to build credibility and trust, communication in the form of words, actions and outcomes must be aligned.

The purpose of communication

At a basic level the role of communication might be seen as responding to the following key questions:

Why is the merger happening?
What will it mean for me?
Where will I be based?
Whom will I be working for?
How will the change be carried out?

But communication is not just passing on information; it has a vital role in all aspects of a merger in:

- reducing uncertainty
- managing expectations
- demonstrating concern
- promoting integration
- building new networks
- building trust and commitment
- encouraging involvement through feedback and two-way communication
- prompting behaviour or 'walking the talk'
- learning.

However, according to Dr Vincent Covello[1], Director of the Center for Risk Communication, there are some basic rules relating to communication during high risk/low trust situations. Although Dr Covello works in extremely delicate arenas such as hostage negotiations or environmental crises, the principles apply equally well to a merger situation where emotions are running high. He identifies the following theoretical constructs:

1 Trust determination theory: trust can only be established by the recipient of the message who 'wants to know that you care before she/he cares what you know'. Trust is built up over a longer period of time but destroyed very quickly. Trust factors include empathy, competence, honesty and commitment.

2 Mental noise theory: people who are upset have difficulty hearing and processing information. Mental noise can reduce the ability to process information by up to 80 per cent. This means that there should be a limited number of messages and frequent repetition.

3 Negative dominance theory: people who are upset tend to think negatively. It is therefore better to avoid negative words such as no, not, never, nothing, none.

4 Risk perception theory: what is perceived is real in its consequences. People's perception of risk is influenced by existing level of trust, perceived benefit, level of control and perceived fairness.

The legal backdrop

In private deals the announcement may be made at any stage and there are fewer restrictions on communication. In public deals, however, the legal position makes it difficult to share information freely with employees.

According to the code for public deal acquisitions in the UK, no stakeholder is allowed preferential information that could affect the share price. The Stock Exchange must be notified before information becomes available to the other stakeholders simultaneously. No communication with employees is permitted before this time, which means that employees will often hear the announcement on the news as they drive into work.

In a public deal there is a minimum 60-day period before approval when the announcement is made public. This may be a good deal longer where the bid is hostile or there are counter bids to consider or regulatory approval is needed. This period can bring uncertainty for employees amid media speculation with little to be done to allay fears under current legislation.

Even in the absence of 'leaks' or rumours in the press, observant employees in a company about to be acquired may notice increased activity in collecting employee data as the company prepares for the due diligence process. HR staff and senior PAs will start to detect unusually secretive activity taking place and internal unease may start to spread.

Early issues to assess

It is important to be clear what the starting point is when planning a communication strategy. This can be done by assessing:

Context

1 What is the prevailing climate in the organizations involved? This will be determined by their experience to date. For example:

- Has there been a long period of uncertainty?
- Is the merger the result of a hostile bid?
- Has the partner company been viewed as a competitor?
- Is the company performing badly?
- Public perception of the organization
- Employee turnover rate
- Will the merger represent security or threat?

2 Is the employment relationship characterized by trust or cynicism?

- Are problems seen as management failure?
- Will a merger be viewed as a positive move for the company employees?
- Are company decisions usually motivated by employee concern?
- Is the merger the latest in a long series of various rescue attempts?

Timing

1 What are the legal restrictions on communication before the announcement of the deal?
2 Will employees hear the news through the press or on the radio while driving into work?
3 How long is the period between the announcement to the completion of the deal?
4 Where are employees based? Are there time zone implications or language translation problems?

Resources

1 What is the budget for communication?
2 Is communication part of the transition plan?

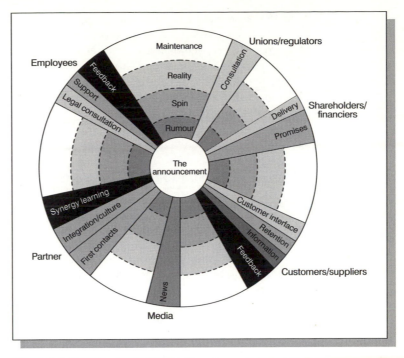

Figure 8.1 The communications web

3 Will communication be handled by a specialist consultant or in-house?
4 If in-house, will the same department handle both internal and external communications?
5 Will communication have a dedicated team from HR?
6 What training is available for those seconded to communication roles?
7 Are line managers experienced in communication?
8 What IT systems will facilitate internal communication? e.g. intranet, e-mail
9 Are both organizations' systems compatible?

The communications web (Figure 8.1) illustrates some (not all) of the issues in communicating difficult messages which are changing over a period of time. The concentric circles provide a sense of what the communication may actually feel like to the recipient. From the announcement at the hub, the immediate aftermath may be the activation of the *'Rumour mill'*. This is often counteracted by the *'Spin'* which represents motivational communication to keep investors and employees on board. *'Reality'* inevitably follows when the true impact of the deal has to be revealed in terms of redundancy, restructuring, re-engineering, re-location, etc. After coming to terms with the reality of the deal the next phase is *'Maintenance'* whereby the organization embeds change and builds continued support.

This maintenance phase is often overlooked and one global pharmaceutical company found that after hiring communication consultants for six months, at the end of that period communication stopped too suddenly without transition back into business as usual. Staff felt they had been abandoned to sort out remaining issues alone.

The changing nature of communication over time underlies the key tasks in meeting the needs of all stakeholders.

The stakeholders

Figure 8.1 illustrates some of the potential stakeholders in a merger. They represent a variety of interest groups requiring different messages. For example, the media may be chiefly interested in a headline-grabbing story of mass closure and redundancy! The first task is to draw up the relevant list for the companies concerned. Where large scale closures are planned, the local community will need to be involved. In the voluntary sector other interest groups will be important. In public services the Government will have a key role.

Once a comprehensive list has been drawn up, a detailed list of individual contacts and e-mail/phone numbers should be collated and maintained as individuals within the company move around during re-structuring.

Figure 8.1 plots some of the forms communication might take with various stakeholders. These range from formal consultation to personal support:

- Legal consultation
- The disclosure process
- Information on whom to contact for what
- Clarifying objectives
- Highlighting organizational values
- Collecting feedback
- Facilitating learning
- Motivating – celebrating achievements
- Retaining customer and supplier loyalty
- Supporting the individual.

Stakeholders each require a different focus for communication but the underlying message should be consistent in all cases, particularly where external and internal communication is handled by different departments. Don't forget that employees may fall into several other categories as shareholders, customers and members of the local community! Also the opinions of one group of stakeholders may heavily influence the opinions of another group.

Internal communication

Internal communication strategy needs particular attention and depends to a large extent on the size of the companies involved. Questions to consider are:

1 How good are we or our new partner at communicating? Do either of us have experience of merger or major change communication?
2 If not, are there any individuals who have such experience from past roles?
3 How robust is our current internal communication system?
4 What vehicles are most commonly used to pass vital information through the organization?
5 How skilled are our managers in communication?
6 What forums or groups exist which might serve as vehicles to harness?
7 Have we used a 'cascade' principle before?

Messages from and to the top

In times of turbulence, all stakeholders like to know that the ship has a captain and signals from the top can set the tone for abandoning ship, reassurance or determination. It can be a real disadvantage where a first class CEO does not have good media presentation skills and investment in media training should be an urgent priority. The ability to communicate a clear vision and objective is essential in the early days of a merger.

Most organizations will hope to front their CEO on the day of the announcement. Other directors may then be involved in taking the message around to various company locations. It should be recognized that these sessions are generally for top down information as staff are likely to be too intimidated to ask questions in a public meeting. Opportunities to ask questions should be provided in a less threatening environment following such meetings.

Subsequent management levels also need the ability to translate objectives and strategy into achievable goals and targets at each organizational level. From the experience of Roffey Park[2], this process occurs reasonably well down to a certain level and then hits a brick wall. Some of the reasons for this are:

- Senior level appointments are made early in the process or even prior to announcement so that these people are able to focus on the job. Further down the organization managers are still in limbo and are still focused on their own position.
- Knowledge is power and some blocks occur where individuals hold on to information as a source of competitive advantage over a colleague.
- As appointments are made, levels of communication are broken and links in the chain not replaced.
- Managers simply do not recognize the importance of communicating to staff or are not skilled in doing so.

Of course, messages must go back up to the top and may also find a sticking point because:

- People are afraid to give negative feedback in a public forum. They may feel it will spoil their chances of progression in the new organization.
- Managers may not wish to pass on bad news and try to maintain a positive spin when speaking to their own senior managers.
- The board may become severely isolated and preoccupied by financial targets. They may not take time to find out what the real organizational temperature is and are blissfully unaware of problems.

Integration

Of course problems in internal communication in a merger are multiplied by two or more. Communication is central to integration success and is a key tool in creating a single organization. Where company employees are to be physically integrated the job is perhaps easier than where sites or divisions remain separate. In some cases, for example, the head office may be combined while branches feel little impact from the merger and continue to work in the old ways, dealing with partner branches as different organizations. In this case some companies are able to use their 'brand' to engage staff in new behaviours. Many organizations now align the external and internal messages using the brand values. Employees become the organization's internal customers and employee and customer satisfaction go hand in hand.

Along with the brand, the logo can be a powerful symbol and acquired employees may feel a great sense of loss for their old corporate identity. Sales forces are particularly affected by change in image. A corporate branding exercise can be an excellent tool for integration.

Communication to promote integration needs to be constantly monitored for effectiveness. For example, one construction company merged two operations into one site but rather than mingle, the employees erected a screen of filing cabinets down the centre and one set of employees sat on one side out of sight of the other company's employees on the other side!

From the acquired perspective

Being acquired may feel to employees as though their own company has failed or been defeated. The feeling may be exacerbated by arrogant contacts by the acquirer's employees who may unwittingly behave as though they are the rescuers. Even where the deal is positioned as a 'merger' one set of employees inevitably feels they are on the losing side. The acquired employees therefore need to be told that their contribution is valued and that their skills and expertise are needed.

The Roffey Park research[2] indicated that acquired employees value having their own managers break the news to them or at least be present when the acquirer first addresses the newly acquired employees. This was partly to have a familiar face around and partly to gauge their own management's reaction to the deal.

The first contact with the acquirer is a particularly sensitive moment and from the Roffey Park research inevitably seems to go wrong. In one case the managing director had gone to the acquired organization well-armed with strategic plans and descriptions of excellent future prospects, but by coffee break he called back to his office to request the HR director be sent down. He realized very quickly that people were not interested in the detail of the business, they first needed to know whether they had a job, where it would be and whether they would be worse off.

At the other extreme, the first glimpse employees had of their acquirer was of men in grey suits walking round the shop floor with clip boards accompanied by their managers. One employee remembers, 'They didn't speak to any of the staff but a few months later we got a video to tell us what was going to happen'. The image of the faceless 'suits' became embedded in the acquired staff's memories.

First impressions are crucial and are difficult to undo. Arrogance on the part of the acquirer is common and lethal. Senior managers should be visible as much as possible and may need coaching in presentation skills and in getting the right first message, with the right tone, across.

Guidelines for first communications might include some cultural awareness:

1 Use an appropriate setting: off-site is fine but may be seen by some cultures as extravagant
2 Choose the appropriate medium: presentations need to be in tune with the audience
3 Dress appropriately: find out what is normal to the audience
4 Be honest: don't make promises that can't be kept
5 Be open: encourage questions and comments.

From the acquirer's perspective

It is often the case that organizations focus their communication efforts on the acquired company in order to reassure them that they will be well looked after, particularly if no job losses are expected in the acquirer's own company. This can sometimes lead to a feeling of neglect back at home.

Nevertheless, the acquirer's employees can also find that they have lost their old organization and that nothing is the same. The Roffey Park case study on the Halifax and Leeds merger, for example, found employees feeling that their Leeds colleagues had been more prepared for change while they had expected to continue as normal. Within six months they realized that their organization had also changed but they had been less prepared.

Cultural issues in communication

The next chapter deals with culture in more depth. However, it is worth noting that in an international merger there may be cultural differences to communication. Consider a short illustration provided by Rosen et al.[3] of German and American styles. Germans tend to be formal in business contexts and reserved towards strangers. They use direct criticism and like to debate content. On the other hand, Americans usually break the ice quickly and adopt an informal approach. They focus on positive feedback and move quickly to action.

Another short example is provided by a manager of an Anglo-French company formed by merger, which subsequently merged with an American company. The new American owners attempted to communicate directly with employees, however junior, in the French company who they felt had specific information that they needed. This direct style was frowned upon by the French managers, who expected any communication to be at management level and any information to pass through them. In this case the English partners were able to mediate between French and American styles.

Communication media

The media available to each organization will vary and may also be a cultural choice. Companies that are highly IT literate may choose predominantly electronic means of transmitting information efficiently but this would hardly be appropriate in a company where the bulk of employees do not have access to PCs. Electronic communication may been seen as impersonal in some contexts but perfectly natural in others.

It is likely that a whole range of methods needs to be identified to suit a range of employees.

For example, Clerical Medical, when acquired by the Halifax on 1 January 1997, took a four-pronged approach to their communication strategy known as PACE. This stands for:

Pulse	in-company magazine
AcTiVate	a business TV service
Connect	face-to-face communication such as team discussions
Echo	intranet site

The four approaches are designed to complement each other. For example, Pulse provides a pre-connect feature to equip staff for discussion meetings. The subsequent evaluation of the effectiveness of this combination strategy was encouraging. Staff understood the role of the various media and a survey showed that:

- 97 per cent read Pulse and 70 per cent filed it for future reference
- 68 per cent watched AcTiVate though there were some doubts about its role
- 86 per cent attended Connect sessions
- 66 per cent had access to or used Echo (32 per cent daily).

Success of the process was attributed to:

- senior manager commitment
- continuing drive and support from central communications
- demonstrating it is working through feedback.

Table 8.1 Advantages and disadvantages of various media forms

Type	Advantages	Disadvantages
Printed material		
Bulletins Newletters	Can reach all employees Can be filed for future reference Can help employees identify with the organization	More impersonal than face to face Resource intensive One-way communication
Electronic material		
E-mails Newletters	Can reach employees with PCs Fast and low resource Can be printed if relevant	More impersonal than face to face Easy to miss an important message
Intranet	Provides a useful reference point with coordinated information	Limited availability in some cases
Videos/TV	Adds a visual aspect Can be distributed widely	Must provide time and facilities to watch
Personal contact		
Roadshows	Motivational Employee involvement Senior level visibility	Not everyone can attend Difficult to cascade motivational information Some employees will feel left out
Helplines	Deal with individual queries Provides support	Needs trained staff Resource intensive
Focus groups/ discussion forums	Opportunities for staff to air feelings Useful barometer for management Can generate synergy and quality improvement	Can turn into moaning sessions May need a staff election process Must have trained facilitators

Preparing for day one

Gearing up for the announcement requires military precision, particularly where the announcement is to be made to the City the same morning. It is a time to test out the emergency call-in list in order to summon managers before the start of business either by a cascading principle or individual phone call. It is not a good time to find out that the list is well out of date and that people have moved house and even moved job. A good activity for HR in the run-up to the announcement is therefore to update all management personnel records and to include mobile phone numbers.

A briefing session for as many managers as possible should be planned for the time of the announcement so that they can be available to answer staff questions as they arrive at work. This is particularly important for customer facing staff who will need to field questions during the course of the day. The staff briefing should be accompanied by a pack of information which they can read at leisure. Where possible, managers should be available to answer any immediate questions. It is also important that as many questions as possible should be anticipated and included in the pack as a question and answer sheet.

Depending on the size of the company, the chief executive may be there in person, a video may be used or directors may visit a site each to convey the news. The logistics for global companies can be extremely difficult and may need to use video, on-line conferences, e-mail, etc. Contingency plans will also be needed in the event of an early leak to the press and an enforced announcement.

Briefing pack

Each member of the staff should receive a personalized briefing pack from the chief executive on the day of the announcement. In a small organization this should be signed in person. The advantage of having a hard copy is that employees can take it home, take time to digest the implications and share details with their families. The pack should contain:

1 A letter from the chief executive saying why and how the merger will take place and what will be the intended benefits to both parties.
2 Brief histories of the companies concerned and the reasons why they will make good partners.
3 A list of as many questions with answers as can be foreseen. In particular what the merger will mean for jobs, where the new Head Office will be, the name of the company, impact on customers.
4 A guide to what the next steps are with any key dates.
5 An organizational chart showing the structure of the new Board if already decided.
6 Copies of press releases and any information prepared for customers.

7 A list of contact numbers to direct external calls or queries to.

8 The press office number with a warning that no employee should speak to the press even if asked for their personal reaction to the news.

9 A staff help line or e-mail address for personal queries.

The follow-up

After the announcement and before the completion of the deal, communication may seem patchy with unnerving periods of silence. Employees may feel in limbo as they wait to hear about their future and many will start to prepare CVs and look around for other possibilities. It is therefore important that key employees are contacted as soon as possible. It is also important to produce a timetable quickly giving key dates by which time decisions will be made.

Communication during this phase should focus on demonstrating an understanding of the psychological impact of mergers and acquisitions. Line managers should be involved in this process as they will know many of the employees personally. Useful initiatives are:

- Providing literature on the natural feelings of employees faced with large-scale change
- Offering workshops to help in dealing with emotions and feelings
- Encouraging joint forums to explore cultural issues with the new partner
- Setting up a helpline for personal advice or a drop-in centre
- Ensuring high visibility of senior managers and HR staff (difficult in such a busy time but very worthwhile)
- Creating the energy for change by constantly demonstrating and communicating the vision and values of the new organization (again difficult in the early days as they may not have been formalized but guidelines are helpful)
- Giving people opportunities to participate.

Gaining feedback and employee involvement

It is essential for the management of the new organization to 'keep its finger on the pulse' of how staff are reacting to the change. The need to manage feedback is often missed early on but it is important to demonstrate that feedback is being heard and understood and where possible acted upon.

In the BP Amoco merger, a weekly telephone survey was used to keep in touch. In BAFS merger of their financial services departments, a full scale attitude survey was undertaken and, in spite of some harsh criticism of management and general dissatisfaction, the results were published and distributed to staff in a glossy brochure with a commitment from senior management to tackle the key issues raised. This brave approach to recognizing that life is difficult during transformational change earned the senior team a good deal of credibility.

Employees appreciate honesty and may be prepared to work through a difficult period as long as they feel their concerns are acknowledged. Feedback is also essential to the board who can become seriously isolated during a merger when they have been preoccupied with legal and financial details as well as their own packages.

Companies can be innovative in the ways they encourage and use feedback. In the GlaxoWellcome merger, employees were encouraged to use a 'graffiti' board, which eventually produced open, honest and explicit commentary to give their managers a sharp reminder of reality. It also acted as a kind of therapy for some employees and introduced an element of fun for others. Communication can be creative!

Role of the line manager

In many organizations line managers have little experience in communicating difficult news or making people redundant. Where the HR presence is small the task may fall to them. Even where managers are used to presenting to groups of staff, particular skills and training may be needed at such a sensitive time.

CGNU provided extensive guidelines to their managers on handling human issues during the merger. An example of how they encouraged empathy is shown in their guidelines on breaking news to groups:

1 Do you know how you will make sure that you are as well prepared as possible to deliver the message?
2 Are you sure that you are clear about the message/information you are presenting? If not, do you know who to ask for more information or clarification?
3 Have you worked through how you yourself feel about the message you are presenting?
4 How will you help yourself to own the message (over which you may have had little input or influence)?

5 How will you help staff feel positive about the message (especially in the situation where it is not a message you personally agree with)?

6 What will you do to help staff to both understand the contents of the message and move forward into the future?

7 Do you know whether the message you are delivering is 'good' or 'bad' news for this group of staff?

Advice to line managers from our own Roffey Park mergers checklist[4] suggests:

- Back up formal communication processes by creating opportunities for staff to discuss the implications of the latest communiqué
- Encourage employees to take advantage of communication processes – look out for individuals who are trying to bury their heads in the sand
- Be prepared to repeat key messages – it is easy for staff to be overwhelmed by merger details and to lose sight of the bigger picture
- Be prepared to handle negative feelings after each major communication round. These events tend to trigger fresh waves of anxiety
- If your organization adopts its partner's communication processes, be prepared for your staff to react badly and to criticize the style of communication. Help them to focus on what is being said instead
- Try to anticipate how your team will react to the latest merger announcement and prepare your own question and answer presentation
- Be honest and open at all times about the extent of your own knowledge.

Summary

It is a common error for senior managers to treat mergers as primarily financial and legally based transactions. From this follows a view of communications that assumes it is enough to state merely the facts and figures of the merger.

Employees receive glossy documents detailing financial ratios, rates of returns, predicted profits and details about their grading, terms and conditions. Top managers then dismantle the communication and feel satisfied with a job well done.

Roffey Park's research strongly suggests that mergers are more than an exchange of assets. They are, in reality, human based transactions. If the merger is to succeed, everyone concerned needs to commit his or her time, energy, emotion, intellect and creativity towards building the new organization. Communication plays a vital role in this process.

Mergers are a balance of opportunities and risks. The opportunities are in the potential synergies and the risks are in lack of communication. Well-informed, motivated and involved employees and managers can mitigate these risks.

Checklist for communication

Did we

- Gain an understanding of employee attitudes and expectations, as well as recognize and address concerns, fears and hopes of employees of both organizations through, for example, attitude surveys or individual discussions?
- Increase people's knowledge about typical reactions and concerns and help them to deal with them, or train their supervisors to support people?
- Sponsor programmes for employees to address resistance to change, grief processes, team building and consensus, stress management training programmes, seminars about merger syndrome?
- Prepare people to meet and work with their counterparts?
- Establish an effective and clear communication structure?
- Reinforce all verbal communications by written statements to avoid confusion?
- Communicate effectively between integrating facilities so that the information required for the integration was obtained in a timely manner?
- Inform people on a regular basis of how the integration is proceeding? Did we communicate regularly even if the content of the message was only to affirm that, at the current time there was little or no information to communicate?
- Communicate a clear vision and strategies, so that everyone has a clear picture of where to head to and how?
- Communicate changes in HR and other issues? Did we let people know what's the plan to proceed?
- Communicate directly to all the employees, e.g. newsletters, e-mails, presentations?
- Facilitate team building and develop an ongoing-timely and continual process of two-way communication?
- Provide people with a possibility to ask questions, e.g. personally, through the intranet or help-line?

- Have a contact person from the acquired organization in place all the time to act as an intermediary for staff of the acquired organization and managers in charge of the integration?

Source: Effective Mergers and Acquisitions: 2000 Roffey Park

References

1 Covello, V. T. (2001): Risk communication presentation (online). Available: http://www.state.me.us/agriculture/pesticides/covello

2 Devine, M., Hirsh, W., Garrow, V., Holbeche, L. and Lake, C. (1998): *Mergers & acquisitions: getting the people bit right*. Roffey Park Research Report

3 Rosen, R. H. (2000): *Global Literacies: lessons on business leadership and national cultures*. London: Simon & Schuster

4 Devine, M., (1999): *The Roffey Park mergers checklist*, Roffey Park Institute

Retaining staff loyalty

Jason and his men plied their oars with vigour, and passed through safe, though the islands closed behind them

Introduction

A common factor in most mergers and acquisitions is that high potential and other key staff are seen by competitors as 'up for grabs'. High flyers often see a merger as an excellent opportunity to break with an organization without detriment to their CV, particularly when they would have to relocate. Currently unemployment rates in the UK stand at their lowest for 25 years and transferable general management skills and particularly IT skills are at a premium.

How then can organizations avoid losing their valuable human resources? What will entice individuals to endure perhaps a year or more of upheaval and work overload for an uncertain future?

The Roffey Park research[1] detected two main waves of loss:

- the first in the run up to the merger when people 'jump ship'
- the second a few months into the merger when people have had time to decide if the new organization is one they wish to work for.

Typically, people are looking at how the merger will affect their opportunities and prospects. If they believe that they will lose out, people start preparing their CVs. Early signals, such as which company's senior management appear to get the top jobs, contribute to individuals' calculations of their own prospects.

Retention and merger strategy

Retention issues should form part of the initial merger strategy. For example:

1 Is the purpose of the acquisition to gain valuable skills, e.g. R&D or IT expertise, in which case what will prevent key employees leaving the organization before completion of the deal?
2 Will the organization post-acquisition have the skills required to manage a more complex organization?
3 What will be the future needs of the organization in terms of delivery of shareholder value?
4 Is the merger or acquisition a cost cutting exercise or a value creating process?
5 Are employees a cost or an asset?

Unfortunately because mergers are generally planned and executed primarily by lawyers and financiers there is a tendency to take a short-term view which culminates with the closure of the deal. This view sees employees as costs and therefore an easy target when reducing overheads. HR is often brought in later in the day to effect headcount reduction and reorganize the remaining resources to achieve economies of scale.

The long-term result of this strategy may be that employees find they are overloaded with merger projects and unable to carry out business as usual because there are not enough people with the right skills remaining.

In particular, management problems can jeopardize the integration phase of a merger. According to Walsh[2], 75 per cent of senior managers in an acquired company leave within three years. Chief executives or chairmen leave in an average of 17 months. He argues that there are three issues that contribute to high turnover:

1 M&As breed uncertainty among top managers. Those who cannot tolerate or reduce uncertainty are likely to leave the organization.
2 The merging of two distinct cultures can often produce 'feelings of hostility' and 'significant discomfort' among top managers. Some are unwilling or unable to adjust to this culture shock.
3 Top managers may perceive that they have lost control and that they are 'losers'.

Translate corporate strategy into structure, roles and skills

As already indicated, it is important to consider the objectives of the merger and to recruit and retain staff with these objectives in mind. Decisions on performance criteria and job roles should be made in line with the new strategy and proposed structure of the organization. It is also useful to be clear from an early stage what new management talents the merger will call for. For example, will people need to be more commercially oriented, have better technical skills, team building and management of change ability etc?

Employees will want to know that appointments are being made 'fairly', but this needs to be carefully defined. Clarify the following:

- In order to achieve a merger of equals, will equal or parallel appointments be made in both companies? What percentage of managers will be selected from each company involved?
- Will the 'best person for the job' be recruited and if so what does this mean in practice? For example, does someone with relevant experience take precedence over another candidate with potential and greater general ability?
- What selection tools will be used? This might include psychometric testing, assessment centres, interviews, etc
- Who will be included in the pool? Will external candidates be invited to apply? Are employees allowed to apply for roles which would mean relocation?

Communicate the right messages early

The first few days following the merger announcement and the official first few days of integration are critical times during which employees take stock of their prospects. Experience suggests that it is important for senior managers (preferably a mix of representatives from both) to be out on site visiting all groups of employees within the first forty-eight hours, even if the structure is not clear and there are many unresolved issues. It is also important that senior managers are prepared for this discussion. They should at least be aware of some of the terms used in both companies and be sensitive to how differences in management style and values will be apparent to employees through what is said and how. Insensitivity on such issues causes employees to question the credibility of the new leadership. Ideally a culture audit carried out before such presentations will alert senior managers to subtle but important differences in operating style.

Similarly, it is important that messages are conveyed about the future direction of the company, even if only in outline form. Typically, employees feel reassured if they believe there is a definite plan of action for the first few months. This helps allay some of the uncertainty that can cause employees to jump ship.

The Roffey Park checklist[3] suggests:

- Don't assume that key employees feel secure about their future in the merging organization. They will probably feel as anxious as anyone, so spell it out that you value their contribution.
- Look out for opportunities to stretch your key employees by giving them new responsibilities or a secondment onto a merger implementation team.
- Be discreet. If you make too much fuss of key employees, the rest of your team may assume their career prospects have been given the thumbs down.

Typical issues of concern to employees in the early phases of a merger

The following list shows a range of issues raised by employees in response to a merger announcement at a regional pharmaceutical company:

- When will I know if I will keep my job?
- Will there be redundancies and if so when will they be announced?
- Why did the merger/acquisition take place?
- What changes are planned and when will they be announced?
- Whom will I be reporting to in future?
- Who will make up the senior management team?
- Will our terms and conditions of employment change?
- Will there be performance appraisals?
- Will there be changes in reporting structure?

- Will my title change?
- Will there be changes in working procedures and practices?
- Will people from the acquiring company be appointed to positions in the acquired?
- What will the new organization be like?
- How do I build good working relationships in the new organization?
- Who can I trust in the new organization?
- Am I being tested?
- What are the plans for the business?
- Will we keep our company name?
- What are the short- and long-term goals for the business?
- How will we find out what is happening or going to happen?
- Are we going to get new job descriptions?
- What is the management style of the new organization?
- Will we be changing our suppliers?
- Will we be changing our customers?
- Will my past record count?
- How will my performance be measured in future?
- What is the culture of the new organization?
- Will I 'fit' in the new environment?

Identify key people

An important first step is to identify who it is important to keep and why. An up-to-date succession plan will assist the process. These may be people who are currently considered to be key employees. Equally, longer-term considerations should, if possible, be taken into account at this stage. Skills and experience, which have so far not been considered as essential may grow in importance in the new company. It is important to identify how skill sets may need to change in the new business environment. Similarly, senior roles should ideally be filled by people with the desired skills, attitudes and behaviours of current and future leaders of the company. The behaviour of leaders in the early days of the merger will influence the development of the new company's culture.

An urgent priority for the HR department is to conduct an HR audit for the new organization. It is important to find out who is likely to leave and who can be encouraged to stay. This is best done in conjunction with the counterpart HR department and line management. It may also be advisable to have the process facilitated by an independent HR consultant to avoid the perception of individual company loyalty. It is important to remember that most employees will be suffering anxiety, fear and uncertainty and may be seeking to end the ambiguity by leaving the company. Key staff in both companies should therefore be identified quickly.

The audit should consider:

For the long term:

- Knowledge management: most organizations find themselves vulnerable to loss of expertise in IT dependent areas, but the audit should identify other areas where technical expertise relies on the experience of key players (see Summary of Priorities : Risk Analysis). Line managers should consider how company knowledge can be safeguarded and passed on as appropriate.
- Achieving strategic objectives for the new organization: early identification of the skills or competencies that will be needed in the new organization and for the future of the industry is essential. This should indicate who are the current employees needed to achieve the strategic objectives.
- Future leadership: will the skills of future leaders be the same as those of the current leadership? It may be useful to revise any leadership competencies or develop a fresh set for the new organization. The top 50 employees of the new organization can be assessed and the net then spread wider. Succession plans should then be reassessed.

For the short term:

- Business as usual: performance usually slumps in the aftermath of a merger as senior managers grapple with the mechanics of the merger and the restructuring of the organization. It is important therefore to identify sufficient operational managers to maintain current performance levels during the merger. If there is not likely to be a role for them after the transition period, generous loyalty bonuses with the promise of subsequent outplacement help are used widely. The Roffey Park research identified best practice where organizations were open and honest about future prospects even when the worst was expected. People respected managers who gave a realistic assessment of their position. Some inevitably were retained in 'body' but not 'spirit' and others behaved unpredictably in a destructive way. Contingency plans are needed to deal with this kind of situation.
- Change agents: organizations fared best who could spare a dedicated resource to manage the merger as a 'project'. For this task people are needed with excellent interpersonal and integrative skills to drive the change. These people could be co-

opted immediately into transition teams who will be responsible for managing the mechanics of the merger. This group of people may well be less concerned about long-term prospects, valuing the experience of merger management and trusting their valuable skills for future employment.

The audit process is often best facilitated by an external consultant who can elicit information from senior management of the individual's parent company. It should cover issues such as the individual's perceived potential, current abilities including strengths and weaknesses, management style, next logical career step etc. The audit should also consider issues such as how the employee is likely to react to the merger, what they stand to gain or lose and the likelihood that s/he will stay with the organization. The audit should also address who could or should replace the employee if they leave and who are the person's key backers, if any.

Find out what staff want

It is worth taking time to consider what employees generally are looking for when choosing an employer. Short-term incentives may buy time but, in the long term, employees will consider a whole range of factors (Figure 9.1).

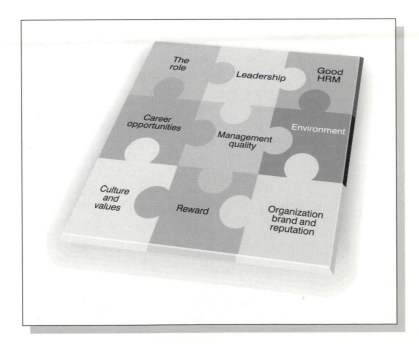

Figure 9.1 The employment relationship

The role

Individuals need to feel that their skills are valued and useful. Where organizational life has become more complex they may need reassuring that they will receive appropriate training and development. Coaching and mentoring schemes can also facilitate cultural integration and understanding.

Where the organization is seeking to become more flexible there may be opportunities for learning new skills, increased autonomy, taking up secondments, working with project teams or even spending time abroad in an international merger. By opening up opportunities, employees may find increased job satisfaction and motivation to stay.

Leadership

Employees will look to their leaders for a clear vision of the future of the organization. In-fighting at senior level can be particularly debilitating leading to a 'fiefdom' mentality. This translates throughout the organization as divisive behaviour which is embedded in the new culture.

Quality of management

It is often said that people leave managers not jobs. In a merger or acquisition, employees may have to adjust to new management but, in all cases, they will be vigilant in assessing whether managers are capable of leading their teams through the transition.

Management style is also important in setting the new cultural tone and it is therefore essential that managers demonstrate the values of the new organization. In particular they need to build commitment and understanding, minimize political behaviour and constantly translate organizational objectives into individual performance targets. By providing feedback, managers can focus their teams on maintaining performance and avoid role ambiguity.

Good HR management

Employees increasingly evaluate organizations on their HR policies, particularly work-life balance, performance management systems, diversity and personal and career development planning processes. Organizations that can demonstrate concern for employees during a merger send a positive message to staff about their future.

In one organization each employee was sent a set of human resources principles which gave reassurance that people would be treated fairly and with respect. Details were provided on how people could apply for other positions in the group if their own position became redundant. In order to implement this, staff information hot lines were set up. In addition, staff could also be given guidelines as to the skills required for the new organization and advice on how to position their application. Some larger groups have set up internal job centres to facilitate job transfer.

Organizational values and culture

By virtue of merger and acquisition employees who have deliberately joined a small, friendly organization may eventually find themselves in a huge global conglomerate. This is a typical scenario for IT specialists who have enjoyed working in a successful and creative environment and are targeted because of this. Such individuals may represent the value of the acquisition but may be disinclined to stay for purely financial reward. They are first likely to evaluate how alien the new culture and values will be before making a decision.

Individuals may feel they no longer 'fit in' in the new organization. A poor person-environment fit (PE-fit) has been linked to low job satisfaction, stress and poor performance.

Compensation and benefits

Reward in terms of pay, benefits and bonuses needs to be market tested and administered fairly. Issues of equity can sour integration efforts very easily. Sometimes status is difficult to assess with titles in one organization bearing little resemblance to titles in the partner organization. The newly merged organizational structure and hierarchy needs to be thoroughly evaluated and adequately rewarded.

Although the basic terms and conditions may not be resolved overnight, any changes to performance related pay or bonuses need to reflect the new organizational values and strategy. Information gathered from the individual interviews may help to identify what is valued. Rewards may include career development opportunities such as a sponsored MBA, which can tie the individual in for several years, sabbaticals, flexible working arrangements to accommodate family commitments.

Some groups may find that their skills are valued more highly in the labour market than in their current position. This is often the case with IT specialists. These groups will need to be brought into line with competitor organizations. Recruitment consultants could offer help on local labour conditions.

Rewards must support the business strategy and culture change and any performance element should ensure that retained employees direct their efforts to key business targets. Some organizations adopt a system of flexible benefits rather than try to provide a package that will suit both sets of employees. This may not be possible in smaller companies but it is worth recognizing that small inequalities can take on significant symbolism during the integration phase. This may come in the form of free lunches, club memberships, car policies, business travel policy and annual leave entitlement.

Working environment

To some organizations relocation may be a barrier to employee retention. Employees may feel strongly about working in a rural site rather than a large town and vice versa. Working conditions and ergonomic factors may also be unappealing in a relocation. Facilities can sometimes be cramped after a merger where one Head Office is chosen to be the main site. Following one large merger team meetings virtually stopped and when the matter was investigated it was usually due to a lack of meeting rooms.

Organization brand and status

The external perception of the organization can give an employee a feeling of pride and be a worthy addition to the CV. Customer satisfaction can be a reward in itself. Organizations that do not have a popular brand will have to work harder at internal marketing and promoting the sense of belonging to a successful company. Enthusiasm is contagious and strong internal positioning of the new company with emphasis on career opportunities and staff development will influence perceptions.

Career opportunities

Other organizations, too, claim that they do the minimum necessary in terms of specific packages for key individuals. They concentrate on identifying career tracks, especially for people who feel they have been disadvantaged by the merger and ensure that individuals have the opportunity to discuss these. It appears also to be important that the training and development intentions of the new company are made clear at an early stage. This does not mean detailed training and development plans but at least a broad plan for training and development with timescales that show that people development will be a priority.

A personal interview with all staff can be an effective way of approaching key players as well as ensuring other staff feel that they have had a voice. One organization which took part in the Roffey Park research set up an HR Merger Programme which divided up the business and prioritized key areas. A team of five personnel staff conducted 5000 individual interviews. They took the opportunity to listen to what people wanted from the merger and to assess the strength of commitment, identifying those who were keen to pursue a career with the new company and willing to relocate if necessary. They also set up a timetable for drawing up new contracts which gave people confidence and milestones to check progress.

This gave the HR team an opportunity to find out what kind of package would motivate the key employees and to make offers that would maximize retention. These may not necessarily involve only pay but may include career opportunities or development. They were also able to respond to some of the questions people had concerning the new organization.

Interviews like these can provide answers to questions such as:

- how can the new management group be motivated and managed?
- how can strengths be utilized and weaknesses addressed?
- how well will the person adapt to the new company's management philosophy and operating style?

Individuals usually find these interviews threatening in prospect, but useful in practice. The issues addressed can include such 'helpful' topics as what job opportunities it might be most appropriate to seek in the new set-up and what developmental steps might contribute most to career effectiveness.

Using retention incentives

Any incentives to retain people during the run-up phase should be announced as early as possible. One international bank offered a general bonus payment named after the new chief executive, which was divided equally between all staff remaining on the closure date for the deal. A further bonus of 25 per cent annual salary was offered to 15 per cent of employees who were identified as being critical to the operation of the bank. The announcement of this deal was made in January with a promised pay-out in June/July, although the final deal did not go through until August. This gave the organization time to establish key motivators for future retention and was very successful as a short-term measure. The organization gained considerable credibility for the speed with which the package was offered.

The real problem with lock-in bonuses is, as one employee told us, 'It buys people to sit on seats but the damage they do during that time is hard to repair. Those of us who stayed had to sort out an awful mess'. Bonuses can also be bought out by competitors and provide no guarantee that people will stay. If a better long-term opportunity is presented it is likely that the individual will leave and, whatever deal has been signed, the company cannot afford to pursue legal action to enforce it at such a sensitive time.

Performance-related earn-outs

This is a mechanism that can be used to encourage owner-managers of acquired organizations to deliver the planned performance throughout the integration period. It makes some element of the offer, whether cash or shares, conditional on achievement of agreed levels of business performance. This mechanism may also provide a means of bridging the gap between an acquirer and an acquired view of future business and therefore company value. It allows for a future price bonus to be paid dependent on the achievement of planned performance levels. Such mechanisms clearly have their merits but do also have some disadvantages worth considering up front. Although they may motivate managers to deliver the planned performance of the acquired company after the acquisition, they can also encourage them to adopt a more parochial position or even actively to obstruct any integration initiatives that puts their earn-out at risk.

The other difficulty with earn-outs is the ability to set performance criteria that are not open to misinterpretation or are liable to need to be renegotiated due to changes in circumstances. This can be a costly renegotiation as the managers may feel they would like an incentive to take on the new goals. One way of minimizing these disadvantages is to limit the time period over which they apply, say, to less than 12 months or to the end of the current operating plan year. It is important that any such deals have the full backing of other shareholders who may see them as unfair if they are not eligible for the 'bonus offer'.

Golden handcuffs

This retention tactic might include share options, loyalty/stay-put bonus payments. They are useful in a crisis situation, such as a merger, but will not solve long-term issues. Disadvantages include:

- Resentment among other staff
- Imbalance in pay strategy and other HR processes
- May keep people in body rather than in spirit
- Easily bought out by competitors.

However, as a short-term measure to assist through the merger and used in connection with other longer-term incentives they may prove of benefit. It must be clear how long the individual should stay to benefit and what the size of the award will be. Some companies offer up to three times the annual salary for some positions and half a year's pay for less critical jobs. Inclusion of a performance element can be targeted at business unit objectives.

Other retention tactics

- Be flexible – a rigid imposition of new reward policy across the board may provoke hostility. It may be worth ring-fencing some benefits for a set period of time. This often happens in the case of returning ex-pats
- Informal, confidential approach of 'a word in your ear' – this depends on a high level of trust and good relationship between individual and senior management
- Additional responsibilities – these may include a specific role in the integration process
- Recognition – the reward and recognition philosophy is part of the psychological contract and reflects organizational culture
- Career development – discuss options for career development with appropriate training and development. The experience of managing through a merger is valuable and can also enrich a CV. Secondments and overseas postings might be attractive
- MBA schemes with pay-back clause if participant leaves within two years
- Use recruitment to replace key people who leave as a strategic opportunity to review what is actually needed in the new organization – and be prepared to integrate new people into the organization with help from mentors etc.

Summary of priorities

- Establish the values of the new organization in dealing with employees: the Roffey Park research[1] showed that individuals do watch how 'people' issues are handled during the transition period of the merger and in the new organization, while they are deciding whether they wish to be part of it. Their personal experience will determine their future commitment to the organization. These issues are dealt with in more depth in Chapter 10, which looks at the evolution of the new corporate culture.

- Risk analysis: identify where the company will be exposed by a shortage of particular skills and knowledge, e.g. technical specialists, managers or groups of key workers. Do any of these areas already have a history of high turnover? How many employees fall into this category? What contingencies can you put in place to avoid exposure in the event of an exodus?

- Are there any key individuals who might leave and take a whole group with them, e.g. popular senior executives or team leaders? Are these people being targeted for specific discussions?

- Decide where the organization is going strategically – what are the implications for skills, knowledge and experience? Profile key roles and identify performance criteria.

- Identify critical people. Who adds the most product and service value from a customer perspective? Who will be difficult to replace? Who will be compatible with the new organizational culture and most likely to stay? Ask senior executives to gather information and select individuals who should be retained. Check their recommendations with other senior managers and, if possible, with an independent recruitment consultant.

- Decide whether to offer retention bonus or other incentive.

- Interview key individuals early in the audit – assess likely willingness to leave/stay and what will motivate them to stay. Prioritize 'key' workers, i.e. current high flyers, essential workers including specialists.

- Sit down with these individuals to discuss a new psychological contract. Involve them in the planning process for the new organization, ensuring they are in the communication link. Reduce ambiguity for them, restore control and make them feel part of the business plan. Discuss the future direction of the company and their future role in it. Clarify status and responsibility issues.

- Discuss rewards and benefits package.

- Develop contingencies, e.g. links with agencies offering temporary help in core skills and find out where specialists are currently working.

- Use structured exit interviews to analyse reasons which may be within the organization's control.

References

1 Hirsh, W., Devine, M., Garrow, V. and Holbeche, L. (1998): *Mergers & acquisitions: getting the people bit right.* Roffey Park Research Report
2 Walsh, J. (1988): Top management turnover following mergers and acquisitions. *Strategic Management Journal,* **9**, 173–183
3 Devine, M., (1999): *The Roffey Park mergers checklist,* Roffey Park Institute

CHAPTER 10

Creating the new organizational culture

Pelias knew he could not harm Jason in festival
time, or offend against the laws of hospitality

Introduction

One of the most important lessons to come out of the
Roffey Park research[1] was summed up by one senior
manager who said, 'You can't paint the culture on
afterwards'. It is a sobering lesson that culture emerges
from the way the merger, transition and integration is
handled. If the process is painful, management and
communication poor, redundancy and appointments
handled badly then it is unlikely that the organization
can suddenly decide to adopt a caring, open and
respectful culture with any success. Examples of organizations that believed they could deal with operational
restructuring first and culture later have found it too
late.

What is culture?

The reason for this is that organizational culture is rooted in the history, structure, environment and leadership of the company. In a merger a new company is effectively born. Perhaps a merger is in fact more like a birth than a marriage. The new organization has genes from both parents but may also suffer from a traumatic birth and lack of good parenting in its early years.

According to Schein[2]:

> Culture is what a group learns over a period of time as that group solves its problems of survival in an external environment and its problems of internal integration. Such learning is simultaneously a behavioural, cognitive and an emotional process.

In popular terms, culture manifests itself in 'how things get done'. Common assumptions arise from recruitment and induction programmes and are reinforced by recognition and reward systems. Critical incidents can also serve to build up case histories which illustrate various principles or shared beliefs. During a merger, critical processes will be:

- Fair appointments
- Sensitively handled redundancy
- Honest communication
- Negotiating terms and conditions
- Performance management
- Handling conflict.

Employees will take note of how these situations are handled and build them into their own understanding of the new organizational culture. Horror stories of bad treatment and poor decisions will pass down into the symbolic 'myths' of the organizational memory! Culturally transmitted knowledge helps employees make sense of particular events and actions and permits a shared sense of experience. For this reason a modern form of cultural analysis is done by 'storytelling', where language and metaphor provide a powerful illustration of deeper underlying assumptions.

Culture, however, should be distinguished from 'climate', which is more like 'mood' and is short term and easier to change. Although the culture will influence the climate, the mood after a merger may be one of anxiety, excitement, gloom or expectancy. These moods may be produced by the 'waves of change' described in Chapter 2 and rise and fall during the various merger stages. A climate survey at any one of the points will need to take into account current activity at local level.

Cultural melange

In some industries, where there have been frequent mergers and acquisitions, cultures have little time to develop and there are legacies of several different backgrounds. Culture may then be stronger between the professional groups of merging companies than inter-departmental groups within the same organization. For example, in one insurance company the brokers who were based in the City had more in common with each other than with their own head office staff who were both based in different counties. Hofstede[3], suggests that people carry several layers of mental programming within themselves which include:

- National
- Regional
- Gender
- Generational
- Social class
- Organizational or corporate.

Culture is also dynamic and shifts to take account of new experiences. Organizations occasionally undertake acquisitions or mergers to achieve a culture shift. During the Roffey Park research, the team came across two organizations that had actively sought to become more entrepreneurial by acquiring companies whose employees were less procedural and less risk averse. In cases like these, it is important that the culture organizations seek to acquire is not lost in the acquisition process. At least one of the companies we interviewed acknowledged that because of the size of the company they had acquired (three times their own size), management had resorted to imposing standard procedures and had thereby lost many of the entrepreneurial managers, while others adjusted to the new owner's strongly entrenched culture.

Other organizations that are likely to continue merging and acquiring do not have the time to carry out intensive cultural programmes before the next merger and tend to develop a flexible and change-oriented culture which attracts employees who can tolerate ambiguity and enjoy uncertainty. Nevertheless, one of the functions of culture, according to Schein, is to reduce anxiety by providing 'automatic patterns' of perceiving, thinking, feeling and behaving which provide meaning, stability and comfort. He maintains that it is the inability to understand or predict events that leads to anxiety and suggests that attention be paid to the following tasks.

External tasks

1 The core mission, functions and primary tasks of the organization vis-à-vis its environments.
2 The specific goals to be pursued by the organization.
3 The basic means to be used in accomplishing the goals.
4 The criteria to be used for measuring results.
5 The remedial or repair strategies if goals are not achieved.

Internal tasks

1 The common language and conceptual system to be used, including basic concepts of time and space.
2 The group boundaries and criteria for inclusion.
3 The criteria for the allocation of status, power and authority.
4 The criteria for intimacy and friendship.
5 The criteria for the allocation of rewards and punishments.
6 Concepts for managing the unmanageable – ideology.

One of the most culturally complex case studies from the Roffey Park research was the creation of the Environment Agency from an amalgamation of over eighty public bodies. Many of the bodies were themselves the product of previous mergers. Initial difficulties in making decisions on office locations and organizational structure reflected deeply rooted geographical differences. The former National Rivers Authority, which had a highly devolved way of working, was used to structures based on river basins, while the waste disposal people related to local authority boundaries. Meanwhile the pollution inspectors dealt with major companies nationally who expected a consistent approach and their culture was of centralized guidance and procedures.

This merger raised issues of whether cultural variation could be accommodated within an integrated organization whose culture still related to the focus of their different areas of business. There were tensions regarding the value of technical expertise against general management and issues that had to be worked through at a local level. One unifying factor was the BSE crisis which demonstrated the real value of an integrated approach to the environment and gave momentum to embedding the changes and cultural shifts.

Selecting a partner on cultural fit

Business leaders need to make sense of their own cultures before they can begin the task of choosing an appropriate partner. There are many different models that can be used. Davis[4] focuses on different business styles, such as an organization's degree of risk-taking and attitudes to power and control. Harrison[5] talks of four different types of culture: role, power, support and achievement. He identifies the strengths, limitations and 'dark' side of each of these cultural orientations.

Deal and Kennedy[6] look at managerial behaviour, risk taking and feedback and describe four different cultures including the 'tough-guy macho' culture and the 'process' or bureaucratic culture. Hofstede's model looks at how work is performed and draws various distinctions, for example process orientation versus results orientation. Rob Goffee and Gareth Jones[7] draw on the sociological tradition and examine cultures along two axes – sociability and solidarity. Sociability refers to relations between people who may regard each other as friends, versus solidarity, which describes task-centred cooperation between unlike individuals and groups and does not have to be sustained by continuous social relations.

Yet another approach is taken by Bridges[8] whose Organizational Character Index (OCI) equates the character or personality of the organization with that of the individuals who make up the organization. It is debatable whether organizations can be said to have personalities as such, but culture change can be influenced by either recruiting heavily one specific personality type or, conversely, by a clear diversity policy.

Cultures are not only reflected in business styles but in the way the organization is structured and its processes operate. Organization elements include whether the structure is centralized, decentralized or divisionalized. They also include the way in which jobs are defined – narrowly and clearly or broadly and flexibly – and the degree of functionality that exists. Organizations respond differently to the requirements of work legislation. They have different working practices and company procedures. Systems, such as the way in which management information is reported, are other facets of the culture. M&As often suffer because of difficulties in trying to rationalize two different IT, financial planning and people management systems such as training and development procedures, terms and conditions, performance management and succession planning.

Organizations contemplating a merger cannot fail to be alarmed by the growing focus on cultural issues as central to merger success or failure. Many companies now include an element of cultural assessment in their due diligence process. Some levels of culture are publicly accessible through *artefacts* such as annual reports, publicity, products, the dress code, advertising and mission statements. Other information on *patterns of behaviour* might be gleaned from former employees of the target who may now be working within the acquirer's organization. This happens frequently in the financial sector where there is a good deal of movement between organizations. Intelligence might include the codes governing management relationships, management philosophy, stories and myths.

Deciphering such information is complex but it is a valuable exercise to begin to gain an insight into how misunderstandings are likely to arise. At the same time, many senior managers are culturally illiterate with regard to their own organization and the pre-merger phase provides a good opportunity to do some self-examination.

Some of the key differences between partners that can cause real problems are:

- Decision-making styles: this is likely to become apparent during the negotiation phase and will probably ring alarm bells at an early stage in the process.
- Hierarchical relationships: it is difficult to match a status conscious and formally hierarchical company with a flatter, egalitarian company. Both sides will find it difficult to provide counterparts for integration discussions.
- Balance of power: which departments are most dominant, which director is most influential and which department gets the lion's share of the organization's resources?
- Management styles: one of the key cultural differences in organizations. Managers with directive styles will find it difficult to motivate employees who are used to a participative style.
- Accountability: how far are individuals within the business held accountable for their own results? In some flat structures accountability may extend to shop floor.
- Customer focus and business philosophy: do employees work for the benefit of the business or for the benefit of their customers? What is the rationale for the company's existence, profit or satisfaction?
- Homogeneity or diversity: are employees encouraged to think for themselves or do they follow a company line?
- Do groups or departments within the organization compete or collaborate when achieving goals and targets?

Various metaphors are helpful in understanding the nature of organizational culture. Trompenaars[9] suggests the following:

1 The family: highly paternalistic; hierarchical and power-oriented.
2 The Eiffel Tower: bureaucratic; highly structured; clear role division and highly regulated.
3 The guided missile: egalitarian; impersonal and task-oriented. Employees highly motivated by the task.
4 The incubator: unstructured; incubating self-expression and fulfilment.

All of the above metaphors, indices and pointers to common issues are helpful in getting a handle on culture but pose a threat of oversimplifying a very complex area. Even in cultures that seem quite similar on paper, small issues can take on enormous proportions when people start to work together.

Developing cultural agility

Rather than be lulled into a sense of security from having selected a compatible partner, it is wiser to develop real ongoing cultural agility in the organization. This is often done more successfully in organizations that are skilled at building strategic alliances. Research at Roffey Park[10] found that in successful alliances employees learn to understand and work between different cultural approaches. To some extent an alliance culture does develop in long-term alliances, but employees must, nevertheless, work with inherent tension between the cultures of their parents.

From our research into mergers, acquisitions and alliances these are some of the ways in which organizations develop cultural agility:

1. Promote self-awareness

- The management group should be clear on their own management style and understand how to relate to managers with different styles.
- 360 feedback is a tool that can help to promote self-awareness among employees and produce a shift to a more open culture.

2. Ensure organizational values are clear

- Values should be demonstrated consistently by leaders and managers.

- Values should translate into individual goals and objectives.
- Values should be reflected by the recognition and reward system.

3. Promote cultural understanding

- Provide opportunities to surface underlying values, assumptions and beliefs, e.g. workshops where employees have the opportunity to explore culture in a creative way using art, metaphors.
- Promote understanding of how the above impact on individual perceptions of other cultures.
- Surface differences with the partner organization using humour and social contexts and create new metaphors.
- Avoid the use of stereotypes in describing employees.

4. Create processes for learning

- Alliances provide excellent opportunities to learn more effective ways of working. Opportunities in mergers are often restricted due to integration processes which do not allow time to explore best practice.

Building a culture that supports the strategy

The real challenge after a merger is to align culture to strategy, which in turn reflects the business environment. For example, an environment that demands speed and results will probably not give priority to building up long-term customer relationships. Similarly a company that is recognized for reliability and consistency over time will not foster a creative or entrepreneurial environment. This is not to say that the market will not shift, requiring a parallel shift in culture. After a merger the organization may find itself in a new environment as a bigger and more complex entity. Some enter the global or international arena and many join a different league of market leaders.

Processes and particularly reward and recognition systems need to support the behaviours required to nurture the chosen culture and strategy. Environments that require individual entrepreneurial or risk-taking behaviour should not be considering team rewards and vice versa. A good example of a market driven shift in strategy can be seen in the high street banks where counter staff have seen their roles change from carrying out efficient customer transactions to cross-selling a variety of bank products. The culture has had to move from one of courteous service to proactive sales and rewards reflect these changes in values.

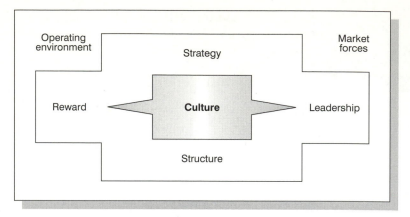

Figure 10.1 The central role of culture

After a merger it is therefore vital that the values which will support the chosen business strategy are made explicit and encouraged by appropriate management and leadership and that they are seen to be valued in the reward system. This inevitably means that much of the work on culture and values will be done at board level, although if employees are not part of the process at any stage there will be a lack of commitment to any new direction. Employees should, at the very least, understand the links between organizational values, strategy and their business environment.

Figure 10.1 shows a central role for culture in supporting strategy while itself being supported by an enabling structure and in turn influencing leadership style and reward. Where these elements form an integrated whole the organization is well-equipped to meet the challenges of its marketplace.

Working cross-culturally

When a merger brings staff from different countries into the same organization, the potential synergies are great but so too can be the difficulties. A recent report by the International Labour Organization[11]) on merger activity in the financial sector acknowledges that cultural aspects constitute a significant obstacle to cross-border mergers in spite of some improvement due to education and training. The report cites the example of Deutsche Bank's acquisition of the Morgan Grenfell Group where the latter was initially allowed to maintain its autonomy. However, when Deutsche Bank was obliged to review its strategy and attempted to impose its own organizational culture and ways of working on Morgan Grenfell, the value of the acquisition was almost totally nullified. Deutsche Bank fortunately learned from this experience to make culture a key part of its integration strategy during the Bankers Trust merger.

Various researchers, such as Trompenaars[9] and Laurent[12], have explored attitudinal differences among managers from different countries. Laurent differentiates managers' views of organizations as:

- Political systems
- Authority systems
- Role formalization systems
- Hierarchical relationship systems.

His results highlight distinctive patterns for managers in each of the various countries. Similarly Hofstede's work[13] on national cultures within IBM in over 50 countries provides four useful dimensions when assessing international deals but can also be useful within different organizations. He identifies:

1 Power distance: the extent to which the less powerful members of organizations expect and accept that power is distributed unequally. Organizational cultures with high power distance are likely to be concerned about structure and hierarchical status.
2 The individualism-collectivism index: the extent to which individual effort is rewarded and respected above teamwork or community effort.
3 Uncertainty avoidance index: the extent to which ambiguity is tolerated which is reflected in willingness to take risks.
4 Masculine–feminine index: the extent to which values tend to favour achievement and competitiveness as opposed to cooperation and mutual support.

The following example from the merger of Cable and Wireless and IDC, Japan, in 1999 demonstrates some of the key factors to be taken into account when determining a cultural integration programme. A cultural survey was conducted within the first two weeks of ownership of the three companies involved: Cable and Wireless, IDC, Cable & Wireless Japan. The survey contained questions relating to:

- Way of executing business
- Inter- and intra-department relationships/communication
- Working environment
- Employee evaluation and reward structure
- Change momentum.

The following significant cultural differences were identified:

IDC	*Cable & Wireless*
Consensus driven bottom-up decision making	Top down decision making
Customer oriented	Profit oriented
Stable and conservative	Change orientated
Casual and cheerful	Formal
Cooperative	Independent
Ageist progression	Performance progression

The integration process continued using this information and considering:

1 The importance of culture
2 The starting points of C&W, C&W Japan and IDC
3 The global telecommunications industry and environment and what corporate culture was desirable
4 Where was the gap between the starting point and the desired culture
5 How could the desired culture be achieved.

By taking time to understand differences and build towards a new future the Japanese and Western management teams now work effectively together developing trust and respect. They actively support a two-way learning process rather than 'ours is best' and stress a 'business as usual' message.

A new culture emerges

Because the manifestations of culture are often symbolic, employees may need consciously to bid farewell to the old before adopting the new. Some American companies go so far as to have a 'wake' and celebrate the ending of an organization.

Producing a new culture is no easy feat. Combining organizations will each have a battery of tactics to protect their respective cultures and prevent 'acculturation' – the process of developing jointly shared meanings and values which help foster cooperation. Larsson[14] identifies four main barriers to acculturation:

- Initial dilution of the combined corporate culture, when fewer shared meanings are developed, causing people to revert to their former loyalties
- Lack of joint socialization mechanisms, when both sets of employees view each other as the newcomers and their own ways as superior

- Separate maintenance mechanisms, when each set of employees maintains their own culture by glorifying the past and vilifying the newcomers
- Collective learned helplessness, when the 'weaker' organization experiences a loss of esteem because of its inability to ward off the takeover.

Larsson's view is that the issue of whether two cultures are similar is less important than events after the merger. Far more important is the socialization process that takes place afterwards. The danger is that culture clashes can become so intense that the organization becomes internally focused, customers become dissatisfied and the business starts to suffer. Developing the new culture therefore has to run alongside a determined effort to build the value proposition for existing and new customers.

A study by Dempsey and McKevitt[15] describes how during the creation of Unison, the UK's largest trade union, from the merger of three other trade unions, explicit initiatives were taken to avoid the new organization resembling any of its predecessors. Institutions had new names, there was a reduction in the use of committees and project team-working and matrix management were developed to foster task orientation and the spanning of boundaries. The integration process was monitored to ensure that no single group dominated the merger. Unfortunately, the cultural integration process was interrupted by a financial crisis and during the subsequent severance programme much ground was lost, revealing persistently strong subcultures. The cultural integration process is still continuing seven years later.

The importance of the micro-level

Although the vision and values may be a top-down process, the real work on culture building starts at the team level where people from the different organizations start to work together and to establish 'ground rules' for how things will get done. Line and team managers are therefore important players in developing new cultural patterns of behaviour.

The Roffey Park checklist[16] suggests the following actions for line managers during the integration period:

- Identify the key tactics used by team members to adhere to their own cultures
- Identify cultural 'hot spots', highly obvious differences in working practices that generate tension and conflict
- Using a culture model, get team members to explore the traits of their culture

- Get your people to identify cultural values or meanings that are important to them and which they wish to preserve
- Challenge team members to identify a cluster of values that everyone can commit themselves to and use as a foundation for working together.

Some of the skills needed by line managers are similar to those required by managers of cross-functional teams. Different functions often have their own embedded cultures and language in the form of jargon which makes joint working difficult.

Culture and values link strongly with work identity and individuals need to feel they can identify with the new organization and their new colleagues. Culture is often described as the 'organizational glue' and should provide a seamless bonding of internal and external facets. A merger or acquisition is a key moment for reassessing the role of culture in organizational life and its value in driving the business forward. The following checklist provides an aid to cultural issues during this time.

Checklist for cultural issues

In dealing with changing cultures, did we:

- Carry out a study of our own (the acquirer's) culture? Did we find out what are the main values and drivers to do business? Did we then consider which aspects of our culture it was desirable and necessary to 'export' to foreign subsidiaries?
- Carry out a cultural audit/due diligence of the acquired organization: get to know the acquired organization and the way it operates?
- Identify the cultural differences and define potential synergies and incompatibilities. Did we decide how the cultural distance was to be resolved?
- Decide the level of cultural integration required?
- Plan how to achieve the desired level of cultural integration, acculturation?
- Provide orientation for managers and employees of both organizations about the history, mission and culture of the other organization?
- Focus on describing a positive but realistic culture? Did we outline, rather than criticize, the cultural differences?
- Encourage the sharing of best practice?
- Support the formation of informal contact networks based on mutual trust?
- Design joint seminars and conferences in a way that promoted informal socialization and the creation of personal links?

- Were management actions, especially communication and transition management, aligned to the direction of the new organization?
- Show people that working together is advantageous?
- Provide opportunities for participation at all levels of the organization?
- Did we take into account different national cultures in judging appropriate approaches to people of different national cultures (see e.g. Hofstede: power distance/level of uncertainty avoidance/ individualism-collectivism /masculinity-femininity)?

Source: Effective Mergers and Acquisitions: 2000 Roffey Park[17]

References

1 Devine, M., Hirsh, W., Garrow, V., Holbeche, L. and Lake, C. (1998): *Mergers & acquisitions: getting the people bit right*. Roffey Park Research Report

2 Schein, E. (1990): Organisational culture. *American Psychologist*, **45**, 2, 109–119

3 Hofstede, G. (1991): *Cultures and Organisations*, London, McGraw-Hill

4 Davis, R. (1968): Compatibility in corporate marriages, *Harvard Business Review*, **46**, 86–93

5 Harrison, R. (1987): *Organizational culture and quality of service*, London, Association of Management and Development

6 Deal, T. and Kennedy, A. (1982): *Corporate Culture: the rites and rituals of corporate life*, London, Penguin Business

7 Goffee, R. and Jones, G. (1998): *What Holds the Modern Company Together?* London, HarperCollins

8 Bridges, W. (1992): *The Character of Organizations: using Jungian type in organizational development*. Consulting Psychologists Press: Palo Alto CA

9 Trompenaars, F. (1993): *Riding the Waves of Culture: understanding cultural diversity in business*. London, Nicholas Brealey Publishing

10 Garrow, V., Devine, M., Hirsch, W. and Holbeche, L. (2000): *Strategic alliances: getting the people bit right*, Roffey Park Institute

11 International Labour Organization (20001): *The employment impact of mergers and acquisitions in the banking and financial services sector*, International Labour Office, Geneva

12 Laurent, A. (1983): The cultural diversity of western conceptions of management, *International Studies of Management and Organization* Vol. XIII, no. 1–2 M.E. Sharpe Inc.

13 Hofstede, G. (1980) : *Cultures Consequences*, California, Sage Publications

14 Larsson, R. (1993): Barriers to acculturation in mergers and acquisitions: strategic human resource implications. *Journal of European Business Education*, **2**, 2, May

15 Dempsey, M. and McKevitt, D. (2001): Unison and the people side of mergers, *Human Resource Management Journal*, **11**, 2

16 Devine, M. (1999): The Roffey Park mergers and acquisitions checklist: a guide to effective people management during a merger or acquisitions.

17. Garrow, V. and Holbeche, L. (2000): *Effective mergers and acquisitions*, Roffey Park

CHAPTER 11

The role of HR

The oracle was consulted

Introduction

Too often mergers and acquisitions are brokered by legal and financial experts without reference to the HR team. The latter then find themselves having to find ways to deliver head count reduction, higher productivity through synergy while ensuring that the company has the right skills to take the new organization forward.

The capacity to do this varies enormously from organization to organization. Some companies have a highly skilled HR team, which is used to working at a strategic level alongside the business. Others have little more than a small personnel function dealing with contracts and pay.

One thing is certain, that it is the people who will make the merger a success or failure in the long term. The areas that HR will have to deal with, outlined in Figure 11.1, will have an impact on the employment relationship and upon subsequent employee commitment to the business.

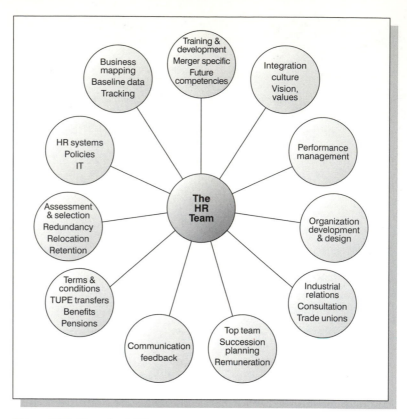

Figure 11.1 The role of HR

Establishing credibility for HR

Mergers can provide an opportunity for the HR team to claim a strategic place in the organization. It is a time to demonstrate that the function can support strategic goals and be instrumental in delivering a high performance organization.

One chief executive recognized the value of HR when he arrived in the acquired organization for the first time to meet his new employees to present a well-prepared five-year business plan. He soon realized that staff were not interested in detailed plans for the organization but in decisions that had an impact on their jobs and security. The CEO rang Head Office and asked the HR director to join him to deal specifically with the people issues raised.

HR should be able to provide the bridge between the business needs and the employees. While the senior team may have exhausted their energies in 'doing the deal', HR needs to plan the longer-term strategy for delivering the deal. The Roffey Park research found that organizations that were strongly HR led, anticipated and overcame many of the integration stumbling blocks that beset other mergers. Some HR teams raised their standing within the organization so that they became key players in subsequent merger discussions.

Soft and hard issues during a merger

Figure 11.1 shows the complexity of a true HR role during a merger. HR may be viewed by the business as dealing with 'soft' issues, but the 'hard' issues risk taking over completely as beleaguered staff turn round a plethora of contracts, rewards systems, benefits and pension schemes. As we have already seen in Chapter 4, employment legislation and the involvement of the trade unions require a meticulous approach to these issues. Industrial tribunals are time consuming and leave a sour taste for those involved as well as those remaining and are detrimental to corporate public image. Nevertheless, even the best transfers can result in a tribunal and it is therefore essential that documentation regarding contracts, consultation and correspondence is kept updated and accessible.

Many HR professionals told the Roffey Park research team that over 75 per cent of HR time is spent on fewer than 5 per cent of the employees. These can include staff in outposts on irregular contracts. One example was the case of an African who, while not directly employed by the company, had always been considered to be invaluable as a 'Man Friday' and had received unofficial compensation for his local knowledge and help.

As with other aspects of merger management, excellent project management skills are a great asset for the HR team. Dividing the work up in terms of accountability and delivery against a strict timetable is a valuable exercise, particularly where joint project groups from both organizations can demonstrate integration principles in their own roles.

While the 'hard' HR issues risk taking over in terms of time and energy, HR professionals should maintain the 'body' but also keep an eye on the 'soul' of the organization. This is a demanding and often emotionally draining process while HR personnel themselves may not be certain of their own future.

Restructuring HR

The question of how HR should structure itself to tackle a merger is a tricky one. It is important to develop a model that will support the strategy of the business and assist in aligning people processes with operational needs.

Some organizations bite the bullet early and restructure themselves in such a way that they are able to support the business directly as new appointments are made. Unfortunately, this may result in difficulties where the restructuring is not completed as quickly as anticipated, so that there are ongoing changes throughout the transition and integration periods. This inevitably leads to discontinuity and employee stress as they take over the workload of colleagues who have moved on or left.

For this reason other organizations leave the HR community until the end of the integration period and guarantee stability until the business is fully established. The risks in this approach are that HR staff may choose to leave rather than to shoulder a heavy workload only to find that there is no job at the end of it. Lock-in bonuses may provide an incentive in such situations but in a buoyant employment market it can be a risky strategy. An additional drawback to this approach is that the business can often seem to be forging ahead at a time when HR is starting to put its own house in order and HR thereby loses its partnership status.

The allocation of projects

Decisions must be taken at an early stage about secondments to project teams. This often causes resentment as merger projects provide valuable experience for professional development and CV building. HR employees who find themselves managing 'business as usual' may feel left out and demotivated.

In many cases the project work is in addition to the 'day job' and both may suffer accordingly. The advantage of this approach, however, is that there is a better transition in handing back merger projects to everyday business needs. Where projects are handled by a discrete team, there can be a lack of ownership as, for example, a new pay and reward structure is handed over to the 'business as usual' team seemingly from out of the blue. Whichever route is taken, it is important that the HR community is informed about which projects are in progress and who is involved in them as well as a clear timetable for outputs.

Where the HR team is small, it may be a sensible decision to outsource some of the projects in order to make the HR team more directly accessible to employees. It is sadly too often the case that when employees most need to talk to someone directly, the HR team is buried under mounds of contracts. Help lines can be a solution but staff need to be well trained and, above all, well informed about the changes happening during the merger.

Areas for urgent attention

Some of the HR roles in Figure 11.1 have been covered in separate chapters as they are vital in the overall merger plan: retaining key employees; communication; legal issues; culture. Other areas may depend on the level of involvement the HR team chooses to have. Where HR are not included it is likely to be due to the senior team's ignorance of what the HR team can offer. In some cases, this means that the HR team has to forge a role for themselves and make themselves an accepted partner to the business teams. This, in turn, may depend on how prepared the department is for merger.

One of the first areas that will need to be addressed is the provision of HR data: how many employees there are; where they are based; what kind of contracts they have; how many vacancies there are; how many contract staff; what liabilities these staff bring and where cost savings might be made. Organizations that have already undergone mergers or acquisitions will undoubtedly be more meticulous in ensuring records are available quickly. For some, 'putting the house in order' can be a sobering experience which stretches HR staff before the merger is underway. Therefore, as soon as there is any rumour of merger, some of this work should be done as urgent preparation.

At the same time the team, whether acquired or acquirer, should be considering some of the softer HR due diligence work that we considered in earlier chapters. HR may not be officially included in the due diligence process but this does not prevent the team suggesting what information they would like to ask for. Raising cultural questions may be the sole domain of the HR team in an inexperienced company. As we have seen in the previous chapter, 'you can't paint the culture on afterwards'. These issues must be surfaced and dealt with at an early stage.

The employment proposition

As we saw in the previous chapter, the key to post-merger success is the ability to align culture, structure, processes and strategy to the operating environment. HR has a key role to play in achieving this alignment. The Royal Bank of Scotland Group provides an excellent example of harnessing business and employee needs. Following their acquisition of NatWest in 2000, the Royal Bank of Scotland Group acknowledged that their source of competitive advantage would be their people. To support the development of a proposition that would allow them to attract and retain people with the appropriate talent, the HR team developed an 'employee proposition' model (Figure 11.2),

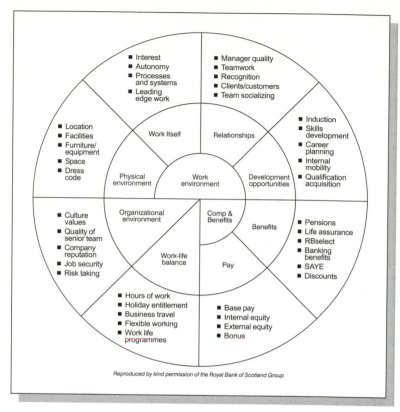

- Interest
- Autonomy
- Processes and systems
- Leading edge work

- Manager quality
- Teamwork
- Recognition
- Clients/customers
- Team socializing

- Location
- Facilities
- Furniture/ equipment
- Space
- Dress code

Work Itself

Relationships

- Induction
- Skills development
- Career planning
- Internal mobility
- Qualification acquisition

Physical environment

Work environment

Development opportunities

- Culture values
- Quality of senior team
- Company reputation
- Job security
- Risk taking

Organizational environment

Comp & Benefits

Benefits

- Pensions
- Life assurance
- RBselect
- Banking benefits
- SAYE
- Discounts

Work-life balance

Pay

- Hours of work
- Holiday entitlement
- Business travel
- Flexible working
- Work life programmes

- Base pay
- Internal equity
- External equity
- Bonus

Reproduced by kind permission of the Royal Bank of Scotland Group

Figure 11.2 The employment proposition

which takes a holistic view of the relationship between the RBS Group and its employees.

This type of tool reminds HR teams of the dangers of focusing too narrowly on one aspect of the relationship. The beauty of the approach is in the broad appreciation of employee issues, which may not be possible to resolve in 100 days and represents an ongoing commitment.

Employee involvement and motivation

An essential task for the HR team is to ensure employees have opportunities to engage with the new organization and begin the process of re-identifying with it. Methods include 'road shows', focus groups, attitude surveys and workshops or a combination of these. It is important for both employees and senior managers, who can become very isolated during a merger, that a temperature check is taken frequently. Outputs from forums can provide valuable learning and encourage employees to contribute ideas and energy to the business. At the same time they have an opportunity to say what things are stopping them from doing a good job.

Developing skills

Mergers present real challenges for organizations to ensure that there are the right kinds of skills to take the business forward in what is probably a more complex environment. The merger may involve HR in organizational development work and many companies find they move permanently into a team-based structure where employees work cross-functionally. This brings the need for team building and development and for good team leadership. A post-merger company often needs managers who can manage ongoing change as well as their functional role. HR must carry out some form of skills audit to establish who is needed and whether additional resources will be required by recruiting externally or whether objectives can be achieved by providing sufficient training and development. A benefit of an early review of training and development is that it demonstrates a commitment to employees and their needs and may entice some to stay in order to acquire new skills.

Dealing with redundancy

While retention is dealt with in a separate chapter, one of the most stressful and difficult tasks for HR professionals is drawing up plans for redundancy. A clear policy should be established and communicated to staff. Decisions need to be made on whether a full review of staffing will be made immediately or whether a 'slotting' process will take place with only those in duplicated jobs being put in job 'pools' either in the same geographic area or in functional pools. Sometimes it is the line manager who will have the face-to-face meeting with those involved and sometimes HR will have the job of breaking the news. The Roffey Park checklist[1] provides the following advice for appointments and redundancy:

- New appointments need to be seen to be fair. Try to ensure that selection criteria are objective, transparent and widely understood
- Stick to company policy and processes. Don't take shortcuts even though work pressure is overwhelming. However, don't dither as this generates enormous resentment and frustration

- Be professional. Don't try to keep everyone on board by 'fudging' redundancies and appointment decisions. Your business will suffer if you fail to match people with the relevant roles and jobs and you will only have to tackle the issue at a later stage
- Treat employees at every level with dignity. Use redundancies and appointments as a way of demonstrating the values and behaviours of the new organization
- Document your processes and be ready to justify your decisions
- Maintain high professional standards. Tell people what is happening and when
- Try to reassure people that their past history and achievements will be taken into account.

Supporting one another

It is a 'hazard of the job' that HR communities find themselves in the firing line from employees suffering from stress and anxiety. Many find it emotionally draining and work hard to do a professional job in difficult circumstances. Where the integration timescales have been cut to the minimum, the workload can be overwhelming and the added worry of having to cut corners adds to the overall anxiety levels. It is therefore essential that HR staff have support from their managers and also take time to support each other. It is not unusual to find a high sickness rate, which adds to the burden on colleagues, and managers must keep an eye on individual workloads. Employees in the Roffey Park research[1] particularly appreciated visits from senior managers and recognition for their efforts. A budget for social occasions and a chance to celebrate what had been achieved were valued.

It is also important to provide opportunities for HR staff to 'have a voice'. They may be involved in staff attitude or climate surveys but their role can make them feel isolated. They are often viewed by staff as a 'management tool' to impart bad news and similarly as a 'prophet of doom' by the management team when trying to offer staff feedback.

Capturing organizational learning

Some organizations in sectors where merger activity is an ongoing fact of life, are trying to build up their internal capability in merger processes. HR can be a key driving force and coordinator of organizational learning.

The difficulties of learning and documenting during a merger are manifold. The time factor and heavy workload are undoubtedly critical and it is tempting to leave evaluation until things settle down. Unfortunately, organizational memories are short and as people leave, much valuable experience is lost. Some organizations now try to put together a toolkit of processes that have worked well. Training and development programmes and materials are valuable, as are examples of communication packs and strategies. Project and progress charts can all be re-used as well as frameworks and policies for recruitment, redundancy and relocation. HR may have the opportunity to provide ongoing training in merger skills for line managers so that they can reflect on their own learning and feel better equipped for next time.

Evaluation

The Roffey Park research found that even where a merger is managed well and people are dealt with properly, there can still be a sense that the organization is no more than the sum of its parts, and that these parts may still not be really working together. The root of the problem often lies in the 'softer' issues such as resistance to the emergence of a new culture, difficulties in internalizing new values and personal transition issues. These things are inherently complex to analyse and are best done by trained facilitators working with groups of employees. The following checklist can be used to evaluate the effectiveness of the integration process at the organizational level, the team level and the individual level.

1. Organizational integration

To what extent do new systems run efficiently? • • •

- Do people understand their new roles and responsibilities?
- Are reporting relationships clear?
- Is accountability clear?
- Do people have the information they need or know where to get it?
- Do people understand and comply with policies and procedures?
- To what extent do new systems run efficiently?
- Do teams have the equipment and resources they need?
- What benefits is the new organization delivering? What has worked well? What has not worked well? Where are the gaps?

Shared values and culture ● ● ●

The area of culture and values links strongly to that of work identity. During the transition phase employees are trying to work out what the organization stands for and whether they want to work for it. Some of the areas to look out for are:

- Are the values of the company clearly communicated and understood?
- What involvement have staff had in creating those values?
- Do staff identify with the company?
- Is there a feeling of organizational pride?
- How far has cultural variation been accommodated within the integrated culture?

Communication ● ● ●

- Is communication actively used to break down organizational barriers?
- Is there good communication between departments?
- Do staff feel part of an integrated organization?
- Is there a climate of openness and transparency fostered by good communication?
- Do staff believe they are listened to?
- What are the mechanisms for two-way communication?

2. Senior team integration

How does the senior team work together? Do they have a clear vision of integration and role model the behaviour to achieve it?

Style ● ● ●

- Is there a consensus of leadership/management style?
- How quickly are decisions made and problems resolved?
- Is there a legacy of a dominant way of doing things?

Structure ● ● ●

- Are roles, responsibilities and accountability clear?
- Is there evidence of frustration in getting things done?

Values/culture ● ● ●

- Do the senior team demonstrate shared objectives, e.g. by the use of similar language when translating strategy into divisional goals?
- What mechanisms reinforce integrated behaviour? e.g. newsletters, events, social gatherings
- Is there evidence of old allegiances, 'fiefdoms' and nostalgia? Do employees introduce themselves as 'ex-company'?
- Do managers model desired behaviour?

3. Team integration

The Roffey Park research shows that it is at team level where the new organizational culture really takes shape. The case studies show that it is at micro-level where differences in working practices and underlying values really get resolved. This requires management with the skills to build new teams. Solutions to differences cannot always be imposed from above. Many issues will need to be discussed and resolved at local level, or networked across teams doing similar work.

Team leadership ● ● ●

- Are team leaders skilled in local change management?
- Has appropriate support/facilitation been provided for teams with difficulties?
- Is integration seen as an active part of this role?

Interpersonal integration ● ● ●

- How far have teams from different backgrounds been integrated, e.g. co-located or able to network electronically or physically?
- Is there any evidence of 'us and them' behaviour?
- Which teams have worked well and why?

Project work ● ● ●

- Do employees feel their schedules are on target?
- Are people enthusiastic about joint projects?
- Do staff get involved in making changes to improve current systems and processes?
- Have new ground rules emerged?

Learning • • •

- Is adequate review and evaluation built into team projects?
- Do teams learn from each other and share success?
- Do teams explore differences and acknowledge new approaches?

4. Personal transition

At a personal level employees experience a sense of loss for their old organizations and their own personal ways of coping and experience can determine their commitment to the new organization. The Roffey Park research found that values and codes of behaviour in the workplace are determined as the integration process plays itself out. For example, if trust is low, people find ways of working which embody lack of trust. Some of the following should be checked out.

Personal feelings • • •

- Have feelings of loss been recognized and respected?
- Do employees feel valued as individuals, from whatever background, both by those who manage them and other staff?

Goal alignment • • •

- Are employees' personal goals aligned with the new organizational strategy?
- Do people feel they have received sufficient communication regarding the integrated goals?
- Do employees respect the people who manage them?

Performance • • •

- Do employees feel they have the necessary skills to do their job?
- Do people know what is valued and rewarded in the organization?
- Are employee development needs being recognized and met?

Fairness and equity • • •

- Do employees perceive that the transition to the new organization has been effected fairly?

- Have appointments been made fairly?
- Have HR processes been harmonized in an equitable way?
- Do individuals believe the workload is evenly shared? What is the perception of work–life balance?

Feedback • • •

- Do employees receive ongoing feedback and coaching to encourage them to work in an integrated way?
- Are there vehicles for employees to express opinions/feelings and make suggestions to improve processes?
- Are there informal networking opportunities?

5. External perception

- Are customers able to navigate their way around the organization? Is the service user-friendly?
- Has integration provided added benefits?
- What is working well and what is not working well? Where are the critical gaps?

Summary

The HR team has to make a choice of how it will work in a merger situation. To some extent this will depend on the skills, experience and size of the department. Some will have to work operationally and others will be able to work strategically alongside the merger transition and integration teams. Where the team cannot cover all the roles in Figure 11.2 it will have to choose the key roles it will play and either outsource or work alongside consultants or enlist support from line managers to fulfil the other roles.

The overriding goal should be to support the business and to be a key player during the merger by being prepared to challenge the senior team and support the long-term health of the organization.

Reference

1. Devine, M. (1999): *Roffey Park mergers and acquisitions checklist*, Roffey Park Institute

The role of line managers in mergers

The Argonauts kept the ship on course through perilous seas

Most mergers succeed or fail depending on whether or not people are willing to work together effectively in the new organization. According to Haspeslagh and Jemison (1991), it is not until two firms have come together and begin to work towards the acquisition's purpose that value can be created. As we have already discussed, human resource issues can easily be overlooked during the negotiation phase by the acquiring company. In the run-up to the new organization, effective planning and project management are essential to handling the initial integration of systems and structures. Transition teams work with the relevant parties to produce the blueprint and work through the logistics. This is tough enough in itself. Yet it is what happens after the big decisions have been taken and the real integration is meant to begin that can make or break the chances of a successful merger. Many of the companies involved in the Roffey Park research[2] admitted that their core business had suffered during the months of transition and that this had led to a tangible downturn in profits.

This is where the role of the line manager becomes critical to merger success. In this chapter we will be looking at how line managers can convert transition management into operational management. Of course, how effective line managers can be is to some extent dependent on how well informed they are about what is going on; on what the integrated business is meant to achieve and how well responsibility for implementation is handed over from transition teams. Line managers are typically at the implementation end of decisions taken by others such as:

- Redefined reporting structures
- Developing the new corporate culture
- Rationalization of product or service support processes and functions
- Integration of premises
- The clarification of new staff requirements
- The need for new skills to be developed by staff
- Harmonization of reward practices
- Harmonization of management information systems.

Transition teams will have sown the seed for integration, but it is line managers who have to translate the strategic plan into reality. Line managers therefore have the twin challenges of managing change, while keeping the business going as usual from the point of view of customers.

Managers as 'enablers' of integration

Making the integration work is not simply an intellectual exercise. The way managers behave during a merger can enhance employee morale and motivation – or the opposite. Roffey Park's research reveals that in mergers, the process is as important as the outcome. The culture and climate of the new organization is determined by the experience of the merger itself. Every day, the actions of leaders and managers at every level help create the style of the new business.

Managers in the acquired business can play a critical role in maintaining loyalty and reducing anxiety among their work teams. A London Business School study[3] into 40 British acquisitions found that employees from acquired firms set greater store by the behaviours and actions of their managers (especially their immediate boss) than the promises or actions made by the acquiring management. Yet on the whole, managers are usually least comfortable with the integration phase of an acquisition. They are just as likely to be prone to the anxiety produced by a merger as everyone else. Managers in an acquired company often neglect human issues because of a general sense of paralysis and uncertainty, while top managers in the acquiring company often fail to make any form of pre-planning for people issues.

In many ways, managers are right to be concerned about their own prospects. According to Walsh[4], 75 per cent of senior managers in an acquired company leave within three years. Just whether these departures have a positive or negative effect on the business is still unknown. However, for the individual, the effects of redundancy can be shattering. A leading outplacement company reports that nearly half of their clients have lost their jobs due to M&A activity. 'The fact is that mergers and acquisitions are displacing younger executives in their peak producing years', says the firm. It argues that these executives often have special need of support because of their relative youth and the profound 'crisis of confidence' that they often experience.

A greater threat for an organization is when employees leave whom the organization would rather retain. A study by Hubbard[5] suggests that there is a link between how well employees' expectations are managed prior to the merger and their intention to stay within the business. Most turnover in mergers occurs at middle management levels. As these people are usually key to the success of the implementation, it is in the organization's interest to manage their expectations well. Managers too need to look after their own career interests, networking hard and establishing their reputation afresh.

Managers' role in the run-up phase

During a period of considerable uncertainty, managers need to maintain a high degree of professionalism – even when things get difficult. London Business School's research[3] found that some management behaviours in the immediate post-acquisition phase were more likely to lead to success. These include:

- In 77 per cent of the successful acquisitions, senior managers demonstrated 'ordered interfaces', deciding quickly which parts of the business were to be kept, sold off, what would be managed by whom and the degree of autonomy they would be allowed
- In 68 per cent of successful acquisitions, managers managed to convince employees that they will not lose financially from the acquisition
- In 64 per cent of successful deals, managers convinced the selling organization that there were clear benefits to the acquisition
- 59 per cent of successful management teams used 'honourable rhetoric', sticking to their promises and assurances.

Controlling anxiety

The period between the announcement and completion of the deal is usually one of considerable anxiety for employees. This period can last weeks, months or in a few cases, years. Nerves are frayed as people wonder if they will lose their jobs and usually the silence from senior management is deafening. This is often through no fault of their own but due to legal and commercial requirements. The actions and approaches of managers at this time appear to have a significant effect on the way staff react to what is happening around them.

The London Business School study, for instance, found that in 68 per cent of the successful acquisitions they examined, managers demonstrated clear vision about the future. The most important effect of this was to reduce uncertainty and get people quickly back to work; 59 per cent of successful management teams made changes with a 'people shape', rather than a mechanistic or theoretical shape. This helped demonstrate a concern for people.

While people want reassurance, bland reassurances may do more harm than good and damage management's credibility. Preparing people for the worst in a realistic way can help prepare people psychologically should things turn out that way. However, this should not turn into a doom-laden scenario, more a conscious acknowledgement that things are definitely changing, even if the actual changes are not yet known. Managers should be supportive, communicate what they know and bring employees into their confidence.

Unfortunately, all too often, managers are unable to help their teams because they focus too much on worrying about their own interests, as self-preservation becomes the dominant theme. Managers start to look for other jobs and it then becomes difficult to keep their own motivation levels high. If managers take an extended holiday during this time, teams feel abandoned. Teams then start to lose trust and commitment and key employees start to jump ship. The following checklist highlights types of effective and ineffective behaviour shown by the managers of acquired companies (after Schweiger and Weber[6]).

Preparing for the merger

- Effective managers try to prevent their staff seeing the other company as 'them and us'. They seek every opportunity to obtain face-to-face contact with their counterpart teams in the other organization.

- Ineffective managers fail to do this, thereby losing opportunities for their staff to begin to become more emotionally attached to the new business.

Commitment and understanding

- Effective managers are highly visible and act as friends to their team, thereby reducing their anxiety and helping them maintain a sense of attachment to the organization. They try to protect their employees and provide a sense of security in the work unit
- Ineffective managers become withdrawn and appear to abdicate any responsibility for their team. They appear more interested in looking after their own career prospects.

Being open and honest

- Effective managers are honest and do not make false promises. They give as much information to their staff as possible and are open about the limits of their knowledge. Their employees therefore feel better equipped to make decisions about the future
- Ineffective managers sometimes lie or fail to honour their promises, making their teams more anxious and less committed to the organization.

Minimizing political behaviour

- Effective managers try to retain a team atmosphere and minimize any destructive political behaviour among team members. They clearly base any difficult staffing decisions on objective performance criteria
- Ineffective managers are seen to protect their 'favourites', leading to divisiveness and competitiveness among the team.

Handling terminations well

- Effective managers handle terminations well, acting as a valuable buffer between the organization and the individual concerned. Remaining team members feel more loyal to the organization and more confident about how they will be treated in the future
- Ineffective managers fail to handle terminations well, making it more likely for remaining team members to feel angry and insecure.

Taking the emotional temperature

During the run-up period, it is vital that managers take the emotional temperature of their teams, spotting signs of strain. Even when they are not directly experiencing change, many employees go through the cycle of shock, anger etc. described in earlier chapters. Managers can watch out for signs of 'merger shock' when people become demotivated and stop performing. For most employees, mergers are a highly personal event. The following questions are at the forefront of people's minds:

- Have I got a job?
- What will my job be?
- Who will I report to/work with?
- Where will I be based?
- What will I get? (i.e. will I lose out?)
- When will this affect me?

Of course, managers themselves will be asking themselves the same questions and may not like the answer, but they still have to help people cope during this extended period of uncertainty. Managers may not be able to take many real steps to reassure staff and it is important to be realistic about what can be done at this time. The following suggestions for managers are from the Roffey Park mergers and acquisitions checklist[7]:

- Even if your team is positive about the merger, don't assume that individuals will not undergo a period of grieving. Be on the alert for this reaction, especially at symbolic events such as the launch of a new name, new corporate logo and identity, any fascia changes, site closures, withdrawal of small items, such as business cards, pens, badges bearing the old corporate logo and name
- Ask people open-ended questions about how they feel about the merger; what do they think will be the benefits and what are their uppermost concerns? Don't assume that you know the answers or how people are likely to react
- Explore people's perceptions of their current owner. Their views may surprise you. For example, in a retail company, non-managerial staff were critical of their parent company, believing that they did not support the business adequately. Consequently, they were very positive about being sold. Their managers had more contact with the parent company, however, and felt betrayed by the decision to sell
- Explore staff's past experiences of mergers. There may be individuals in your team who have valuable and positive experiences of a merger. Ask them about the lessons they

learned from the experience. Think about encouraging them to become valuable champions of change during the coming months

- Make every attempt to request and expect from the merger team a timetable of events so that your people can anticipate when changes such as reorganizations, relocations and redundancies will affect them personally
- Be as honest and open as possible, even when you don't know what's happening yourself. Don't make the mistake of trying to protect your staff by denying bad news. This will only make them feel more anxious and out of control. They will certainly not forgive you for lying to them
- Take your own needs seriously and build support networks for yourself, especially if you have to take difficult resource decisions.

Managing the transition

The immediate transition period of mergers always seems to generate a huge workload, especially for managers. Managers may be managing the departure of staff and the reallocation of existing staff to other duties while trying to maintain 'business as usual'. They will be managing 'survivors' – dealing with winners, losers and high flyers. They will be in the front line of communications, keeping people informed and involved in what's happening. In a real sense they are at the cutting edge of culture change and need to be able to create both a supportive environment and a stretching performance challenge. Their contribution involves:

- Controlling anxiety
- Handling exits
- Integrating staff and building new teams
- Providing clarity of direction, gaining buy-in and removing role ambiguity
- Contributing to the development of the new culture
- Managing performance
- Preventing deterioration in operational performance
- Managing staff expectations
- Communicating effectively
- Helping people cope with change
- Motivating staff
- Developing new skills and approaches.

The list of ways in which managers can help develop the new organization goes on and on and managers themselves may feel ill-equipped for the challenge. They may need to identify sources of support to help them manage the transition. The line manager's workload needs to be focused and managed. The bottom-line is that managers need to be able to help their teams become motivated to high performance in the new organization. The following areas all have an impact on creating a highly motivated, high performing workforce.

Handling exits and appointments

Resource decisions are an inevitable aspect of mergers. The process of allocating people to jobs and selecting people for redundancy can take months and prolongs the uncertainty for everyone. All employees – both those who will stay and those whose jobs will go – should be told the criteria for selection and the process should be seen to be fair.

The Roffey Park research suggests that it is vital for managers to be involved in decisions about which jobs are to go and in the hiring process. Decisions and management behaviour are studied closely by teams at this time and managers need to be able to strike a balance between fighting on behalf of their own team and taking a corporate view without 'selling out' their own team. It is important to treat people with respect and care, especially if their job is going. Similarly, new appointments must be seen to be fair. Managers will be liaising with HR or Personnel on these issues and should ensure that selection criteria are objective, transparent and widely understood.

Managing survivors

Can line managers manage team morale? This is always debatable. However, there are certain indicators of team morale which managers should be alert to and attempt to address if morale is low. As a team's position becomes clearer and the composition of the team begins to stabilize, managers need to guard against what Marks and Mirvis[8] have termed 'survivor sickness'. Survivors typically adopt one of three mindsets which can eventually become counter-productive:

- *Employees who are 'the ready'*: these individuals have achieved the hoped-for job change or promotion and are full of energy and enthusiasm. Unfortunately, however, these same people are often overly aggressive and act in a patronizing or overbearing way. This behaviour can generate enormous resentment and upset in the emotionally charged atmosphere of a merger.

- *Employees who are 'the wanting'*: these individuals are survivors who did not receive the job they wanted in the new organization or who were demoted. While some will adjust to their new situation, others might become angry or depressed.
- *Employees who are 'the wrung out'*: these individuals have the same job as before the merger but their work environment has changed forever. They are easy to overlook, yet they are often working through difficult emotions and reactions. Some employees might feel frustrated that nothing much has changed. Others might feel frustrated by both small and major changes in their work context. If they fail to work through these reactions, these employees can eventually become demotivated, lacking purpose and direction.

Managers can help by giving people opportunities to work through their feelings, without making false promises. It is important to re-orient people whose jobs may have changed.

Ideally, managers should attempt to ensure that team members' interests are being respected. If people have lost out in the merger, it is useful for manager and employee to work together to identify some aspect of the job, or specific responsibility, which might compensate for what has been lost. It is vital that people receive appropriate training or other high quality resources to enable them to acquire the skills and tools for their new role.

Celebrate the changeover

There is a great temptation for people in the acquiring company to assume that they will not be affected, that only the acquired company will be subject to change. However, it is important that people from both companies recognize that things have changed forever. When the Leeds and Halifax Building Societies merged to form Halifax PLC, staff from the Leeds offices held parties/wakes when their shop fronts were rebadged with the new company name. It was not until a year or so later, when the integrated company was clearly working differently from either of the two predecessor organizations, that staff from the previous Halifax Building Society realized that they should have held a wake too. They simply had not realized that, though they had retained the name, many other things would change.

Keeping people focused on performance

Mergers interfere with one of the main ways in which people build a sense of loyalty and pride – they make it harder for people to understand how they can be successful. With all the uncertainty, it is very easy for people to start under-performing. This is a time when everyone feels that there is not enough communication and no clear focus. Business systems and policies are in a state of flux. Work progress can easily start to drift and inertia can set in. However, people can become revitalized if there is a clear sense of purpose and specific tasks which are given high priority by the manager. People need to know:

- Who's in charge and whom do I need to please?
- How will my performance be measured?
- What are the boundaries of my job?
- How much informal power will I have?
- How can I start to be successful in this new set-up?

Managers can provide some answers to these questions by keeping people focused on performance, even if they are themselves unclear about the organization's strategy. This may require a manager to have the courage to create their team's own vision and goals in the absence of an organizational vision and goals. As has been said elsewhere, 'it is easier to ask forgiveness than ask permission'. Managers need to help staff be as clear as possible about the business strategy, about their roles, responsibilities and accountabilities. Managers can also help provide further clarity by focusing people on developing high performance. This will involve establishing priorities and new performance standards, agreeing new objectives, introducing new management controls and ensuring that customer needs are met without disruption from the merger.

In some organizations, taking such risks might be considered a step too far. However, managers can provide some clarity through interim performance management, setting performance targets which are achievable, time-bounded and have some stretch to them. The aim here is not to go for perfection and a number of just-in-time temporary processes may be needed to keep the business going in the transition period. Managers should try to engineer some quick wins for their teams, preferably genuine and useful successes which can be celebrated. As people start to believe that they are part of a winning team, they usually start to regain their motivation and sense of belonging.

Keeping business as usual going alongside the changes

The success of mergers is usually judged on early results, often gained from economies of scale. It is generally assumed that staff are the main casualties of mergers. In some cases, the real sufferers are customers who experience a decline in service or quality in the run-up and aftermath of a merger. Of course, customers generally have choices and, if they are unhappy, usually switch to another supplier. The main reasons why customers defect are:

- Poor standards of customer care. Disgruntled or frustrated staff often communicate their feelings when dealing with customers over the phone or face-to-face. When staff are preoccupied with their own feelings, they may fail to follow through on customer requests, leading to customer dissatisfaction. This is made worse when two standards of customer care are obvious after the merger.
- When customers hear news about the merger it is usually because they have picked up the sketchy details of the plan in media reports. Often staff are no better informed and can give customers the impression that the company is in chaos.
- Concern that they will no longer receive the goods or quality that they had before.

Line managers must discuss and agree with teams from day one what are the non-negotiables with regard to customers. A common (high) standard should be aimed for and performance carefully monitored. Staff may need help in rehearsing specific customer situations post-merger and many companies provide communication prompts for people dealing directly with customers.

Real synergies are usually achieved by a focus on value creation, which usually entails merging production and other processes. This takes a long time and the pressure to create dramatic improvements in the early days can be intense. However, haste is not necessarily the best approach and a planned transition to new processes should sit alongside existing processes so that it can be phased in appropriately. Managers should involve themselves in planning for the introduction of new processes so that an end-user perspective is integrated into the process design.

Building integrated teams

Mergers typically result in people from different organizations working together. Some may be brought together into integrated teams such as in marketing, operations, sales. They will have different ways of doing things, different approaches to dealing with their customers and may well have strong residual loyalty to their previous employer. There may well be culture clashes which are obvious in power struggles, misunderstandings and confusion. One key element of a manager's role in building an integrated team is managing differences in corporate culture. Often, the differences in corporate culture, as described earlier in this book, remain as an ongoing source of conflict and mutual irritation. The challenge for line managers is to create a context in which people do not see themselves as 'winners' and 'losers' but as part of a successful new team.

One way of tackling culture clashes is help people explore characteristics of their culture such as:

- Process versus results orientation
- Managerial behaviour
- Feedback mechanisms
- Risk taking
- Use of power
- Decision-making processes
- Accountability
- Customer handling processes.

It is then important to help team members work out the cultural 'hot spots' which are likely to generate tension. Ideally, though, this cultural auditing should not take place in isolation but be related to what the team is designed to achieve. The 'best of both' philosophy does not always produce the most useful outcome if the new organization's strategic ambitions are different from those of the predecessor bodies. Ideally, the team should be challenged to find new and better ways of operating to meet ambitious business needs.

If problems persist, it may be necessary to get specialist help from a facilitator or HR professional who can help people work together compatibly and work through any interpersonal conflict. The aim should be not only to address dysfunctional group behaviour but also to realize a team's potential. Some teams benefit from team-building activities from the earliest possible date and line managers may need to negotiate the resources to provide this. A key element of building an integrated team is creating a real sense of belonging and team spirit. As one recently merged manager put it, 'people used to like working for Company X and they were proud to be able to tell people whom they worked for. In this new set-up, feelings towards the organization are neutral at best. People don't feel motivated to go the extra mile like they did before'.

The challenge is to build mutual trust and support and overcome resistance to change. One company which has provided managers and team members with the tools to do this is First Quench.

First Quench, formed from the merger between two rival high-street chains, Victoria Wine and Thresher, developed a culture change programme called Alchemy. The aim was to accelerate the embedding of the new culture throughout the company which has many diverse locations. The Alchemy process begins with a two-day course which is designed to take the values down to the shop floor. The first day is company-focused, discussing the vision and values, including an exploration of the effects it would have if people did not 'live' the values. The second day concentrates on what is important to individuals, building their self-belief and setting their personal and business goals. The techniques used include accelerated learning and neuro-linguistic programming.

The effect of the programme is to build trust between employees and managers. Business development manager Simon Thornton has a team of 31 branch managers. 'Alchemy was a godsend for me. It has brought the staff together, but the trust element has had the most impact. People have become bolder. They can make decisions on their own. They know what makes a profit and what needs to be done'. One shop reported a post-Alchemy profit increase of 42 per cent on the year.

Internal communications are aligned to the Alchemy language of praise and positive attitudes. There are employee suggestion and reward schemes, many of them cheap and cheerful but effective, such as a simple 'Thank you' card. Many reward schemes have emerged spontaneously – one manager took his team to his house and cooked them a meal.

Alchemy provides a tool for achieving the vision. It has improved the quality of interaction between employees and with customers, changed behaviours in line with the company values and created an atmosphere of trust and respect. The 'wow' factor and 'celebration' are terms common throughout the company[9].

Monitor how the change process is working

Managers are at the sharp end – they really should know how things are going, even without attitude surveys etc. In the flurry of activity, followed by long periods of no news, which is typical of mergers, it is very easy for misinformation to occur, for morale to drop and for key people to contemplate leaving. Managers should be prepared to channel the information they pick up to more senior management so that preventative or remedial action can be taken. Similarly, in the rush to introduce new practices post-merger, not all initiatives are well-conceived. Managers should be prepared to challenge poor practice at whatever level so that the organization does not resort to its lowest common denominator.

Manage your own career

As well as managing others, managers have a responsibility to themselves. Many managers find the uncertainty aspect of mergers very difficult to cope with. For some, mergers represent a real threat to security and career prospects. Conversely, some people find that a merger opens up new avenues of opportunity than had previously existed in the old company. While there is no denying that some management and other jobs do disappear in mergers, managers can help themselves by thinking of the benefits of repositioning themselves. If you want to stay in the company, then how and to what would you wish to be re-recruited? If you are leaving, what will you want your next role to bring you and what can you learn from the merger experience? In particular, how can you engineer being in the right place at the right time for the right job?

In the Roffey Park mergers and acquisitions checklist, Marion Devine[7] offers the following helpful advice:

- Think about becoming a member of a merger taskforce or joint working team involved in some aspect of the integration. Use this to hone your change management skills and to get a new view of the overall business
- Consider opting for any secondments or temporary project teams where you can extend your personal network of contacts and learn new skills – but make sure you still have a job to return to afterwards
- Look for any opportunities to network with more senior people – attend events such as questions and answer sessions, presentations, dinners – and bear in mind that senior people need access to insightful feedback about what is happening at grass roots level
- Look for any career fast tracks – for example, in order to move quickly, some companies cut out swathes of bureaucracy. Members of the merger committee need up-to-the minute feedback and more junior managers can suddenly find that

they have direct access to directors. This can be an invaluable opportunity to forward their own careers and gain a better understanding of strategy and policy.

Summary

The line manager's role is not an easy one but, if done well, can contribute to merger success. For managers mergers can offer as many opportunities as threats. There are opportunities to develop new skills and work with different people and to find new ways of operating. The main challenges of managing change while keeping business going as usual call for good problem-solving, organizational and team-building skills. Motivating new teams to high levels of performance involves overcoming all the many causes of conflict and turning difference into a source of potential synergy. This requires good strategic leadership and team-building skills. So line managers need to be able not only to deal effectively with the short-term hot spots, but also help identify and release the potential of the new organization. In that sense, they can help the organization achieve more than the planners dared to dream.

References

1 Haspeslagh, P.C. and Jemison, D.B. (1991): *Managing Acquisitions, creating value through corporate renewal*, Free Press, New York

2 Devine, M., Hirsh, W., Garrow, V. and Holbeche, L. (1998): *Mergers and acquisitions – getting the people bit right,* Roffey Park Institute

3 Hunt, J. (1987): *Mergers and Acquisitions,* London Business School, Egon Zehnder

4 Walsh, J. (1988): Top management turnover following mergers and acquisitions, *Strategic Management Journal,* **9**, 173–183

5 Hubbard, N. (1999): *Acquisition: strategy and implementation,* Basingstoke, Macmillan Business

6 Schweiger, D. and Weber, Y. (1989): Strategies for managing human resources during mergers and acquisitions : an empirical investigation, *Human Resource Planning,* **2**, 2

7 Devine, M. (1999): *The Roffey Park mergers and acquisitions checklist,* Roffey Park Institute

8 Marks, M. and Mirvis, P. (1985): Merger syndrome: stress and uncertainty, *Mergers and Acquisitions,* Summer 1985

9 Tyler, E. (2000): Golden Hello, *People Management,* 9 November

Conclusion – reaping the benefits of mergers and acquisitions

He lulled the monster to sleep, and obtained
the Golden Fleece, and immediately set sail
with Medea

So what really is a successful merger? Is it one which
increases stock value in the short-term or is it one which
also produces a sustainable, flexible organization capable of realizing greater returns over time than either of
the constituent predecessor organizations would have
been capable of alone? Talk to City analysts and they
will give an unequivocal answer – one which increases
shareholder value in the shortest possible time. Talk to
customers, employees and other stakeholders and their
answers may be different.

In publicly quoted companies, company practice is
usually focused on achieving short-term returns even
though the shareholder, customer and employee may
actually gain more if a longer-term approach were
taken – assuming that there is a clear and effective
strategy to achieve revenue enhancement over time. By
most standards, the timeframe for achieving real

financial success is longer than the first quarter, i.e. cash investment typically has a payback period of three years or less, so there usually is the opportunity to go for the bigger wins if the will is there. In public sector mergers, the complex process of integration often takes so long that the next policy change has occurred before any of the benefits of the merger have worked their way through the system.

To judge by the way in which many management teams place their priorities, doing the deal is seen to be more important than realizing its longer-term value. So frenzied can deal-making become that companies become lumbering giants made up of many different entities which management teams struggle to pull together before the next deal is done. Is it any wonder that the main beneficiaries of merger mania are the advisers and analysts who offer advice at the de-merger stage, when the assets have failed to realize their combined value?

Mergers are a major gamble for the acquirer. The premium paid to close a deal represents the acquiring company's confidence that they can create additional value through the combination and/or deployment of intellectual property. If this gamble backfires, value was wasted rather than added and the premium paid represents a loss. Michael Porter suggests that acquisitions on average are value-destroying for the acquirer. He found that half the acquisitions of 33 leading US companies were subsequently divested within a five to ten year period[1].

De-mergers abound. Kingfisher for example is de-merging Woolworths, B&Q and Comet, while selling Superdrug to a Dutch company for £280 million. Examples of companies divesting themselves of assets at less than they paid are legion. For example, Emap, the magazine and radio group, extricated itself from a major US investment at a huge loss after just two years. (Emap had paid £950 million for Petersen in 1999. They sold the troubled division to Primedia, a rival US magazine publisher for just £366 million in June 2001.)

What makes for a successful merger?

In theory, if a merger is to succeed, the main causes of merger failure have to be avoided. One of the main causes of failure as we have seen is poor merger logic and an inappropriate deal structure based on inadequate information. Therefore, the logic behind any deal should be built on challenging the acquirer's assumptions about how they would acquire a business for less than it is worth. In developing an appropriate deal structure, the focus should be on gathering information about the right things

– relevant to the deal logic. This will typically include the nature and location of talent, the expectations of customers, the interests and likely intentions of key employees. This focused approach to due diligence takes time but should not be skipped because of difficulties obtaining the information or pressure from the deal-makers.

Another key cause of merger failure is unsuccessful integration, often caused by culture clashes or management attitude combined with a lack of adequate planning. Often the challenges of integrating the operational elements such as production technologies and computer systems are underestimated, as are the difficulties of aligning employees' beliefs and ways of working. Here speed of integration may help rather than hinder. A number of studies have shown that successful acquirers act quickly, using a disciplined project management process. On measures such as profitability, productivity, cash flow and gross margin, quick integration tends to lead to better results than slow integration. However, each merger is different and requires bespoke treatment according to how much autonomy is required and how much interdependence exists.

Of course making a success of a merger where there is a good fit of cultures, a sound strategic fit and good market conditions ought to be straightforward. In principle, executives ought to have an idea of the benefits they expect from any single merger and how those benefits are to be obtained. Yet so often the potential value of the deal is undercut by a lack of vision as to what can be achieved with the combined organization once the deal has been cut and the savings made. The end result is that companies pay too much for an asset whose synergies they have been unable to actualize. According to Stuart Wallis, chairman SSL International plc, 'Strategic planning is not about building up from today; it is about articulating the ultimate position the company wishes to achieve'[2].

1. A well coordinated integration process, focused on building a high performance culture

Realizing the value of the merger is likely to involve two significant phases of major activity. Much of this book has been focused on phase one, in the immediate aftermath of the deal. During this period, as we have seen, there is a mass of activity, requiring many disparate projects to be carried out and coordinated, just to make the integration work effectively. Typically this involves bringing together the main 'mechanics' of the organization.

In successful mergers, integration teams consist of people from both organizations. They develop their own maps or timelines, building in points for a pause to review and reflect. They develop clear language and parameters. They make sure that there is sufficient resource for what needs to be done early enough. They develop strategies for dealing with merger fatigue. They ensure that there are effective handovers between transition and operational activities, so that line managers are able to play their part in integrating the organization effectively. Integration teams should engage front line managers in the process of weaving together existing processes, systems and policies into a single integrated operating system. Activities include the mapping and analysis of processes, systems and policy.

The aim at this point should be not only to integrate processes but also to build a high performance culture which should enable the combined asset to start realizing some of its potential value. Communications are treated as a high priority and maintained beyond the initial integration period. In successful mergers, the best people are chosen for jobs and management teams are prepared to look outside for more complex jobs or where the skills internally are in short supply. Since mergers allow blue-chips to gain access to leading edge expertise, capitalize on a shared customer base and enter new markets, M&A activity is likely to be an ongoing feature of corporate life. Therefore, all the integration activity in phase one should be carried out with flexibility factored in. The way in which the IT infrastructure and service delivery are designed should enable future M&As, or divestments, not mitigate against them. The organization's approach to e-business for example should be well thought through and designed into new systems and processes.

Similarly, mergers provide the opportunity to build a culture which is market, rather than product oriented. In such a culture, the drive to provide superior customer value and the continual quest for new forms of competitive advantage create the context for employee involvement and innovation. In such a culture, the key capabilities include the ability to read what is happening in the marketplace and to anticipate shifts. Relationship management and strategic thinking are then enabled by a shared knowledge base, using information technology and other processes, such as story telling. Cultural values are likely to include placing a premium on knowledge sharing and co-creation, being externally rather than internally focused and on forming close relationships with key customers. This kind of culture will typically be underpinned by resources, structures and reward systems which reflect the cultural values.

In phase 2, once the organization is functioning as a combined entity, continuous improvement, in which systems can be re-engineered and networks optimized, enables some of the operational benefits of the merger to start to be realized. However, to achieve revenue enhancement which exceeds any gains made through the initial post-deal savings, a more radical approach is called for, typically requiring bold strategic vision about what can be achieved. Success in phase 2 calls for real leadership on the one hand and a willingness by employees to be flexible on the other. The latter depends to some extent on how the integration in phase 1 was carried out. If the people you depend on for success in phase 2 have become demotivated or have left the organization as a result of how the merger was handled, phase 2 becomes largely academic. So the focus in all the integration activities should be on building an organization which is capable of achieving challenging business objectives.

2. In successful mergers, the focus is on revenue enhancement/maximizing potential

Whatever the importance of the strategic planning and integration processes, many longer-term benefits are not known before the deal. If the focus is mainly on saving costs, as in many financial services mergers, progress tends to be slow. Philippe Haspeslagh[3] suggests that a year into the integration, managers should have started to realize the potential of the capabilities and resources of the new organization. To exploit fully the main potential benefits of the deal, executives need to identify ways to maximize business potential and effectiveness. A second wave of change is required in phase 2 to keep the momentum going beyond the first phase of integration, consolidation and performance improvement. This is the time to aim for the bigger strategic goals which are made possible by having the benefits of an adaptable employee base and flexible systems. This will therefore involve another major period of change, new direction and management effort.

According to Haspeslagh, more detailed and ambitious strategies can be developed, though these should focus as much on the 'how' as on the 'what'. 'People need the education and the tools to help them change. They need to be measured and rewarded not only for what they achieve but also for how they manage. Whether around the discipline of the six sigma, or through the operationalization of value based management, the key to the second phase is to initiate and sustain a change process in support of a new culture of performance'.

When Thresher, then part of Whitbread Plc, acquired Peter Dominic in the early 1990s, the increased market reach was an early benefit of the deal. However, with major potential competitive challenge about to occur when the personal import restrictions on alcohol and tobacco were lifted in the EU, Thresher recognized the potential of the combined organization to operate differently. An operations development project (ODP), spearheaded by the then Head of Operations, Brian Wisdom, and the HR controller, Chris Johnson, involved reviewing most aspects of operations, including information flow and structures.

The review, which involved staff in one brand, led to a period of organization redesign, staff development and operational 're-energizing'. The financial benefits of the project were such that the company was not only able to withstand the onslaught of cross-Channel trade but subsequently acquire Victoria Wines, thus forming First Quench. Though it would no doubt have been tempting not to embark on the change journey again with the ODP, the project allowed the company to move from a defensive to a strategic position in the marketplace and better to realize the value of the asset[4].

3. Successful mergers have effective leaders

According to Stuart Wallis[2], deals work best when management teams get to know each other and understand each other's position at the earliest stage, preferably before talks leak to the press. The business logic around anticipated synergies and savings should emerge from this base of good sense and mutual respect. The merger between the Bristol and West Building Society and the Bank of Ireland was an example of an extended courtship with a purpose. Management teams came to know each other well enough that they were able to carry out the negotiations with each other's needs in mind, as well as their own[6].

Wallis suggests that the relationship building is important as is taking time to assess the opportunity. Management overload usually results in a failure to spend sufficient time doing this, which makes it harder to realize the benefits of the deal, even assuming the deal is not over-valued in the first place. Executives need to identify the important issues for a successful merger, including the main 'hot spots' and the similarities. They need to identify who will do the investigative work and oversee the integration. They need to work out the key elements and stages to move each company from where they are now to where the new company wants to be. They need to figure out how the two companies will develop together, especially if they have very major differences in culture and background.

Once the deal has been done and major effort has been put into the process of merging, integration fatigue can set in. Leadership needs to create an air of urgency around each task and to take a hands-on role in completing integration tasks. According to Philippe Haspeslagh[3], another critical aspect of sustaining the organization's stamina for change is making sure that the executive team is a team. Unless the executive and management teams really buy in to the new culture and performance expectations, no-one else will either. Haspeslagh suggests that it may be necessary to replace some players after the new structure has been tried out. He suggests that up to 30 per cent 'do not measure up to the merger task'. New people, preferably outsiders who have allegiance to neither of the two former sides, should be brought in to improve management quality.

Leaders have a key role in managing employee expectations and it is critical that senior management constantly repeats those messages they want employees to understand. Senior executives need to be visible and make frequent visits to different locations to ensure that people feel they know what is going on. Answering people's questions openly and honestly can lead to trust building and is an important element of staff motivation during the changes.

4. In successful mergers, the human and organizational issues are handled effectively

In a survey published in *Organizational Dynamics*, Jim Markowsky found that the main causes of failure in business change programmes were as follows:

- Inadequate leadership: 42 per cent
- Organizational/cultural: 27 per cent
- People issues: 23 per cent
- Information technology: 4 per cent
- Other: 4 per cent.

Mergers represent for most employees some of the biggest changes that they will experience at work. Uncertainty and delays often lead to paralysis through politics. Morale, customer service and productivity can nose-dive. Many people will need support through the merger process and the very people they would usually turn to – line managers – are usually too busy to help and they are often experiencing the same uncertainties.

Workshops which provide people with information about the merger and its possible implications can be helpful in gearing people up to the realities of change. The AA, for example, when acquired by Centrica, ran workshops which were open to all employees to help them cope with change and think about how to position themselves within the new company. Similarly, some organizations run workshops for managers to help them to help their teams to cope with the change. Mergers provide real opportunities for developing leadership and management capability at all levels in the organization. Given that management behaviour is usually the most telling message about how the new culture is shaping up, managers have to be careful to ensure that their words are backed up by their deeds.

Effective communications are paramount not only during the run-up and transition but also in the longer-term integration phase. In many ways, early contacts set the tone and 'ambassadors' need to be sensitive to the messages they are sending. There needs to be an evolution from one-way (i.e. 'tell') communications in the early phase to two-way involvement. Using the many forms of communication at their disposal, leaders can set the tone for the new organization and its potential. Focus groups, hot lines, attitude surveys all have their role to play. People need to know what their part in the new organization will be – not only their role but the skills and approaches required for success in the new organization. A strategic and tactical approach to communicating with all stakeholder groups is vital to ensuring that people remain interested and become involved in shaping the new organization.

People will be affected by mergers in many ways. Ideally the structure design should flow from customer to process to roles to posts. The best people for the job should be selected, rather than aiming for even-handedness in terms of staff numbers. Determining who is best for a post may involve taking into account not just skills but values and 'fit' with the new organization. Resourcing issues should be handled as transparently as possible. For some companies, the approach taken is to 'slot' the chosen candidates into some roles while making other roles open to application from a talent 'pool'. Other companies use external assessment processes to validate their decisions, given that management's knowledge of employees may be limited, or to ensure that the genuinely best person gets the job. Whichever approach is taken, people need to know so that they can best position themselves in the circumstances.

Individuals whose jobs have gone should be treated with respect and the 'survivors' given chance to come to terms with departures. Then the focus should be on building for the future, with individuals offered training if need be to help them thrive in new roles. There is a point at which teams need to design their own roles. Some integrated teams may need team building and other processes to help them function effectively as quickly as possible. People should be given conscious opportunities to learn from each other.

As we have seen, creating the new organization and its culture evolves from the earliest stage, emerges from the transition and becomes more apparent when there are deliberate attempts to identify organizational values and mission statements. Our experience suggests that values should reflect the new practices rather than being simply aspirational statements which can lead to employee cynicism. Better perhaps to have one core value linked with one clear statement of strategic intent and let the organization and its leadership focus on making that work before producing well-intentioned wish lists of desired behaviours. Trust can be built and the aim should be to get the process right for individuals every time. People need to feel that they have survived and thrived in a merger if they are going to be flexible and open to further change as the wider strategy evolves.

Conflict is perhaps an inevitable part of change and managers need to anticipate this. There are usually profound differences in the combining organizations' strategies, structures, cultures and politics. These differences can become divisive when people are feeling unsure of the future and can become stumbling blocks. It helps if groups of managers brainstorm what they believe will be the top few conflicts they will encounter and outline some strategies for handling each conflict. Facilitators can be used when conflicts arise and open and honest discussion will often serve to diffuse the issue, rather than denying it. Employees who relish conflict should be dealt with swiftly so as to avoid the organization becoming torn apart by internal battles.

Similarly, boredom with change and inertia is to be anticipated in a change effort which lasts some time and which has long periods when not much is happening that is new. Again, managers can helpfully brainstorm ten practical quick-win actions and who should do these pieces of work, so that a sense of progress is reinforced. Managers can also anticipate some of the risks they will have to manage and filter them by likelihood and impact. They can again identify ways of managing specific risks, preferably by working with colleagues so that good ideas are spread quickly.

The human resources agenda is a complex one, particularly with respect to employment contracts, aligning pay and conditions and the role played by workers' councils or trade unions. Good planning and project management, together with expert advice may be needed to ensure that appropriate processes are applied. Mergers provide unparalleled opportunities to build a high performance culture. This involves consciously designing structures, governance systems, competencies and reward systems so that they reinforce the new direction. This may entail cutting across established practice and may require effective negotiation with employee representatives in order to break with tradition.

5. In successful mergers, success is defined and measured

Success criteria post-deal typically fall into two categories – financial and the 'intangibles', such as organizational capability and whether the new board is working together effectively. In financial terms, the sum of the whole should be worth more than the parts. Financial measures would include ongoing summaries of the actual achieved synergies and the economic value of those already achieved. Measures typically include revenue growth, profit growth, market share growth, return on invested capital, economic value added etc. However, it may take years for the real benefits to begin to flow and it may be advisable not to go public with ambitious figures on savings in the short term.

Galpin et al.[5] suggest that there are three other key areas, in addition to finance, in which measures should be developed. First, there are integration measures which assess specific integration events and would include, for example, brief surveys of task force members and employee focus groups. Second, operational measures are necessary in tracking any merger-related impact on the organization's ability to manage its 'business as usual'. These would include statistics that reflect sudden changes in the number of productivity or quality related issues.

Third, process and cultural measures are used in determining the status of merger-driven efforts to redesign business processes or elements of the organizational culture. In reality, most value is created after the deal by people at all levels in both organizations being willing to collaborate in activities which lead to increased value of the firm. This is where a focus on the intangibles is critically important. The 'soft', cultural aspects of the organization need as much attention as the operational integration. Differences in organizational culture can be bridged by effective leadership yet typically there is a leadership void, causing issues to remain unresolved. Measures can be developed to ensure that a continued focus is maintained on these issues. Examples would include periodic feedback identifying pressure points with respect to how things are done in the new organization.

Philippe Haspeslagh[3] suggests six areas of activity which contribute to merger success or otherwise during the integration phase:

1 Clarify the leadership and discipline interface management
2 Get management back to work and be back in the market
3 Find out reality and remedy the glaring weaknesses
4 Clarify and create buy-in for the integration logic
5 Develop a common purpose and harness complementarities
6 Align communication internally and externally.

Each of these areas of activity can be measured in ways which not only provide tracking information (lag indicators) but help create the culture which the organization needs (lead indicators). Marks and Mirvis[6] suggest that there are many benefits to tracking the process of integration. One such benefit is that tracking keeps managers focused on what this merger is meant to achieve while executives are contemplating the next merger.

Other benefits are that tracking helps managers to:

• Work out whether the transition is going to plan
• Identify 'hot spots' before they flare out of control
• Ensure a good flow of communication
• Become aware of the need for corrective action
• Demonstrate interest in the human side of change
• Involve more people in the integration process
• Send a message about the new company's culture.

Setting measures can help transform merger activities into learning opportunities or a chance to reposition entire functions through the value that they bring. Teams involved in the merger process, such as HR, should develop their own guiding principles or success measures. One HR team whose organization is on the acquisition trail has identified their own success measures by answering the question, 'What do we want to be known for?'

• To develop core capability in merging
• To capture opportunities
• To create a meaningful partnership with representative groups
• To retain key individuals
• To become recognized externally as the Best Place to Work.

Having a sense of where you have come from and where you are now is important in recognizing some of the more subtle benefits of the merger. The same HR team took a photo of themselves and their counterparts at the start of the integration process and again when the process was completed. In a very graphic way, individuals were able to see how far they had travelled over the previous few months.

6. In successful mergers, rich learning is experienced and shared

One of the characteristics of an organization which makes a difference to the business, according to Dave Ulrich[7], is one in which there is a good flow of ideas. Mergers give unparalleled opportunities for skills transfer in a constructive and deliberate way.

The merger process itself provides many opportunities for rapid and deep learning – for deal-makers and those carrying out due diligence; for planning and transition teams as they struggle to design the organization and integrate processes; for line managers as they learn to integrate teams while keeping the business going as usual. The adrenaline flows as people grapple with complex issues and carry out tactical problem-solving. The common practice is that this learning rarely gets shared beyond the groups in question, so that when individuals with specialist knowledge move on, their knowledge goes with them.

Some organizations are increasingly seeking to widen the pool of people involved in managing the merger process so that there is less risk of losing the knowledge. Others are deliberately documenting their learning in generic integration guides so that knowledge is safeguarded for another team. It is usually helpful to have some continuity between merger projects, so that at least one experienced individual joins any new transition team to ensure that things are not missed. Resources should be committed to documenting lessons learned during the integration process. One financial services organization wanted to understand their own processes before embarking on more acquisitions. They employed a researcher to document their merger-related decisions and to investigate the impact of those decisions on the integration process.

Mergers also provide opportunities to create knowledge-rich cultures, in which the classic deterrents to knowledge sharing, such as lack of advantage to the individual, can be addressed through career routes etc. New learning processes dedicated to capturing and leveraging the intellectual property of the combined organization should be created at this time. As John Brown, CEO of BP noted, 'The wonderful thing about knowledge is that it is relatively inexpensive to replicate *if* you can capture it'[8].

Since people expect change during mergers, why not use the opportunity to introduce good practices which perhaps did not exist before? Some companies for example have built in review processes so that they focus not only on the progress of tasks but on learning. They set up cross-functional teams which create the context for knowledge sharing. They encourage individuals to belong to at least two teams in the internal supply chain so that there is an increased understanding of the needs of different groups. The first step is usually to create integration teams from both companies to tackle integration challenges. Many organizations treat conflict as problems to be solved and a potentially powerful source of energy which can be harnessed to the organization's interests. They create knowledge inventories of the combining organizations and set up 'learning communities', actions learning sets or special interest groups dedicated to the cross-fertilization of ideas across organizational boundaries.

As a merger reaches the end of its integration phase, and the 'we are one' phase is a reality, it is time to take stock and work out what went well and what could have been done differently. Unless this happens, there is a risk that managers will repeat the same mistakes again and lessons will remain unlearned. Developing a sustained merger capability depends on the quality of learning that is gained from each merger experience.

Capabilities for success

To bring about a successful merger is not easy; nor is it just a matter of luck. It's about being able effectively to choose the right merger strategy and manage the people implications of that strategy. If by the way you implement the merger strategy you destroy the foundation of your intellectual property – the commitment and goodwill of key employees – yours will become just another failure statistic. Success calls for a number of apparently contradictory capabilities in leaders:

- It's about being strategic in terms of growth possibilities and tactical in terms of seizing opportunities
- It's about being expert at managing mergers as a project, both the 'mechanics' and the cultural integration, while being open-minded about what unforeseen possibilities can be created from the merger

- It's about being able to treat a merger as an intellectual exercise, while experiencing it as an emotional one
- It's about being prepared to make tough decisions but also about being aware of people's feelings and able to build trust
- It's about leading with vision and consistency while recognizing the different starting points of both organizations
- It's about setting high aspirations while sorting out local issues
- It's about walking the talk as well as communicating through formal channels
- It's about going for the best possible outcomes for the business, its customers and employees while recognizing that some of these will be incompatible
- It's about being good at coping with ambiguity, while helping people to go through change successfully.

In conclusion, any merger or acquisition represents a major strategic undertaking. The change must be driven by real leaders who are committed to achieving the preferred outcomes. Understanding the dynamics involved becomes critical and will increasingly become a key requirement for directors and others who aspire to chief executive roles. Senior management needs to pay as much attention to the people and cultural issues as they do to the financial and operational strategies. They need to commit huge energy to communicating with all stakeholders and involving the people affected in the change.

When undertaking a merger or acquisition, management teams need to move quickly. Strong project management needs to be in place and measures established to navigate towards the desired results of the merger. Management teams therefore need to have their strategies clearly formulated and a good understanding of their own company culture before they embark on the acquisition trail. Because, reverting to the story of Jason and the Argonauts, Jason successfully overcame all manner of obstacles to capture the Golden Fleece, but his ship ended up being beached so that he never returned to his home port, thus snatching defeat out of the jaws of victory. Lessons of mythology suggest that a strategic map may be useful if one does not wish to share Jason's fate!

References

1 Porter, M. (1998): Clusters and the new economics of competition, *Harvard Business Review*, Nov–Dec
2 Wallis, S. (2000): When deals work. In *Managing Mergers and Acquisitions*, IBM Global Services

3 Haspeslagh, P.C (2000): Maintaining momentum in mergers, *European Business Forum*, Winter

4 Holbeche, L. (1999): *Aligning HR and Business Strategies*, Butterworth-Heinemann

5 Galpin, T.J. and Herndon, M. (2000): *The Complete Guide to Mergers and Acquisitions*, Jossey-Bass, San Francisco

6 Marks, M.L and Mirvis, P.H. (1998): *Joining Forces, Making One Plus One Make Three in Mergers & Acquisitions*, Jossey-Bass, San Francisco

7 Ulrich, D., Ashkenas, R., Jick, T. and Herr, S. (1998): *The Boundaryless Organization*, Jossey-Bass, San Francisco

8 Thomas, M. (1998): *Mergers and Acquisitions*, Hawksmere

Glossary of terms

ARD   Acquired rights directive

CEO   Chief executive officer

CFO   Chief financial officer

Competition Commission   An independent public body over-seeing company mergers and acquisitions, formerly known as the Monopolies & Mergers Commission

COO   Chief operating officer

Due diligence   Exercise prior to completion of a purchase contract to validate a company's assets, liabilities and trading position

DAX 30   Index of top 30 listed companies on the German stock exchange

EGM   Extraordinary general meeting of shareholders, usually set up for a specific purpose

Escrow account   Funds paid by one party to a third party agent for a limited period of time to provide a guaranteed fund to cover liabilities

FTSE 100   Index of top 100 listed companies on the London stock exchange

Goodwill   The difference between a company's true value and its net worth

Indemnity   A guaranteed financial solution against a specific liability

IPO   A company's first sale of stock to the public

IPR   Intellectual property rights, ownership rights related to the knowledge and expertise related to a particular subject area

M&A   Mergers and acquisitions

NDA   Non-disclosure agreement, a confidentiality agreement restricting disclosure of information

Net worth   The worth of a company measured in terms of a company's total assets less its total liabilities

OFT   Office of Fair Trading, an independent watchdog overseeing fairness of trading practices

Opening balance sheet   The opening balance sheet is the balance sheet of a company at the point of acquisition

Opening operating plan   The operating plan for a company at the point of acquisition

P-E ratio   Price earnings ratio, the ratio of a company's stock price and its earnings per share

Private finance initiative   Initiative funded by private finance to deliver a public service on behalf of public body

PPP   Public private partnership, joint venture of public body with a private company to deliver a public service

Price-sales ratio   The ratio of a company's stack price and its revenues per share

Reverse takeover   An acquisition, where the management of the acquired company assumes effective control of the joint company

SAR   Substantial Acquisition Rules

SPO   Secondary public offering, further offerings of shares in a listed company subsequent to the initial offering

TUPE   Transfer of Undertakings (Protection of Employment), regulations that protect existing employee rights following a merger or acquisition

Warranties   A guarantee that information disclosed is accurate

Information security terms

Content filtering   Software that monitors the content of mail and other internet traffic

Message encryption   Solutions that encode and decode messages for secure transmission

Network firewalls   Solutions that control the flow of information through a gateway between two networks

Index

Other Roffey Park books and research reports

Devine, M. (2001) *Mergers & Acquisitions Checklist.* £11.00
Devine, M. and Hirsh, W. (1998) *Mergers and Acquisitions: getting the people bit right.* £50.00
Evans, C. (2000) *Developing a Knowledge Creating Culture.* £30.00
Garrow, V. (1997) *A Guide to the Implementation of 360 Degree Feedback.* £7.61
Garrow, V. Glynn, C. Tarpey, S. and Whatmore, J. (2000) *Contemporary Approaches to Teamworking.* £30.00
Garrow, V. Devine, M. Hirsh, W. and Holbeche, L. (2000) *Strategic Alliances: Getting the People Bit Right.* £60.00
Garrow, V. and Holbeche, L. (2001) *Effective Mergers and Acquisitions.* £50.00
Glynn, C. and Holbeche, L. (2001) *The Management Agenda 2001.* £30.00
Glynn, C. (2000) *Work Life Balance, Careers and the Psychological Contract.* £20.00
Glynn, C. (1999) *Enabling Balance, the Importance of Organisational Culture.* £30.00
Glynn, C. (1999) *Towards Global Leadership, Recruiting and Developing International Managers.* £40.00
Hamilton, F. (2000) *Interpersonal Conflict at Work.* £30.00
Holbeche, L. (1998) *High Flyers and Succession Planning in Changing Organisations.* £50.00
Holbeche, L. (2000) *The Future of Careers.* £50.00
Kenton, B. and Moody, D. (2001) *What Makes Coaching a Success?* £30.00
Lammiman, J. and Syrett, M. (1998) *Innovation at the Top: Where Do Directors Get Their Ideas From?* £50.00
Lammiman, J. and Syrett, M. (2000) *Entering Tiger Country: How Ideas are Shaped in Organisations.* £60.00

To purchase any of the publications listed above please contact Pauline Hinds on 01293 851644 or e-mail pauline.hinds@roffeypark.com

Roffey Park has over 50 years experience of developing innovative approaches to management development and understanding the human dimension of organisational issues. Areas of expertise include organisational and management development at all levels, managing change, training developers and interpersonal skills development. Roffey Park offers a wide range of services including short residential open programmes, in-company development and consultancy, weekend workshops, an MBA, Post Graduate Diploma in Management and MSc in People and Organisational Development.

Roffey Park Institute, Forest Road, Horsham, West Sussex, RH12 4TD, United Kingdom
Tel: +44 (0) 1293 851644; Fax: +44 (0) 1293 851565
www.roffeypark.com; e-mail: info@roffeypark.com

Roffey Park Institute Limited is a Charity, Registered No: 254591 VAT No: 201–9601–03